MATH WISE!

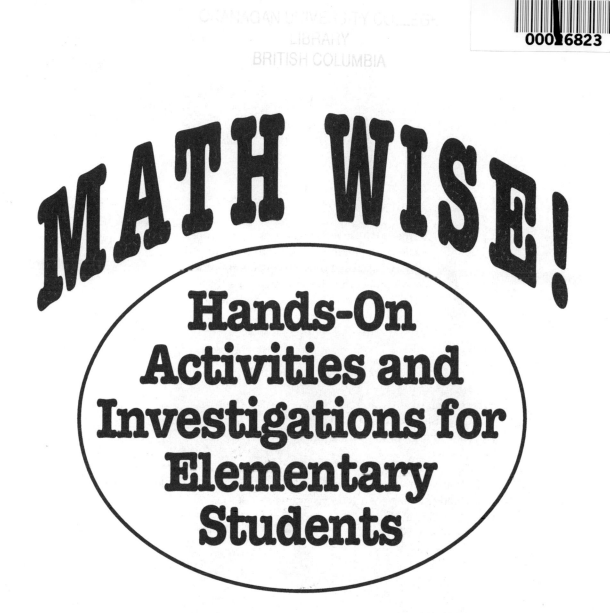

Hands-On Activities and Investigations for Elementary Students

JIM OVERHOLT

illustrations by Cris Guenter

THE CENTER FOR APPLIED RESEARCH IN EDUCATION
West Nyack, New York 10994

10 9 8 7 6 5 4 3 2

Library of Congress Cataloging-in-Publication Data

Overholt, James L.
    Math wise! : hands-on activities and investigations for elementary
students / Jim Overholt ; illustrations by Cris Guenter.
        p. cm.
    ISBN 0-87628-555-8
    1. Mathematics—Study and teaching (Elementary)   2. Mathematics—
Study and teaching—Activity programs.   I. Title.
QA135.5.0933 1995
372.7´044—dc20   95-6989
                                                                                          CIP

ISBN 0-87628-555-8

 **The Center for Applied Research
in Education,** Professional Publishing
West Nyack, NY 10994
A Simon & Schuster Company

PRINTED IN THE UNITED STATES OF AMERICA

ABOUT THIS RESOURCE

Student learners in today's society must be able to do more than achieve correct answers through computation; they need to understand basic concepts and to experience a wide variety of mathematical applications. *Math Wise!* was written to provide activities and investigations that will help each learner *truly understand* the mathematics that he or she is expected to deal with. It contains a wide variety of learning experiences that have been arranged according to difficulty level. The focuses include numbers and counting, computation, estimation, problem solving, geometry, logical thinking and other mathematical strands; whenever feasible, the provided activities have been dealt with in either concrete hands-on or visual formats. An added bonus is that the included tasks can be characterized as *informative, interesting,* and *fun!*

CONCRETE/MANIPULATIVE ACTIVITIES

Whenever possible, and especially when "new" concepts are being developed, each learner should work with hands-on, 1-to-1 correspondence materials. Thus, a number of the activities set forth in this book call for the use of easily obtained manipulatives such as straws, paper clips, sugar cubes, and beans. For example, one problem in the "Paper Clip Division" activity asks the learner to show 44 divided by 7. The result might appear as that shown in the illustration.

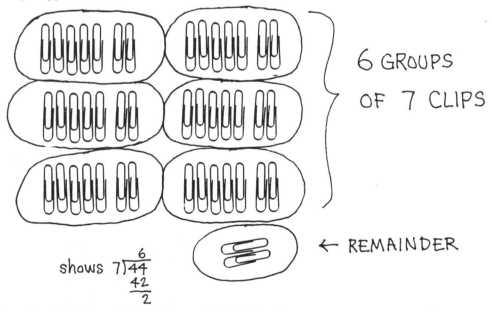

6 GROUPS
OF 7 CLIPS

← REMAINDER

shows $7\overline{)44}$ with 6 above, 42 below, remainder 2

In another situation "Punchy Math" suggests that the learners use a paper punch, scrap paper, and a pencil to show $3 \times 7 = \underline{\ ?\ }$. The outcome, after folding, punching, looping, and labeling shows 3 groups of 7. If turned sideways, it can also show 7 groups of 3, or $7 \times 3 = \underline{\ ?\ }$. The resulting punched holes are clearly concrete; however, the looped segments also provide a visual component that corresponds directly to the abstract number relationships.

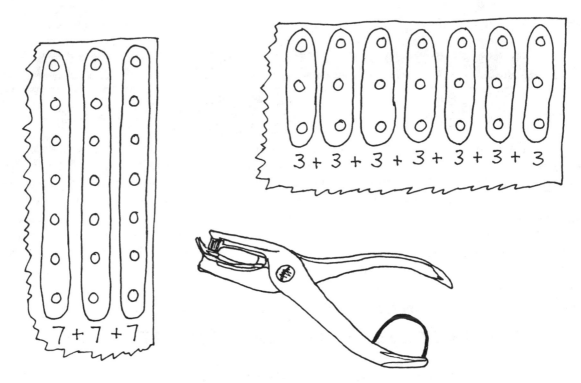

Manipulative experiences, such as these, provide a basis for true understanding by learners. Because they are so important, a number of similar activities are contained in each section.

VISUAL/PICTORIAL ACTIVITIES

For many learners, visual representations or pictures can also provide keys to comprehension. When first utilized, such representations should show the entire situation and involve 1-to-1 correspondence. For example, "Cross-Line Multiplication" for $3 \times 5 = \underline{\ ?\ }$ shows 3 lines crossed by 5 lines to yield 15 intersections. Of course, by turning the drawing sideways $5 \times 3 = 15$ is also shown.

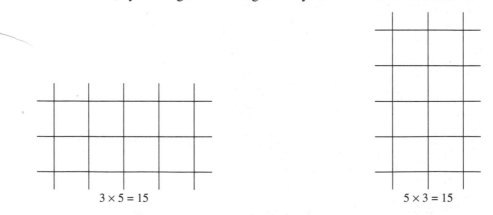

Another visual investigation is "Mystery Object Guess." To begin, various small three-dimensional items are gathered together and kept hidden. The leader selects one, places it (still hidden) on the overhead projector, and displays a single view of it on the screen. Then the players, either by cooperative group or individually, are allowed a designated number of guesses as to what the object might be and the reasons why they think so. The leader does not respond until all guesses and reasons have been stated. Furthermore, if no correct guess was stated, a view of the object from a different perspective is shown on the screen, and the process continues. For example, two views of an item are shown below. What object do you think is being displayed and why?

View #1   View #2

Visual activities, such as this, may combine elements of spatial thinking, problem solving, geometry, logical thinking, etc. In View #1, the object displayed appears as a small circle with a bump on it. In View #2, it seems to be a rectangle with a smaller rectangle extending from it. Did you guess that the object was a cap for a ball-point pen? (*Note:* The pen cap appears as a circle with a bump on it when standing on end, and as a rectangle with a smaller rectangle as an extension when on its side.)

ABSTRACT PROCEDURES

One goal of mathematics education is to have learners progress to points where they are able to work with abstract mathematical procedures and concepts. When possible, such knowledge should provide for both the mechanics and a true understanding of what is happening.

In "Post-it™ Mental Math" one player has Post-it™ numerals placed on his or her back without being allowed to see them. The other group members, after viewing the numerals, physically act out computations related to them. Based on these physical clues, the Post-it™ player must mentally determine and state the numerals posted. In the situation that follows, the Post-it™ player has made a first guess based on the fact that the other players had completed five sit-ups in unison. Since he did not guess the actual posted numerals, the players might now decide to show the product of the numerals by running in place and counting in unison 1, 2, 3 . . . 36 for each time their left foot touches the ground. The Post-it™ player will then be allowed to make a second guess as to the numerals on his back.

"Calculator Solution Logic" is another activity that calls on learners to utilize their knowledge of abstract computation processes together with problem-solving and logical-thinking abilities. It is played most effectively as a group activity that utilizes an overhead projection calculator. (*Note:* The calculator must have an automatic constant feature. To check, try the following problem.) To play, the teacher or leader enters (in secret) a problem such as 90 divided by 90 equals 1 and displays the 1 on the overhead screen. The learners are then told that the number they are to find, with the fewest possible guesses, is between 1 and 100. Furthermore, as their guesses are entered, the calculator will give them clues. When the correct number is identified, the calculator will again display 1. For example, if 40 were guessed and entered (enter 40 =) the display would read .44444444; if 50 were tried, the display would become .5555555; for 75, it becomes .8333333; for 88 it becomes .9777777; and for 90 the display is 1, so the hidden number has been determined!

A FINAL WORD

Learners will very often find the activities and investigations from this book to be *informative* and *interesting,* and often just plain *fun.* But in any event, they will be helped to *understand* the mathematics that they are expected to master. As such, *Math Wise! Hands-On Activities and Investigations for Elementary Students* will prove to be a most valuable supplement to any mathematics program.

ABOUT THE AUTHOR

James L. Overholt, Ed.D. (University of Wyoming, Laramie) has been exploring the use of manipulative and visual materials available for mathematics instructions since the 1960s. As an elementary and secondary school teacher in Minnesota and Wyoming, and then as a university professor, his investigations have taken him into K-12 classrooms and to adult mathematics learning workshops. He is currently Professor of Education at California State University, Chico.

Dr. Overholt regularly conducts mathematics education courses and workshops for preservice and inservice teachers at the elementary and secondary levels. His earlier published books include *Math Stories for Problem Solving Success: Ready-to-Use Activities for Grades 7–12* (The Center for Applied Research in Education), *Dr. Jim's Elementary Math Prescriptions* (Scott, Foresman & Co.), *Math Problem Solving for Grades 4–8* (Allyn & Bacon, Inc.), *Math Problem Solving for Beginners through Grade 3* (Allyn & Bacon, Inc.), *Outdoor Action Games for Elementary Children* (Parker Publishing Co.), and *Indoor Action Games for Elementary Children* (Parker Publishing Co.).

ABOUT THE ARTIST

Cris E. Guenter, Ed.D. (University of Wyoming, Laramie) has been exhibiting her artwork since 1972 and teaching since 1978. As a K-12 art and gifted and talented teacher in Pennsylvania and Wyoming, and now as a university professor, her creative endeavors and pursuits in arts education have made her a consultant in arts education for several school districts and a keynote speaker on the arts in northern California. She is currently an Associate Professor of Education in fine arts/curriculum and instruction at California State University, Chico.

Dr. Guenter regularly conducts fine arts, education, and creativity courses and workshops for preservice and inservice teachers at the elementary and secondary levels. She is an active member of The California Arts Project and its efforts for statewide staff development in the arts. Her paintings, prints, and photographs have been exhibited in seventeen national and international juried exhibitions in the past seven years. In 1994 she published a chapter, "Fostering Creativity through Problem Solving" in the book *Changing College Classrooms* (Jossey-Bass).

SUGGESTIONS FOR USING MATH WISE!

HANDS-ON ACTIVITIES AND INVESTIGATIONS FOR ELEMENTARY STUDENTS

The *Math Wise* activities in this book provide a varied collection of interesting and understandable tasks that learners in grades K–8 (and beyond) will benefit from. While many of these activities can be dealt with in any order, it is generally advisable to designate tasks that are appropriate for specific situations. With this in mind, several features of this book were designed to serve as guides when selecting appropriate activities.

- The **Contents/Index** categorizes each activity in five ways:
  1. by *Section*—Making Sense of Numbers; Computation Connections; Investigations and Problem Solving; and Logical Thinking and Some Puzzles
  2. by *Descriptive Titles*—such as Everyday Things Numberbooks; Paper Clip Division; Peek Box Probability; and String Triangle Geometry
  3. by *Grade Level*—K–2, 2–4, 4–6, 6–8, and 8–Adult
  4. by *Activity Type*—Concrete/Manipulative; Visual/Pictorial; or Abstract Procedures
  5. by *Learning Format*—Total Group; Cooperative; and/or Independent
- With each activity, a key noting the most appropriate grade levels, the kind of experiences learners will take part in (Concrete/Manipulative, Visual/Pictorial, and/or Abstract Procedures), and the working arrangement (Total Group, Cooperative, and/or Independent) is provided. For example, the key to "Silent Math" (see below) indicates that: (1) the activity is best suited for students in grades 4–8; (2) the activity might be worked on by a Total Class or in Cooperative Groups; and (3) the learners will have Visual and Abstract experiences.

SILENT MATH

Grades 4–8

☒ Total group activity
☒ Cooperative activity
☐ Independent activity

☐ Concrete/manipulative
☒ Visual/pictorial
☒ Abstract procedure

- Each activity begins with a **Why Do It** statement that denotes what mathematical concepts the students will be learning and/or practicing.
- A **You Will Need** statement specifies any supplies or equipment necessary for the activity. Such items (as paper clips, index cards, straws, etc.) are easily obtained and free or inexpensive.

- The **How to Do It** section notes what a leader must do to get the activity started. It also suggests whether the investigation works best as an independent activity, as a cooperative project or as a total group venture; many will work in either format.

- The **Examples** illustrate how the activity might progress and/or display typical outcomes.

- An **Extensions** section at the end of each activity contains sample *questions, situations,* or *suggestions* that might be completed by the learner(s). In most instances the learners (or the leader) can and should also propose similar tasks of their own.

- Where appropriate, *black-line masters* have been provided immediately following the associated activity. Thus, such items as gameboards, workmats, dot paper, playing cards, graph paper, etc., are readily available.

- The learners should be encouraged to keep records of the methods attempted as well as their solutions. Keeping a math journal is one possibility; a math file with work samples is another.

CONTENTS/INDEX

Section I

MAKING SENSE OF NUMBERS

This section introduces learners to many number concepts and relationships. A variety of situations involving 1-to-1 correspondence, basic number combinations, place value, mental math, fractions, large numbers, and decimals are provided. As such, students may develop conceptual understandings or practice essential mathematical skills through activities, investigations, and/or games that make use of manipulative experiences, visual portrayals, and/or relevant abstract procedures.

In addition to the number sense experiences set forth in this section, a number of activities from other portions of this book can be utilized to extend and enhance learner understandings. Some of these are *Punchy Math, Bounce It, Beat the Calculator,* and others from Section II; *Peek Box Probability* and *Restaurant Menu Math* in Section III; as well as *Duplicate Digit Logic* from Section IV.

TOOTHPICK STORYBOOKS

Grades K–3

☒ total group activity
☒ cooperative activity
☒ independent activity

☒ concrete/manipulative
☒ visual/pictorial
☒ abstract procedure

Why Do It: To discover 1-to-1 counting, number conservation, and basic computation relationships.

You Will Need: Several boxes of flat toothpicks; both white and colored paper (pages approximately 6″ by 9″ work well); glue; and marking pens or crayons.

How to Do It:

1. Have young students explore and share different arrangements they can make with a given quantity of toothpicks; that is, if the number were 4, they could arrange their 4 toothpicks in a wide variety of different configurations, and all still yield 4 toothpicks.

2. After exploring for a time, the students should begin making *Toothpick Storybooks*. They might first make number pages; for instance, on a white paper a numeral, perhaps 6, is written and on a colored paper 6 toothpicks are glued (to avoid a sticky mess, dip only the ends of the toothpicks in the glue). When the students are ready, the same procedure is followed for equations and the corresponding toothpick pictures. (*Note:* Students sometimes portray subtraction by pasting a small flap on the colored page that covers the number of toothpicks to be "taken away." Furthermore, they seem to enjoy lifting the flap to rediscover the missing portion.)

3. When a number of toothpick diagrams have been finished, they can be stapled together into either individual or group *Toothpick Storybooks*. Finally, each student should be asked to tell a number story about one of the diagrams; his or her story should make reference to both the toothpick figure and the written equation or number. They might also take them home and share with an adult.

Example: Shown below are possible toothpick diagrams for 4; 3 + 5 = _?_; and 7 − 2 = _?_.

Extensions:

1. Multiplication facts, and even larger problems, can be portrayed with toothpick diagrams. For $6 \times 3 =$ _?_ the player might show ||| ||| ||| ||| ||| ||| = 18. In a similar manner for $4 \times 23 =$ _?_ it is necessary to show 4 groups of 23 toothpicks to yield 92.

2. Division might also be shown with toothpick diagrams. If, for example, the problem calls for 110 to be divided into sets of 12, the player would need to form as many groups of 12 as possible, plus take into account any remainder. (*Note:* The student might also complete such a problem using Partitive Division. See *Paper Clip Division* in Section II.)

NUMBER COMBINATION NOISY BOXES

Grades K–3

☐ total group activity   ☐ concrete/manipulative
☒ cooperative activity   ☒ visual/pictorial
☒ independent activity   ☒ abstract procedure

Why Do It: To provide students with a visual (or concrete) aid that will help them understand number combinations and to practice addition and subtraction facts.

You Will Need: Ten (or more) stationery or greeting card boxes with plastic lids; approximately 50 marbles; and pieces of styrofoam or sponge that can be trimmed to fit inside the boxes. Cut the foam to the shape of a divider (see illustration) and glue it to the box bottom. Use a marking pen to write the numeral on the divider, plus the appropriate number of dots and the number word on the edges of the box. Insert the correct number of marbles and tape the plastic lid on. Construct *Noisy Boxes* for the numerals 0–9 (or beyond).

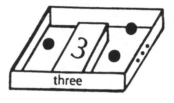

How to Do It: Allow the players to work with each of the *Noisy Boxes*. A player needs to tip or shake a Noisy Box such that some or all of the marbles roll past the divider. Once this is done the player is to record the outcome, shake the box again and record the new outcome, etc. Play continues in this manner until no further combinations are possible. (See Example below.)

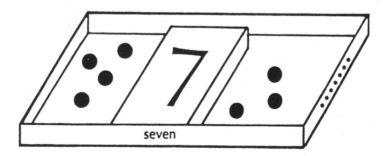

Example: The recorded number combinations for the **7's** Noisy Box should include the following:

4 + 3 = 7	0 + 7 = 7	7 − 0 = 7	7 − 4 = 3
3 + 4 = 7	2 + 5 = 7	7 − 1 = 6	7 − 5 = 2
5 + 2 = 7	1 + 6 = 7 *or*	7 − 2 = 5	7 − 6 = 1
6 + 1 = 7	7 + 0 = 7	7 − 3 = 4	7 − 7 = 0

Extensions: Should any player have difficulty utilizing a Noisy Box at the visual level, have that individual temporarily take the plastic lid off. Then he or she can touch and physically move the marbles from one side of the box to the other. Nearly all students will experience success as a result of such direct concrete experience.

EVERYDAY THINGS NUMBERBOOKS

Grades K–4

☒ total group activity ☒ concrete/manipulative
☒ cooperative activity ☒ visual/pictorial
☒ independent activity ☒ abstract procedure

Why Do It: To discover that our daily lives are full of things that come in numbered amounts.

You Will Need: A supply of paper that can be stapled into booklets and pencils. Scissors and glue sticks or paste may also be desired.

How to Do It:

1. As a group, discuss things in everyday life that are generally found as singles or 1's: 1 nose for each person; 1 trunk per tree (most trees); 1 beak on a bird; 1 tail per cat; 1-A-Day Multiple Vitamins, etc. Then provide each player with a sheet of paper and have them write a "2" at the top. Each player should list as many things that come in 2's as they can think of: 2 eyes, ears, hands, legs for each person; 2 wheels on a bicycle; 2 wings per bird, etc. Do the same for 3's: 3 wheels on a tricycle; 3 sides for any triangle; a 3-leaf clover, etc. The players might also paste pictures representing numbered amounts on their pages. Have the players complete a page (or more) for each number up to 10 or beyond. Have a discussion as to their suggestions and perhaps construct large class lists for each number. Finally, this might also be a homework activity, and it might continue for several days.

2. At first some numbers seem unusable, but wait and you will be delighted with the suggestions that come forth. For instance, how about 7 or 8; start with 7-UP for 7, and 8 sides on a STOP sign for 8. Players will often continue to make suggestions, even after the activity has ended!

Example: The following is a partial Numberbook listing for **4.**

Extensions: For more able players consider situations such as these.

1. What items can commonly be found in 25's, 50's, 100's, and/or any specified number? Is there any number amount for which an example cannot be found?

2. Find examples of fraction numbered amounts. (*Hints:* How many segments typically found in an orange? How many pieces do restaurants usually cut their pies into?)

UNDER THE BOWL

Grades K–3

☐ total group activity
☒ cooperative activity
☒ independent activity

☒ concrete/manipulative
☒ visual/pictorial
☒ abstract procedure

Why Do It: To provide students with a visual (or concrete) aid that will help them understand basic number combinations and to practice addition and subtraction facts.

You Will Need: A bowl or small box lid and small objects such as beans, blocks or bread tags for each player.

How to Do It: Allow the players a brief free exploration time with their bowls and objects. Then have the players begin with a small number of objects and give beginning instructions. For example, with three beans, the players might be told to put two beans under the bowl and place the other on top of it. Then they should say aloud (to a partner or chorally as a class), "the one bean on top of the bowl and the two beans under it make three beans altogether." Continue in this manner until the students understand the procedure and then ask them to also keep a written record of what they have done; for the example with three beans, noted above, they should record $1 + 2 = 3$ (and, when able, they should also record $2 + 1 = 3, 3 - 2 = 1$, and $3 - 1 = 2$). Whereas initially the players should use only a few objects, they might go on to use as many as 20 or 30 or even 100 objects.

Example: The players shown above are working with 7 beans. Thus far they have worked and recorded their findings for 1 bean on top of the bowl and 6 beans under it. They are now beginning to do the recording for 2 beans on top. Next they might put 3 beans on top and record their findings, etc. (*Note:* An important feature of this activity: Should a student become confused about a number combination, he or she may count the objects on top and then lift the bowl and either visually or physically count the objects underneath. This serves to quickly clarify understandings for individual students.)

Extension: When working as partners, an interesting variation is to have one student make a combination and have the other try to figure out what it is. For instance, student #1 might put 3 beans on top of the bowl and some others under it. He then states, "I have 11 beans altogether. How many beans are under the bowl and what equations can you write to tell about this problem?" Student #2 should, hopefully, respond that there are 8 beans under the bowl and the equations are $3 + 8 = 11, 8 + 3 = 11, 11 - 8 = 3$, and $11 - 3 = 8$.

CHEERIOS® & FRUIT LOOPS® PLACE VALUE

Grades K–5

☒ total group activity   ☒ concrete/manipulative
☒ cooperative activity   ☒ visual/pictorial
☒ independent activity   ☒ abstract procedure

Why Do It: To provide students with a concrete (or visual) experience that will help them understand place value concepts.

You Will Need: Several boxes of Cheerios® and one of Fruit Loops® breakfast cereal; a supply of string or strong thread; two paper clips per student (to temporarily hold the cereal in place); and needles for each group or each student. (*Note:* If you do not wish to use needles, the activity can be accomplished by utilizing waxed or other stiff cord.)

How to Do It: Following a place value discussion of 1's, 10's and 100's, challenge the students to make their own place value necklaces (or decorations). Ask them, for instance, to determine the "place value" of their own neck and, when they look puzzled, ask, "How many Cheerios® on a string will it take to go all the way around your neck?" Then note that they will be stringing Cheerios® and Fruit Loops® on their necklaces in a way that shows place value. That is, of each 10 cereal pieces to be strung, the first 9 will be Cheerios®, and every 10th piece must be a colored Fruit Loop®; that way they will be able to count the place value of their neck as 10, 20, 30, etc. As students finish their necklaces, be certain to have place value discussions about them.

Example: The partially completed Cheerios® and Fruit Loop® necklace shown above has the place value of two 10's and three 1's or 23.

Extensions:

1. Try making and discussing other personal place value decorations such as wrist or ankle bracelets or belts.

2. An interesting group project is to estimate the length of your classroom (or even a hallway) and make very long Cheerios® and Fruit Loops® chains. When doing so be sure to initiate place value discussions about 100's, 1000's, and even 10,000's or more. (*Hint:* When making such long chains it is helpful to have individuals make strings of 100 and then tie these 100's strings together.)

INCREDIBLE EQUATIONS

Grades K–6

☒ total group activity
☒ cooperative activity
☐ independent activity

☐ concrete/manipulative
☐ visual/pictorial
☒ abstract procedure

Why Do It: To develop number sense and to cite mathematical connections.

How to Do It: In this activity each player must name a specified number in a different way. Keep a permanent record of these many ways of naming the same number by writing your *Incredible Equations* on a large piece of newsprint or butcher paper; or use the chalkboard if you only wish a short-term record.

Example: The following are *Incredible Equations* for the number 21 that one group of players devised.

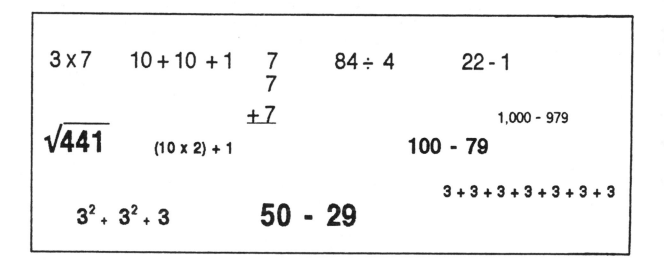

3×7 $10 + 10 + 1$ $\begin{array}{r} 7 \\ 7 \\ +7 \\ \hline \end{array}$ $84 \div 4$ $22 - 1$

$\sqrt{441}$ $(10 \times 2) + 1$ $1{,}000 - 979$ $100 - 79$

$3 + 3 + 3 + 3 + 3 + 3 + 3$

$3^2 + 3^2 + 3$ $50 - 29$

Extensions: *Incredible Equations* may be quite simple addition or subtraction problems or they may be more complex situations involving multiple operations, exponents, etc.

1. Each day develop and list equations to correspond with the calendar date. Students should also build these numbers with manipulatives. For example, 21 might be built with two bundles of 10 straws rubber banded together plus a single straw.

2. Restrict players to certain operations. For example, players might be directed to use only addition and subtraction.

3. Players, who have had sufficient experience, could be required to use all four basic operations. Advanced players might be expected to utilize parentheses, exponents, square roots, etc. (Be certain to use the proper left-to-right Order of Operations: Parentheses; Exponents; Multiplication and Division; Addition and Subtraction.)

4. Calculators might be utilized to create truly *Incredible Equations*. For example, each player might be required to use at least five different numbers together with a minimum of three different operations.

NUMBER CUTOUTS

Grades K–8

☒ total group activity   ☒ concrete/manipulative
☒ cooperative activity   ☒ visual/pictorial
☒ independent activity   ☒ abstract procedure

Why Do It: To develop number sense and to emphasize mathematical connections.

You Will Need: Graph paper (find 1-inch and 1-centimeter masters on the following pages); scissors; glue or bulletin board pins; and a pencil.

How to Do It: Cut out and label rectangular numbers from 1 to 100. Choose either square-inch or square-centimeter graph paper to complete in as many ways as possible the rectangular area cutouts for each number. Arrange them in order on a bulletin board or glue them to a large sheet of poster paper. Examples for the numbers 1 through 6 are shown. Also, do as many of the Extensions as you can. Keep a record of your findings.

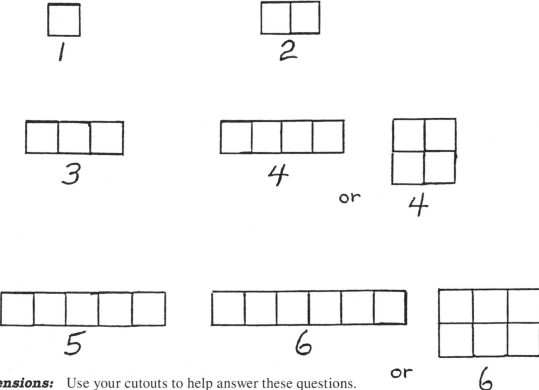

Extensions: Use your cutouts to help answer these questions.

1. Which of the number cutouts for 1 through 6 can be shown in more than one way?

2. Which numbers from 1 through 6 might be called square numbers? Why? Cut out three square numbers that are not shown above.

3. Show the number 12 with as many rectangular cutouts as possible. How about the number 16?

4. Which numbers from 1 to 100 can be cut out in only one way? What are these numbers called?

5. What do your cutouts show about multiplication?

6. What else did you find that was interesting? Use your number cutouts to explain.

NUMBER CUTOUT GRAPH PAPER (cm)

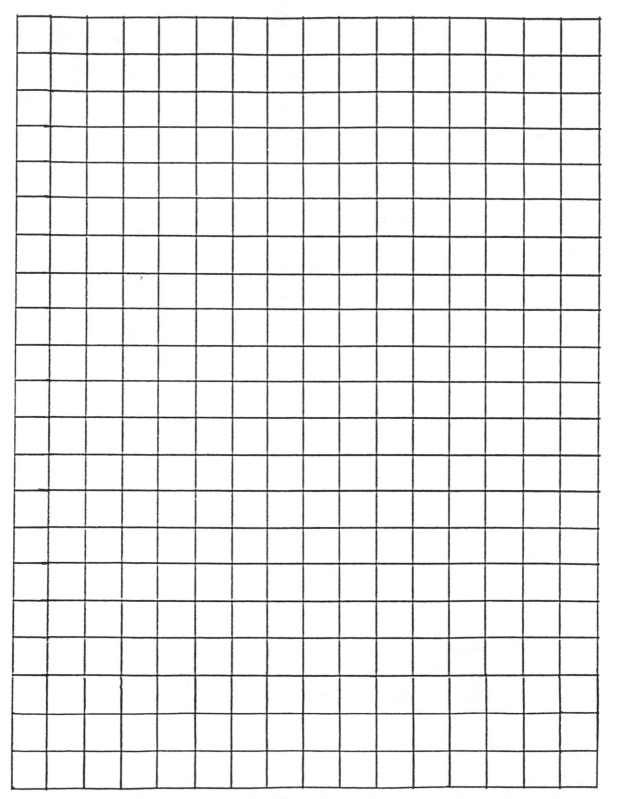

NUMBER CUTOUT GRAPH PAPER (inch)

BEANS AND BEANSTICKS

Grades K–7

☒ total group activity   ☒ concrete/manipulative
☒ cooperative activity   ☒ visual/pictorial
☒ independent activity   ☒ abstract procedure

Why Do It: To bring about 1-to-1 concrete and visual understandings of place value and computation concepts.

You Will Need: A supply of dried beans; popsicle sticks (or tongue depressors); and clear drying carpenter's-type glue (Elmer's™ Glue-All permanent glue works well). Single beans will serve for the numbers 1–9, but thereafter 10's beansticks and/or 100's flats (or rafts) will be needed. The 10's beansticks are to be constructed by gluing 10 beans to a stick; and the 100's flats by gluing ten of the beansticks together with cross supports (see the illustrations below). The beansticks and rafts will be more durable if a second bead of glue is run over them several hours after the first gluing dries. Finally, the students can and should (for reasons of ownership and pride) construct the beansticks themselves; or, if necessary, older students can do the construction and then use them to instruct young students.

How to Do It:

1. The players should first use individual beans to show a variety of single-digit numbers. Next the 10's beansticks should be incorporated to display numbers with two-digit place value, and when three-digit numbers are dealt with the 100's rafts are to be utilized. Example 1, below, shows such place value exhibits.

2. Examples 2, 3, 4, and 5 cite methods for using the beans and beansticks to add, subtract, multiply, and divide. Please pay particular attention to the situations where trading (sometimes called renaming, regrouping, borrowing, and/or carrying) is necessary. Finally, players should keep a written record of the problems, processes, and outcomes they determine.

Example 1:   The numbers 3, 25, and 137 are displayed using beans and beansticks.

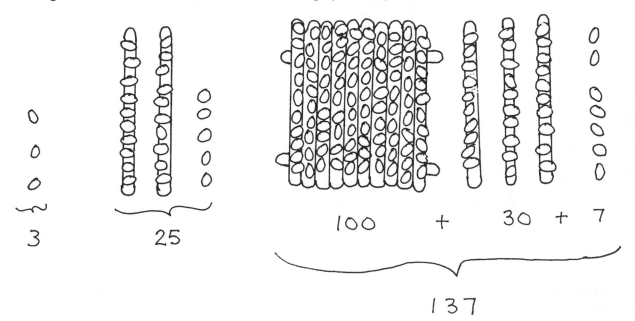

Example 2:   The problem $16 + 12 = \underline{\;?\;}$ is solved below (in equation format) by simply combining the 1's beans and then the 10's beansticks. As such, it is not necessary to trade.

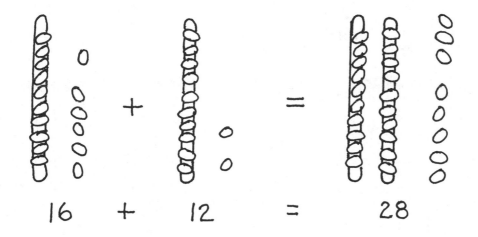

$$16 \quad + \quad 12 \quad = \quad 28$$

Example 3:   The problem $21 - 6$ does require trading. Notice, since 6 cannot be subtracted from 1, one of the 10's beansticks is traded for 10 single beans; now 6 can be taken away from 11. Thus, the player ends with one 10's beanstick and 5 single beans; or $10 + 5 = 15$.

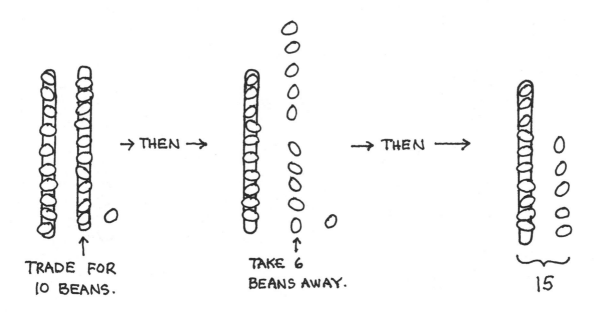

Example 4:   Trading is necessary to solve the problem $3 \times 45 = \underline{\;?\;}$. Notice that 10 of the 15 loose beans need to be traded for a 10 stick; and also that 10 of the beansticks are traded for a 100's flat.

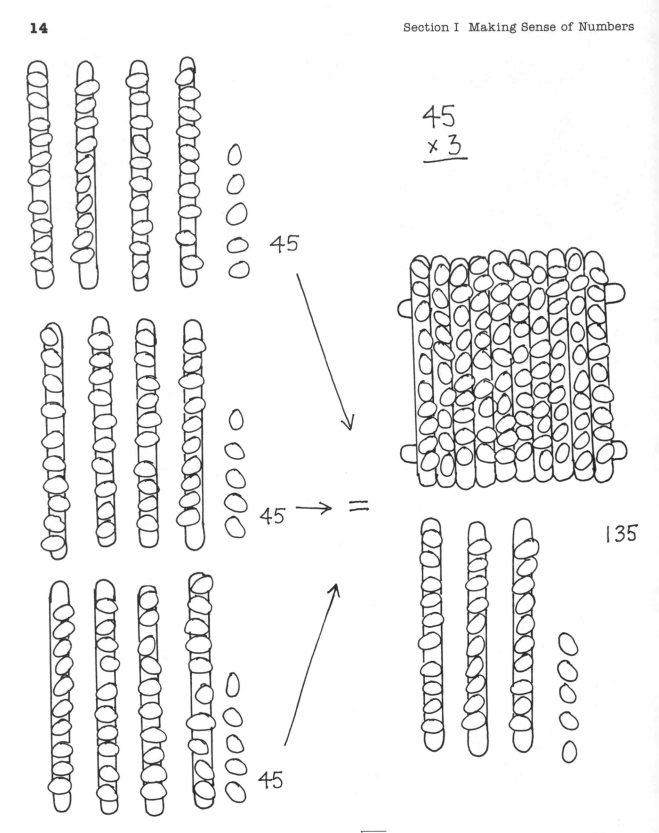

$$45$$
$$\times 3$$

45

45 → =

45

|35

Example 5: A player worked the division problem $27\overline{)123}$ and stated that the answer was 4 with a remainder of 15. When asked to "prove" that the answer was correct, the player used beans and beansticks to show the following. Was 4 groups of 27 beans with a remainder of 15 beans the correct solution?

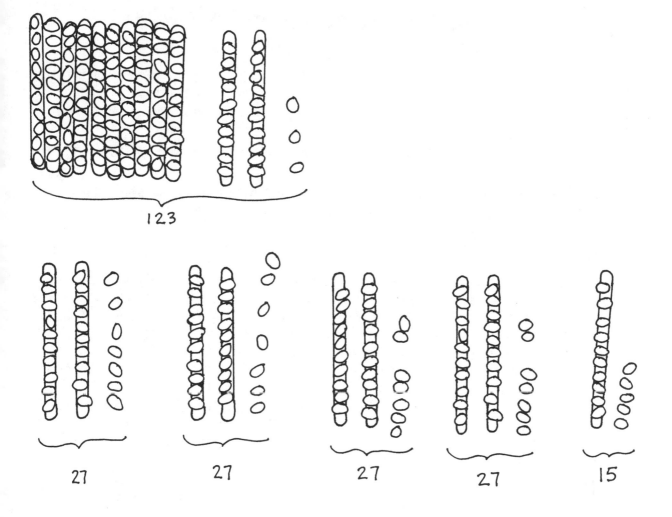

Extensions: Beans and beansticks may also be utilized with both larger and smaller numbers.

1. If numbers into the 1,000's are to be worked with they can be built by stacking the 100's flats. That is, each 1,000 will call for 10 of the 100's flats to be piled together.

2. At times it is also helpful to utilize visual representations for the beanstick problems. For example, the number 253 might be quickly illustrated as follows:

3. Decimals might also be portrayed (in reverse order) with beansticks. For instance, if the 100's flat = 1, then each 10's stick would = .1 and each single bean would represent .01. As such, decimal computations might be displayed in the same manner as those shown in the whole number examples above.

CELEBRATE 100 DAYS

Grades K–5

☒ total group activity
☒ cooperative activity
☒ independent activity

☒ concrete/manipulative
☒ visual/pictorial
☒ abstract procedure

Why Do It: To bring about greater understanding of number and numeral concepts from 1 to 100.

You Will Need: A roll of wide adding machine paper tape; marking pens; 100 straws; rubber bands; and cans with 1, 10 and 100 written on them. For the culmination activity, a wide variety of items that can be counted, separated or marked into 100's will be needed. (*Note:* These items should be free or inexpensive and many can be brought from home.)

How to Do It:

1. Begin the first day of school by taping a long length of paper tape to the classroom wall (perhaps just above the chalkboard and the width of the room). Since this is day 1, write a large numeral **1** at the left end of the tape and tell the students that a numeral will be added (perhaps during the morning opening exercises) for each day they are in school. Continue in this manner until day 5, at which time note that every 5th number will be circled (counting by 5's). Also, on the 10th day, note each 10's number will have a square placed around it; notice that 10, 20, 30, etc., have both circles and squares. This ongoing activity will continue until **Day 100.**

2. Use the 1, 10 and 100 cans together with straws and rubber bands to help students understand the 1-to-1 connection with the numerals on the wall tape. When writing the numeral 1 on the wall chart, have a student put 1 straw in the 1 can; on day 2 put a second straw in the can. When day 10 is reached, put a rubber band around the 10 straws and move then to the 10 can, etc.

3. When **Day 100** is reached, it is time for a celebration! On that day it becomes each student's responsibility to do, make, count, separate, mark, or share 100 of something. It will prove to be a fun learning experience! (See the Extensions below for some possible 100's ideas.)

Example: The illustration below shows the wall tape numerals and the straws in the number cans for the 23rd day of school.

Example: These students are **Celebrating Day 100** by showing 100 in their own ways!

Extensions:

1. Create *Incredible Equations* or do a *Words to Numbers* activity or one for *Calendar Math* that corresponds to the day being considered (these activities are from Section I). Also consider making a *Dot Paper Diagram* or completing a *Computer Paper Edge* activity (from Section II).

2. Have the students each collect 100 aluminum soda cans as part of a class project. Donate the money from such an endeavor to a worthy project, such as the purchase and/or training of a seeing eye dog for a blind person.

PAPER PLATE FRACTIONS

Grades 1–7

☒ total group activity   ☒ concrete/manipulative
☒ cooperative activity   ☒ visual/pictorial
☒ independent activity   ☒ abstract procedure

Why Do It: To provide students with concrete (and visual) exposure to basic fraction concepts. Able students may also have direct experiences with fraction equivalence.

You Will Need: About 200–300 lightweight paper plates (use varied colors if available) will be needed for a class of 30 students. Each student will need six plates plus scissors and a crayon or marking pen.

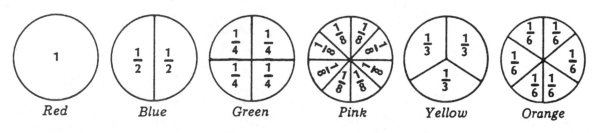

Red   *Blue*   *Green*   *Pink*   *Yellow*   *Orange*

How to Do It:

1. Instruct the students to take a red plate and mark it 1 for one whole amount. Next have them fold or draw a line through the center of the blue plate and use scissors to cut along this line. Ask how many blue parts there are and whether they are equal. Since there are now 2 equal portions, a 2 should be written on each part and then a 1 above each 2 to indicate that each is 1 of 2 equal parts. Note that we commonly call each ½, but this really means 1 of 2 equal parts. Continue this process with each green plate being cut into ¼ths, which means 1 of 4 equal parts; each pink plate into ⅛ths, etc.

2. As students become ready have them use their Paper Plate Fractions to explore equivalence concepts. Initially, direct them to use fraction pieces of the same sizes, match them to the red 1 whole plate, keep records of what they find, and share their findings with the whole group; they will determine that ½ and ½ = 1 and that ¼ + ¼ + ¼ + ¼ = 1, etc. After such explorations with 1 whole, help them to compare fractions to fractions, again by doing physical matches. They will soon discover that ¼ and ¼ make ½, and that ⅛ + ⅛ = ¼, but that ⅙ths and ¼ths don't match up, etc.

3. If students have mastered the concepts noted above, they may be introduced to a game called PUT TOGETHER ONE WHOLE. To play the students will need their paper plate fraction cutouts and a spinner (see below). They will use their red 1 whole paper plate as their individual gameboards and, with each spin, they may choose whether or not to lay the corresponding fractional part on top of the red plate. The object is to put together enough of the proper fractional pieces to equal exactly ONE WHOLE. In the example noted below, the fractions spun so far were ¼, ⅓, ⅛, ½ and ⅙. Player #1 opted not to use ⅓ or ⅙, and Player #2 did not use ⅛ or ½. Thus, in order to exactly equal ONE WHOLE, Player #1 needs ⅛ and Player #2 needs ¼.

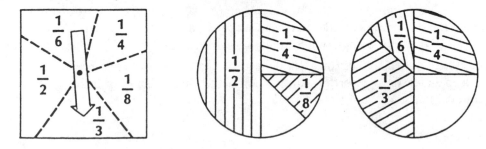

Example: The students shown below are talking about their discoveries with ¼ths and ⅛ths as these fractions relate to 1.

Extensions:

1. The paper plate activity could be expanded to provide experiences with other common fractions such as ⅑, ¹⁄₁₀, ¹⁄₁₂, and ¹⁄₁₆.

2. Advanced students might explore and show the meanings of decimal fractions as .1, .01, and .001. Challenge them, for example, to show whether they would get more to eat if they were to get .2 or .123 of a pizza, etc.

BEAN CUPS TO 1,000

Grades 2–7

☒ total group activity
☒ cooperative activity
☒ independent activity

☒ concrete/manipulative
☒ visual/pictorial
☒ abstract procedure

Why Do It: To experience number and place value concepts in concrete, visual, and abstract formats.

You Will Need: A bag of dried beans (approximately a quart); 100 or more small cups (6-oz. clear plastic are ideal; paper Dixie Cups will work); and a Place Value Workmat approximately 2′ by 4′ in size (sample shown below). If the activity is to be played separately at either abstract or visual levels, cards will also need to be made up (see examples below).

How to Do It:

1. Explain to the students that they will be counting sets of 10 beans and putting them in cups until they reach 1,000 (or more). Begin by spilling a quantity of beans onto the surface beside the Place Value Workmat. Have each player put 10 beans in a cup and place all of their cups in the Tens grid of the Workmat. Continue by counting together by 10's to find the first 100, the second 100, etc.; stack those sets of 10 cups to show 100's and place them in the Hundreds segment of the mat. Keep a "running" record of the numeral value of the beans counted (e.g., when a class of 28 students have each filled a 10's cup the total = 280). Continue in this manner until ten cup stacks of 100 are achieved; then move the ten 100's = 1,000 to the Thousands section of the Place Value Workmat. Note that they are now displaying one group equal to a Thousand and zero groups of Hundreds and Tens and Ones or 1,000. Finally, if player interest continues and more beans are available, the counting and recording may continue.

2. Following the initial group activity for 1,000, the students should regularly work individually or in small groups to show a variety of numbers with bean cups on the Place Value Workmat. At times they should be instructed to build numbers (e.g., 47, 320, 918 or 1,234). In other instances bean numbers may be built by one student and another must determine what the number is and write it in numerals. Additionally, similar visual and abstract level activities are noted in the Extensions below.

Example: The players below have shown the number **1,325** with beans and bean cups.

Extensions:

1. Use two Place Value Workmats and a pair of dice as two teams (or individual players) compete to *Get to 1,000 First.* To start, one team rolls the dice and adds its total, perhaps 5 + 6, and as a result they get to place a 10's cup of beans in the Tens section and 1 bean in the Ones portion. Then the other team takes a turn with the dice and puts the rolled number on its Mat. Each team, at its turn, adds to its previously rolled totals. The first team to get to 1,000 (or any preset number) wins the game.

Pictorial level (option)

2. Advanced players should also make use of visual and abstract level cards to complete the 1,000 activity and any of the other related number and place value options. At these levels it will be necessary to "trade"; that is, when ten of the 1's cards are accumulated they will be traded for one 10 card, and likewise when ten of the 10's cards are amassed they will be traded for one 100 card, etc. For instance, abstract level cards showing 325 are illustrated on the Mat below. Visual (Pictorial level) cards, designed to be utilized in a similar manner, are shown above.

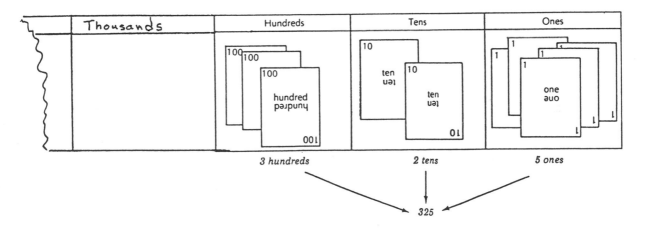

3. Other activities that correlate well are *Beans and Beansticks, Celebrate 100 Days, A Million or More,* plus *Dot Paper Diagrams.*

PLACE VALUE UP, DOWN, OR EQUAL

Grades 3–8

☒ total group activity   ☐ concrete/manipulative
☒ cooperative activity   ☒ visual/pictorial
☐ independent activity   ☒ abstract procedure

Why Do It: To help clarify student understandings of place value, number, and estimation concepts through active involvement.

You Will Need: Initially an overhead projector with pens or a chalkboard and chalk will serve to write the numerals to be considered. To augment discussion and provide further clarification, the hands-on items from the *Beans and Beansticks* activity (noted earlier in this section) and/or overhead Place Value Dots transparency (see master copy) may be helpful.

How to Do It:

1. Explain to the students that a numeral will be displayed and a place value statement(s) will be made about that numeral. If the statement made about the numeral's place value is too high, they are to stand UP; if it is too low, they must sit DOWN; and if it is exactly right, they should use both hands to make an EQUAL sign. When doing so the players may function individually or they may work cooperatively and make group decisions. For example, 47 is displayed and the leader states, "This number has a value of at least seven tens." Since the statement is incorrect and the value stated too large, the players should stand UP.

2. In addition, if the students become confused, it is often wise to use either visual or concrete displays to help clarify the situation. For instance, the example noted above citing 47 might be displayed and discussed by using four of the 10's beansticks and seven loose beans for 47 as compared to seven of the 10's beansticks which shows 70. A similar visual display might also be shown by utilizing Place Value Dot Transparencies.

Example: When shown the number 325 Vicki and Omar both responded correctly to the leader's place value statements about it.

Extensions:

1. For beginners try statements such as 13 has three tens and one one (UP); or 10 straws rubber banded together plus another 10 straws banded together plus 4 loose straws are 24 straws altogether; etc. If there is confusion (and quite frequently there is) be certain to have the students actually construct the numbers with concrete objects like straws and rubber bands or beans and beansticks.

2. Allow the students to use either a transparency or paper copies of the Place Value Dots master (shown on next page) to build and display visuals of the numbers being considered.

3. Advanced students might be challenged to display very large numbers. To do so the dot paper provided with the activity *A Million or More* (located later in this section) may be utilized.

PLACE VALUE DOTS MASTER

Make 5 copies of the pattern for each student set. Cut along the solid lines.

FRACTION COVER-UP OR UN-COVER

Grades 3–8

☐ total group activity   ☒ concrete/manipulative
☒ cooperative activity   ☒ visual/pictorial
☐ independent activity   ☒ abstract procedure

Why Do It: To provide students with conceptual experiences with fractions in a game-like setting.

You Will Need: Begin with a die marked ¼, ⅛, ¹⁄₁₆, ¹⁄₁₆, blank and blank (write on stickers or pieces of tape and stick them to the die); gameboards marked 1 for each player or team (minimum of two players or teams); and several fractional pieces of each size (as shown below). Later, after students have become proficient with this entry-level game, provide gameboards with other shapes or dimensions and/or die with varied fractions, decimals, or even percentage as noted in the Extensions section below.

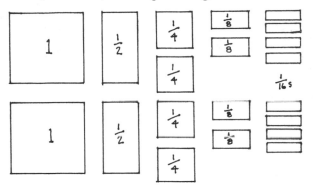

(Use construction paper or tagboard to make Cover-Up or Un-Cover gameboards and fractional pieces such as these. The fraction parts should be labeled and you may wish to make each of the sizes a different color.)

How to Do It:

1. To play *Cover-Up* a pair of players will each need a gameboard. The fractional pieces are placed nearby in a pile from which either may draw depending on their die rolls. They then each roll the die once to see who will begin; the player with the greater fraction starts. Player #1 rolls the die and whatever fraction turns up determines the size of the piece she draws from the pile to cover a portion of her gameboard. In turn, Player #2 rolls the die to find out how much of his gameboard he may cover. Play then continues with Players #1 and #2 alternately taking turns until one of them exactly covers his or her gameboard to equal 1. (*Note:* When rolling the die, if a blank turns up it counts as zero and no piece is put on the gameboard. *Also:* Students may, and probably should, trade in combinations of smaller fraction pieces for larger ones as the game progresses; they might, for example, replace ¹⁄₁₆ plus ¹⁄₁₆ with a ⅛ piece, or ⅛ + ⅛ for ¼, etc.)

2. *Un-Cover* is played in a reverse manner. To do so each player, or team, covers his or her gameboard with the ½, ¼, ⅛, ¹⁄₁₆ and ¹⁄₁₆ pieces. Then with each roll of the die a player may take off a fractional part. Perhaps on his first try Player #1 rolls ⅛; he may remove the ⅛ piece or he might instead take off ¹⁄₁₆ + ¹⁄₁₆. (*Note:* As this game progresses it will be necessary to trade in pieces a number of times. For example, part way through the game, if Player #2 has only the ½ fraction piece on her gameboard and she rolls ¹⁄₁₆, she must first trade in the ½ for ¼ + ⅛ + ¹⁄₁₆ + ¹⁄₁₆ before she can remove ¹⁄₁₆.) The game continues in this manner until one player is able to remove fractional pieces that equal exactly 1.

Example: The students shown below are playing *Cover-Up*. Thus far Justin has rolled ¹⁄₁₆, ¼, and ⅛. Currently Angelica has gotten ¼ + ¼ (which she traded in for ½) and ⅛.

JUSTIN   ANGELICA

Extensions:

1. To expand player understandings, change the shape of the gameboard and/or the fractional pieces. They might have experiences with squares, rectangles, triangles, octagons, circles, etc. A few possibilities are shown below.

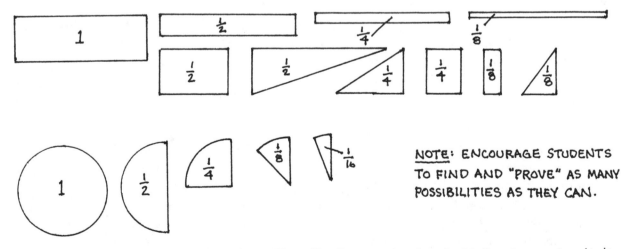

NOTE: ENCOURAGE STUDENTS TO FIND AND "PROVE" AS MANY POSSIBILITIES AS THEY CAN.

2. For players who are quite adept, *Cover-Up* or *Un-Cover* can be played with fractions such as ¹⁄₉, ¹⁄₁₀, ¹⁄₁₂, and ¹⁄₁₆; or even with those like ⅜ and ⁷⁄₁₆. In fact, very able students might be challenged to role two dice at each turn. As such they would be required to add (or subtract) two fractions, such as ¹⁄₁₂ and ⅜, and then determine exactly how much to *Cover-Up* or *Un-Cover*.

3. *Cover-Up* and *Un-Cover* can also be utilized with decimal fractions and/or percentage.

POST-IT™ MENTAL MATH

Grades 3–8

☒ total group activity
☒ cooperative activity
☐ independent activity

☐ concrete/manipulative
☐ visual/pictorial
☒ abstract procedure

Why Do It: To enhance mental math skills, stimulate logical thinking, and act out the associated computations.

You Will Need: Large size Post-it™ Notes (or index cards and masking tape) and a marking pen.

How to Do It:

1. Explain to the students that a numeral will be written on each of two Post-it™ Notes and placed on the back of a chosen Post-it™ player without him/her being allowed to see them. The chosen player must then turn her/his back to the other group members, so that they may see the two written numerals, and then turn to face the group again. A leader then calls for the group members to physically act out computations related to the two Post-it™ numerals. It now becomes the job of the Post-it™ player to mentally determine and state which numerals are posted on her/his back.

2. Assume that the two numerals are 4 and 9. The leader might call on the group members to do sit-ups to show the difference between the numerals and to count 1, 2, 3, 4, 5 in unison as they do so. The Post-it™ player is then allowed one guess as to what the numerals on his/her back are. If the response given is correct, the round is over and a new Post-it™ player is chosen; if not, the leader calls for another computation activity with the same two numerals. For example, the leader might call for the group members to show the product of the numbers by running in place and counting in unison 1, 2, 3 . . . 36 for each time their left foot touches the ground. This round might even continue by acting out the sum of the two numerals and/or the quotient. If the Post-it™ player is able to guess the correct numerals after one or two tries she/he gets to select the new Post-it™ player; if not, the leader makes the selection.

Example: The group members shown above have just completed 5 sit-ups as a subtraction computation clue to which single-digit numerals are on the Post-it™ player's back. The Post-it™ player is now making a first guess as to what the two numerals might be.

Extensions:

1. Beginners might work with a single numeral and just practice acting out that number value. Later they might play *One More* where the acted out number value is one more than the number on the Post-it™ player's back; as such, if the group members complete 6 hops, the Post-it™ player must respond 5 to be correct (other options include *One Less, Two More,* etc.).

2. Advanced players might work with three single-digit numerals on the Post-it™ player's back. If the chosen numerals are 4, 6, and 9, for example, the group players might be asked to subtract the smallest number from the largest and add the remaining number ($9 - 4 + 6 = 11$) and act out the answer; or they might multiply the largest by the smallest and then divide by the middle size number ($4 \times 9 \div 6 = 6$), etc.

DRAWING FRACTION COMMON DENOMINATORS

Grades 3–8

☒ total group activity
☒ cooperative activity
☒ independent activity

☒ concrete/manipulative
☒ visual/pictorial
☒ abstract procedure

Why Do It: To gain a visual perspective of what a common denominator is and why it is used.

How to Do It: Use graph paper or draw your own grid to show fraction common denominators. The "secret" is to use the denominator (bottom) numbers in any pair of fractions and to draw a rectangle that is the length of one and the width of the other. For example, if the fractions are $\frac{1}{3}$ and $\frac{1}{4}$, then draw a rectangle that is 3 by 4, which shows 12 square units. See Example 1 below.

Example 1: For $\frac{1}{3} + \frac{1}{4} =$ _?_ draw rectangles that are 3 by 4 = 12 units. Then shade in $\frac{1}{3}$ of the total which is $\frac{4}{12}$; and $\frac{1}{4}$ which is $\frac{3}{12}$. Next move the $\frac{4}{12}$ and the $\frac{3}{12}$ onto a single rectangular grid for a total of $\frac{7}{12}$. (*Note:* When you move the $\frac{4}{12}$ and the $\frac{3}{12}$ onto one grid it is necessary to reposition some of the $\frac{1}{12}$ pieces so they do not overlap.)

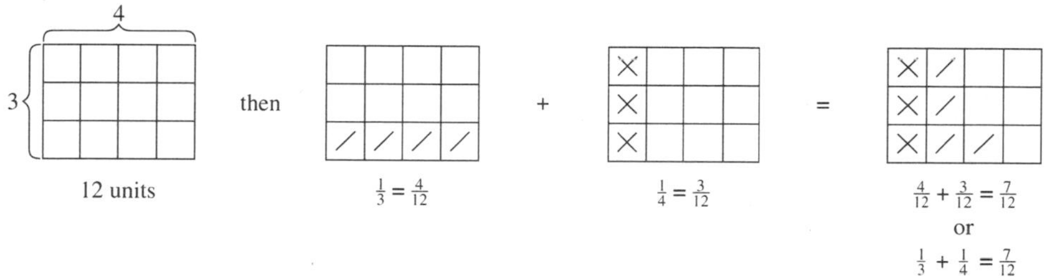

Example 2: Now try a slightly harder problem. For $\frac{1}{6} + \frac{2}{3} =$ _?_ draw a rectangle that is 6 × 3 = 18. Shade in $\frac{1}{6}$ which is $\frac{3}{18}$; and $\frac{2}{3}$ which is $\frac{12}{18}$. Combine these to get $\frac{15}{18}$, which is correct, but not in lowest terms.

To reduce the $\frac{15}{18}$ to lowest terms look for ways to group units; in this case both the 15 and the 18 can be grouped into 3's. As such, draw loops to show the 15 as 5 groups of 3 and the 18 (the entire rectangular grid) as 6 groups of 3. Thus, 5 of the 6 loops are marked. Therefore, $\frac{15}{18}$ can be renamed (reduced to) $\frac{5}{6}$.

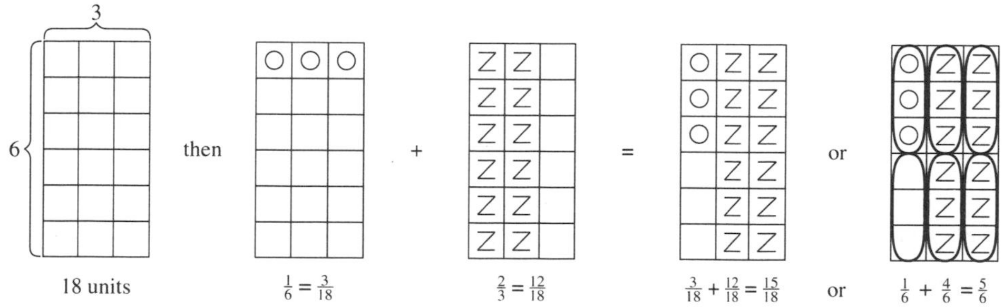

Extensions:

1. Draw diagrams for $\frac{1}{2} + \frac{1}{3} =$ _?_.
2. Show $\frac{2}{5} + \frac{1}{2} =$ _?_.
3. Show $\frac{1}{2} + \frac{1}{6} =$ _?_ in lowest terms. (*Hint:* Use groups of 4.)
4. Show $\frac{1}{4} + \frac{1}{6} =$ _?_ in lowest terms.
5. Try several problems of your own or "prove" the results to some assigned fraction problems.

CALENDAR MATH

Grades 3–8

☒ total group activity   ☐ concrete/manipulative
☒ cooperative activity   ☐ visual/pictorial
☒ independent activity   ☒ abstract procedure

Why Do It: To practice a variety of computational skills and to discover interesting patterns.

You Will Need: A calendar page for each player or group of players (or players can write their own on a grid like the one below); pencil and paper; and colored pencils or crayons.

How to Do It: Get a calendar page or make one of your own. Find out how many days are in this month. If you are making your own calendar page, number it beginning with the first day as 1 and ending with the last as 28, 29, 30, or 31. Then do some investigating starting with the questions in the Extensions section, and then see what more you can discover on your own. Share your findings with some other players.

Sunday	Monday	Tuesday	Wednesday	Thursday	Friday	Saturday

Extensions:

1. Add the dates for the first two Tuesdays together and get _____ .

2. Subtract the date for the second Friday from the third and get _____ .

3. All of the Monday dates added together equal _____ .

4. Subtract the first Wednesday from the third Thursday and you get _____ .

5. Multiply the date of the second Wednesday by that of the third Wednesday and get _____ .

6. Color some patterns on your calendar. For example, count off by 2's (2, 4, 6, 8, etc.) and share the pattern found. Use a different color and mark in the multiples of 3. Were any of the numbers marked as both 2's and 3's? Why did that happen? Try coloring in some other number multiples and share what happens.

7. Play *Corner to Corner* with 1, 2, or 3 players. You will need a large calendar page, different colored markers, and about 40 small cards marked as here.

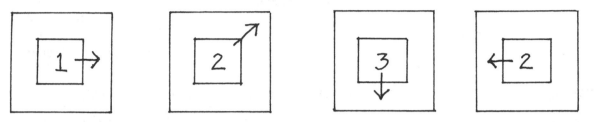

(Move 1 space right)   (Move 2 spaces diagonally)   (Move down 3 spaces)   (Move left 2 spaces)

Shuffle the cards and pile them upside down next to the calendar page. Have each player put his/her marker on a calendar corner number. Also decide who will go 1st, 2nd, etc. Then as turns are taken each player will select one of the cards and devise and solve a math problem using those two calendar numbers. For example, on the calendar shown below Ryan's red marker is on the 5 and the card he drew indicated that he must move down two spaces to the 19. He then needs to decide on a math problem using those numbers; perhaps $19 - 5 = 14$. If the other players agree that he is correct, Ryan gets to move his marker to the 19. Play continues in this manner. The first player to reach the corner opposite his/her starting place is the winner.

NUMBERS TO WORDS TO NUMBERS

Grades 3–8

☒ total group activity	☐ concrete/manipulative
☒ cooperative activity	☐ visual/pictorial
☒ independent activity	☒ abstract procedure

Why Do It: To practice writing numbers as numerals and as words and to compare accuracy with an interesting activity.

You Will Need: At the onset the leader will use the chalkboard and chalk or an overhead projector and pens; the players need pencil and paper.

How to Do It:

1. At the onset the *Numbers to Words to Numbers* activity should be played by the entire group. Begin by asking the players to select a number. Once decided, everyone should write it in numeral form on their papers and underline it; the leader should do the same on the chalkboard (see Example 1 where 63 was chosen). Next, write that number as a word. Count the letters in that word and write the word for the "new" number. Continue this procedure until the number word "four" continually repeats.

2. Further formats for utilizing these procedures with young students, in groups and/or with advanced players are cited in the Extensions below.

Example 1: The number chosen is 63.

1. Number picked: **63**
2. Written form: sixty three
3. Counted letters: 10
4. Written form: ten
5. Counted letters: 3
6. Written form: three
7. Counted letters: 5
8. Written form: five
9. Counted letters: 4
10. Written form: four ←(NOTE: About here
11. Counted letters: 4   the players will real-
                                    ize that 4 will con-
12. Written form: four   tinue to repeat.)

Example 2: The number chosen is 57.

1. Number picked: **57**
2. Written form: fifty seven
3. Counted letters: 20
4. Written form: twenty
5. Counted letters: 6
6. Written form: six
7. Counted letters: 3
8. Written form: three
9. Counted letters: 5
10. Written form: four (repeat)
11. Counted letters: 4
12. Written form: four (repeat)

Example 3: In this situation an error was made by one of the players when spelling the number word. Notice how the compared *Number to Word to Number* outcome sequences vary! The number chosen was 45. *Which player made the error?*

Player A

1. Number picked: **45**
2. Written form: fourty five
3. Counted letters: 10
4. Written form: ten
5. Counted letters: 3
6. Written form: three
7. Counted letters: 5
8. Written form: five
9. Counted letters: 4
10. Written form: four

Player B

1. Number picked: **45**
2. Written form: forty five
3. Counted letters: 9
4. Written form: nine
5. Counted letters: 4
6. Written form: four

Extensions: Utilize the *Numbers to Words to Numbers* process for practice in several formats and at a variety of academic levels.

1. Primary students might practice with numbers no more than 20. They may also need to follow the leader a number of times as he or she works through this process, at the chalkboard, or on the overhead projector.

2. When familiar with the procedure, the players may practice and check their work in pairs (or in cooperative groups). That is, each individual (or group) will work independently with the selected number and then compare outcomes.

3. Advanced players might try more complex numbers. For instance, try 1,672,431 which in written form is one million six hundred seventy two thousand four hundred thirty one. (*Hint:* Remember to use "and" only to denote a decimal point.)

LET'S HAVE ORDER

Grades 2–8

☒ total group activity
☒ cooperative activity
☐ independent activity

☐ concrete/manipulative
☐ visual/pictorial
☒ abstract procedure

Why Do It: To reinforce place value number order concepts.

You Will Need: A set of large numeral cards 0 through 9 for each team. (If duplicate digits are to be included, several copies of each numeral card will be needed.)

How to Do It: Form teams with ten players. Pass out the numeral cards (or have players make their own) and put one person in charge of each. Also designate locations where each team's numeral-carrying players are to report and display their "ordered numbers" (chalkboard locations marked One, Ten, Hundred, etc., work well). To begin, the leader calls out a number, perhaps 402, and then, after the teams have held a brief conference, says "Let's Have Order!" The team members with the needed numerals then move directly to their teams' designated location and display the numeral cards in proper order. Each team displaying 4 in the Hundred position, 0 with the Ten, and 2 in the One location score 3 points (1 point for each numeral in a proper position). If greater competition is desired, the scoring might also provide a bonus point for the team that first displays the proper answer.

Example: The number called out for these teams is four hundred two.

Extensions:

1. Young player responses might be limited to numbers with two (or three) digits.

2. Call out numbers in place value terms only and have the players show the numerals and state the "standard" number names. The leader, for example, might call for five thousands, six hundreds, three tens, and zero ones.

3. If numbers with duplicate numerals are called out, allow the player in charge of that numeral to decide whether he can "reach" far enough. That is, for a number like 303 the player in charge of 3's could stand behind the 0's player and "reach" a 3 out to either side of her. However, for a number like 25,432 the 2's player would need to put another team member in charge of one of the 2's.

4. Ask advanced players to deal with large-number numbers, perhaps into the billions or more. For example, how might three hundred twenty billion ninety one million sixty two thousand seven be shown?   (320,091,062,007)

REJECT A DIGIT

Grades 3–8

☒ total group activity   ☐ concrete/manipulative
☒ cooperative activity   ☐ visual/pictorial
☐ independent activity   ☒ abstract procedure

Why Do It: To provide logical thinking experiences with place value concepts as they relate to computation situations.

You Will Need: A spinner with the numbers 0 through 9 (an easily made paper clip spinner is described in *Spin Your Own Homework*) for each group of players; plus pencils and paper.

How to Do It:

1. When first introducing *Reject a Digit* you might have the players attempt to get the largest (or smallest) numeral. To do so they first need to draw digit boxes and a reject box (see example) on their individual record-keeping pages (or duplicated copies may be provided). In the example shown below, the students are each attempting to get the largest numeral containing 1's, 10's, 100's, and 1,000's. The rules they follow are: (1) Each time the spinner stops all players are required to write the number that comes up in a digit box or in the reject box; (2) Only one numeral can be written in the reject box; (3) Once a numeral is written it cannot be moved; (4) The spinner is spun once more than the number of digit boxes, which allows one rejection.

2. Once players are familiar with the basic procedure, *Reject a Digit* may be played in a wide variety of computation situations (see the Extensions for suggestions). However, what is equally important are the ensuing discussions of player findings. Allow the students to comment on what happened, what worked or did not work, why they think a certain outcome resulted, what might have been done differently, how a change in rules might affect the outcomes, etc. In this way the players will gain experience not only with place value and computation concepts, but also with logical thinking.

Example: In this game of *Reject a Digit* the students had each been trying to get the largest numeral. The spinner stopped in succession on 8, 4, 9, 3, and 2. Dan won, of course, but the discussion to follow is likely more important; of concern might be what numbers were achieved, why a number was put in a certain place-value location or rejected, etc. (*Note:* It appears that each of these students chose logically, but some luck was also involved. Can you envision why the students placed the numbers as they did?)

Extensions:

1. Play the activity for addition, subtraction, multiplication, or division. In each of the situations below it is necessary to spin six numerals; five are to be placed in digit boxes and one is to be rejected. Then, in each situation the computation must be completed for the largest or smallest answer or the one nearest to a target number.

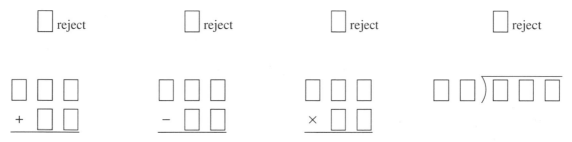

2. Spin a selected number of digits (perhaps four) and challenge the players to devise all possible problems of a certain type (as addition) with them. For example, if the numbers happen to be 1, 2, 3, and 4, some possible arrangements might include:

1	12	31	43	1	123	etc.
2	+34	+42	+21	23	+ 4	
3				+4		
+4						

3. Calculators may prove helpful, especially for problems with large numbers of digits. Also, for able players, consider problems with more than 8 digits (most calculators have only an 8-digit display).

A MILLION OR MORE

Grades 4–8

☒ total group activity   ☐ concrete/manipulative
☒ cooperative activity   ☒ visual/pictorial
☐ independent activity   ☒ abstract procedure

Why Do It: To obtain a visual concept of how many a million is and to further develop place value concepts of how many thousands and hundreds are in a million.

You Will Need: Dot paper sets for 10,000 (master on page 40), 1,000, and 100, plus possibly 10 and/or 1 (it is sometimes easier to have the players draw 1 and 10 dot amounts with their pencils).

How to Do It:

1. Begin by examining and comparing 1 dot, a 10-dot strip, and a 100-dot square. Then bring out the 1,000-dot strips and ask how many of the 100-dot squares would make the same amount; how many of the 10's strips? Make the same types of comparisons with a 10,000-dot page. Now have the players figure out how many of the 10,000-dot pages it will take to make a million. Once they have determined the number of pages needed, have them "make" a million by posting 100 such pages side by side on a large bulletin board (if possible, the best arrangement is as a single row) or on butcher paper.

2. Once the Million Bulletin Board is in place, have the players find exact dot locations for numbers between 1 and 1,000,000. When doing so be certain to establish a precise counting/location procedure; it is suggested that the players always begin at the lower left-hand corner and count up to 10, then go to the bottom of the next column and proceed from 11–20, etc., until the first 100's dot square has been completed. If the number being sought is more than 100, the player may count squares of 100 from the bottom up. Also, each full column = 1,000 and each full page = 10,000.

Example: The dot diagram at the left displays the number 1,234.

Extensions: Once the players have grasped the basic number and place value concepts for numbers up to *A Million or More,* it is fun to extend those ideas to everyday life experiences.

1. A whole class activity, or even one for the entire school, is to have the players bring "statistics" and place them on the Million Bulletin Board. That is, they must clip a "statistic" (number data) between 1 and 1,000,000 from a newspaper or magazine, or obtain such information from radio or television and bring it to school. The data clipping must then be glued to an index card or, if gotten from radio or TV, transcribed and written on an index card together with the inscription LOCATED BY (STUDENT'S NAME). Then place the information card on the bulletin board and use push pins and yarn to connect it with the exact dot. For instance, they might bring data that shows an automobile priced at $19,995 or the average price of a home in a certain area to be $189,623 or a typical teacher salary to be ???

2. Include space on the Million Bulletin Board (likely to the far right) for a *More Than a Million* category. In it the students can place data cards with items like the number of albums sold by popular music stars or the salaries of some professional athletes, etc.

3. Also included on the Million Dot Board (likely to the far left at the bottom) might be a category *Less Than One.* In it would be data relating to fractions or decimals between 0 and 1 (e.g., a ½ price sale, a soda can contains .354 liters) or even negative numbers (e.g., it was −20 degrees F. in Alaska).

10,000 DOTS

SMALLEST AND LARGEST

Grades 4–8

☒ total group activity   ☐ concrete/manipulative
☒ cooperative activity   ☐ visual/pictorial
☒ independent activity   ☒ abstract procedure

Why Do It: To enhance estimation understandings, mental math skills, logical thinking, and to provide computation practice.

You Will Need: Number charts, such as the one shown on page 42 (see master copies) need to be duplicated for the players. However, if played as a group activity, a single copy of the appropriate chart displayed with an overhead projector or on the chalkboard will suffice.

How to Do It: When first introducing a *Smallest and Largest* chart activity, the leader should note any game rules, demonstrate how to complete one or two problems, and discuss reasonable estimates, mental math procedures, why certain numbers were chosen, etc. For instance, in the Example below, zeroes were allowed, but not in the first digit of a number. After completing an easy problem and a more difficult one together, the players should individually, or in small groups, try a problem on their own. The procedures used and the solutions decided upon should be discussed and brief notes should be recorded. Finally, when the players have successfully completed the listed problem situation, they should devise some of their own, record their findings (in the rows at the end of the chart), and share their procedures and outcomes with the entire group.

Example: Two of the problem situations on this ADDITION *Smallest and Largest* chart have been dealt with. Most players were able to master the problem situation in the first row quite easily, but the second problem required more analysis for varied reasons (e.g., some players thought, when seeking the smallest sum, that the first number should be 111 and the second 1,111). The discussion which followed was, perhaps, the most important aspect of the activity.

ADDITION—SMALLEST AND LARGEST

Number of digits in first number	Number of digits in second number	Estimated smallest sum	Actual smallest sum (show work)	Estimated largest sum	Actual largest sum (show work)	My notes
1	1	2	1 +1 2	18	9 +9 18	*My partner and I agree.*
2	2					
2	3					
3	3					
3	4	1200	100 +1000 1100	11,000	999 +9,999 10,998	*At first I forgot about using zero.*

Extensions:

1. Play the activity for subtraction. Unless the players are to deal with negative answers, be certain that the first number has more (or larger) digits than the second.

2. To avoid confusion when working with division, designate the first number as the dividend and the second as the divisor.

3. The activity might be made more challenging by restricting the digits to be utilized (e.g., in certain cases only 6's, 7's, and 8's might be allowed).

4. Calculators may prove helpful, especially for problems with large numbers of digits. Also, for able players, consider problems with more than 8 digits (most calculators have only an 8-digit display).

ADDITION—SMALLEST AND LARGEST

Number of digits in first number	Number of digits in second number	Estimated smallest sum	Actual smallest sum (show work)	Estimated largest sum	Actual largest sum (show work)	My notes
1	1					
2	2					
2	3					
3	3					
3	4					

SUBTRACTION—SMALLEST AND LARGEST

Number of digits in first number	Number of digits in second number	Estimated smallest difference	Actual smallest difference (show work)	Estimated largest difference	Actual largest difference (show work)	My notes
2	1					
3	2					
4	2					
4	3					
5	4					

MULTIPLICATION—SMALLEST AND LARGEST

Number of digits in first number	Number of digits in second number	Estimated smallest product	Actual smallest product (show work)	Estimated largest product	Actual largest product (show work)	My notes
1	1					
2	2					
3	2					
3	3					
4	3					

DIVISION—SMALLEST AND LARGEST

Number of digits in dividend	Number of digits in divisor	Estimated smallest quotient	Actual smallest quotient (show work)	Estimated largest quotient	Actual largest quotient (show work)	My notes
2	1					
3	1					
3	2					
4	2					
4	3					

SLICED CHEESE FRACTIONS AND DECIMALS

Grades 4–8

☒	total group activity	☒	concrete/manipulative
☒	cooperative activity	☒	visual/pictorial
☒	independent activity	☒	abstract procedure

Why Do It: To provide an interesting hands-on activity that will help players clarify fraction and decimal concepts.

You Will Need: A supply of sliced cheese; wax paper; and table knives. If you don't have cheese, you may instead utilize the diagrams on the following page (or graph paper) together with pencils or crayons and scissors.

How to Do It: Use a clean knife and cut a piece of sliced cheese into decimals or fractions as asked in the Questions and Extensions section below. Be sure to wash your hands and cut onto a piece of waxed paper if you wish to eat your fractions and decimals when finished.

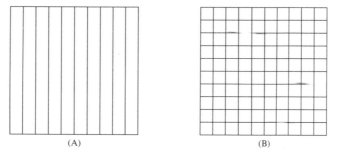

(A)   (B)

Questions and Extensions: Cut up cheese slices to find solutions to these questions. Check your solutions with the answers noted below.

1. Cut a cheese slice into 10 equal strips as shown in Figure A above. One of your strips is what fraction of the whole slice? What is the decimal name for the same cheese strip?

2. How many of your cheese strips make up half of the total slice? This fraction could be called ½ or _?_/10? What is the decimal name for the same amount of cheese?

3. Now make 10 opposite cuts in your cheese slice so that it looks like Figure B. How many small cheese squares do you have? What is the fractional name for each? The decimal name? How many of the small squares are the same as one strip? Therefore, the fraction for one cheese strip could be written as _?_ or _?_ or in decimals as _?_ or _?_.

4. Count out 25 of the small squares. What is its decimal name? The same 25 small squares would have the fraction names of _?_ or _?_. Next, if you count out 40 small squares, the decimal names would be _?_ or _?_ and fraction names for them would be _?_ or _?_ or _?_.

5. Compare and then eat .01, .1 and .14 of your cheese slice. Altogether you just ate the decimal _?_ or fraction _?_ of your cheese slice. Now compare .35 and ²/10 and tell exactly how much larger one is than the other. Eat these amounts also. The amount remaining has the decimal name _?_ or the fraction name _?_.

SLICED CHEESE ANSWERS: (1) ¹/10; .1   (2) 5 strips = half of the slice; ⁵/10; .5   (3) 100 small cheese squares = ¹/100 = .01; 10 small squares = 1 strip, ¹⁰/100 or ¹/10 = .1 or .10   (4) .25 = ²⁵/100 or ¼; .40 or .4, ⁴⁰/100 or ⁴/10 or ²/5   (5) .25 or ¼; .35 − .20 = .15; .20 or ¹/5.

WORKMAT FOR *SLICED CHEESE FRACTIONS AND DECIMALS*

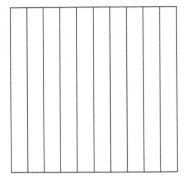
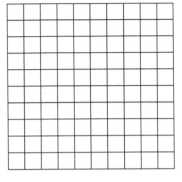

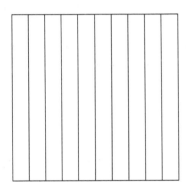
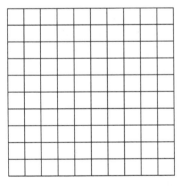

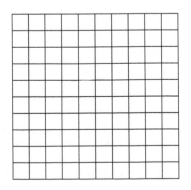

TARGET A NUMBER

Grades 4–8

☒ total group activity
☒ cooperative activity
☒ independent activity

☐ concrete/manipulative
☐ visual/pictorial
☒ abstract procedure

Why Do It: To jointly reinforce place value understandings and computation skills. Reasoning and communication skills will also be enhanced.

How to Do It:

1. Begin by selecting geometric shapes, perhaps ○, □, △, and ◇ at the start. Also decide which operation will be used (+, −, ×, ÷). Each player then decides individually where to place his or her shapes within an arrangement specified by the leader (see the Example below). Then select a Target Number and begin play.

2. To begin, the leader notes the first shape to be considered and rolls a die (or uses a spinner) to determine the number to be placed in that shape. Play continues in the same manner for the remaining shapes. When all of the shapes are numbered, the players use the specified operation and complete their computations. As a group, discuss the varied problems and solutions found. The player(s) achieving the Target Number, or being the closest to it, wins the round.

Example: 3 − ○, 1 = □, 4 = △, and 6 = ◇. The preceding numbers were rolled in order and matched with the specified shapes. The Target Number was **850** and the operations was **×**. The problems and solutions determined by three different players are shown below. Who won this round?

Extensions:

1. Use only a few geometric shapes and/or limit the operations (perhaps only + or −) if you wish the *Target a Number* games to be quite easy. For more complex games increase the number of shapes utilized.

2. Allow the students to save the numbers until all have been rolled. Then let them individually arrange their numbers to see if they can "hit" the target number!

3. Have the players place their numbers as rolled, but allow them to +, −, ×, or ÷ as an individual choice.

4. Use the *Target a Number* procedure with fraction operations as $\dfrac{○}{□} \times \dfrac{⬡}{△} =$

5. Try using parentheses and brackets such as ○△ + (□ × ◇) − (△ ÷ ○) =

FRACTION × AND ÷ DIAGRAMS

Grades 4–8

☒ total group activity   ☐ concrete/manipulative
☒ cooperative activity   ☒ visual/pictorial
☒ independent activity   ☒ abstract procedure

Why Do It: To help students gain a visual perspective of what happens when fractions are multiplied and divided.

You Will Need: Obtain a supply of graph paper (or make duplicate copies from the *Number Cutouts* activity found earlier in this section) and distribute two or three sheets to each student. Colored pencils are optional, but will help to make the student diagrams more appealing. Furthermore, for initial instruction, you may wish to utilize large demonstration size graph paper or an overhead projector transparency grid and colored pens.

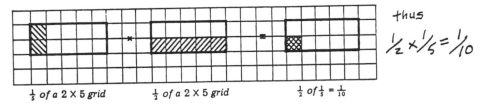

thus
$$\tfrac{1}{2} \times \tfrac{1}{5} = \tfrac{1}{10}$$

$\tfrac{1}{5}$ of a 2 × 5 grid $\tfrac{1}{2}$ of a 2 × 5 grid $\tfrac{1}{2}$ of $\tfrac{1}{5} = \tfrac{1}{10}$

How to Do It:

1. Use the large graph paper or an overhead transparency grid and pens to work through several problems with the students. For example, with the problem $\tfrac{1}{2} \times \tfrac{1}{5} =$ _____ (illustrated above), begin by helping the students to understand that, since the denominators are 2 and 5, they will need to utilize a 2 by 5 grid. Then mark a column of $\tfrac{1}{5}$ and a row of $\tfrac{1}{2}$ and note, where they overlap, that $\tfrac{1}{2}$ of the $\tfrac{1}{5}$ portion equals 1 out of the 10 grid spaces. Thus, it has been shown that $\tfrac{1}{2} \times \tfrac{1}{5} = \underline{\tfrac{1}{10}}$. (*Note:* Some students find it helpful to think of this situation as $\tfrac{1}{2}$ of $\tfrac{1}{5} = \tfrac{1}{10}$.)

2. A similar process is followed when dividing a fraction by a fraction. The students in the example below are dealing with the problem $\tfrac{1}{4} \div \tfrac{1}{3} =$ _____ . Notice, particularly, their thoughts about the division process. Finally, the slightly more complex issue of multiplying (or dividing) a mixed number by a mixed number is illustrated in the Extensions section.

Example: These students are working cooperatively on drawing a diagram for ¼ ÷ ⅓ = _____.
Their thinking, including a "nice" application, is noted above.

Extensions: When ready, students might be asked to visualize and diagram mixed number situations
such as those that follow.

1. The problem $1\frac{1}{3} \times 2\frac{1}{4}$ = _____ might be dealt with as:

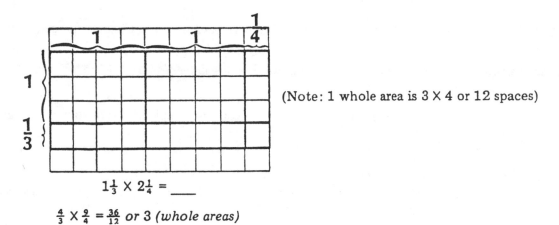

(Note: 1 whole area is 3 × 4 or 12 spaces)

$$1\tfrac{1}{3} \times 2\tfrac{1}{4} = \underline{\quad}$$

$$\tfrac{4}{3} \times \tfrac{9}{4} = \tfrac{36}{12} \text{ or } 3 \text{ (whole areas)}$$

2. However, the same numerals utilized in a division setting yield quite a different result. In this situation $1\frac{1}{3} \div 2\frac{1}{4}$ = _____ might be illustrated as:

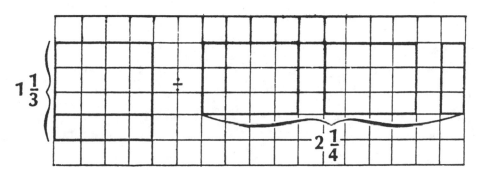

$$(16 \text{ squares}) \div (27 \text{ squares}) = \tfrac{16}{27}$$

or

$$1\tfrac{1}{3} \quad \div \quad 2\tfrac{1}{4} \quad =$$

$$\tfrac{4}{3} \quad \div \quad \tfrac{9}{4} \quad =$$

$$\tfrac{4}{3} \quad \times \quad \tfrac{4}{9} \quad = \tfrac{16}{27}$$

FRACTION CODES

Grades 4–8

☒ total group activity	☐ concrete/manipulative
☒ cooperative activity	☒ visual/pictorial
☒ independent activity	☒ abstract procedure

Why Do It: To provide students with conceptual experiences with fractions (or percents or decimals) in a code setting.

You Will Need: A prepared Fraction Code Message and pencils or pens.

How to Do It: The first time *Fraction Code* is attempted provide the players with a prepared code message (see Example) that they must solve. They may work independently or in cooperative groups as they try to determine the message from clues such as use the first ⅓ of the word *frenzy*, the first ⅜ of *actually*, and the last ½ of mo*tion* to form a word (fr + act + ion = fraction). After working with several sample coded messages they may devise some of their own (see Extensions).

Example: The players might be asked to solve the Fractions and Smiles code below. A portion is already solved. Can you decode the rest of the message?

Fractions and Smiles

Last ½ of take	_ke_	First ¼ of opposite	_____
Last ⅖ of sleep	_ep_	Last ⅓ of stable	_____
First ⅗ of smirk	_____	First ⅔ of wonderful	_____
First ¼ of leap	_____	First ⅗ of whale	_____
Last ⅗ of being	_____	Last ⅕ of generosity	_____
First ½ of item	_____	First ⅖ of ought	_____
First ⅓ of matter	_____	Last ¾ of care	_____
First ¼ of keep	_____	First ⅓ of use	_____
First ⅕ of especially	_____	Last ⅓ of abrupt	_____
First ⅒ of perimeters	_____	Last ½ of do	_____
First ⅒ of equivalent	_____		

The message is: _Keep (smiling it makes people wonder what you are up to)_

Extensions:

1. To expand player understandings, devise coded messages that must be solved using percentages (or decimals). For example, they might determine a breakfast food from clues such as: use the first 50% of the word *chip*, the middle 33⅓% of *cheese*, the final 25% of *poor*, the first 40% of *ionic*, and the first 25% of *step* (ch + ee + r + io + s = Cheerios®).

2. If able, challenge the students to devise their own Fraction (or decimal) Codes. As an alternative, they might be allowed to deal with spelling or vocabulary words in this manner.

COMPARING FRACTIONS, DECIMALS, %, ETC.

Grades 4–8

☒ total group activity
☒ cooperative activity
☐ independent activity

☒ concrete/manipulative
☒ visual/pictorial
☒ abstract procedure

Why Do It: To help students understand concepts and compare the relationships between fractions, division, decimals, percents and a variety of applications of each.

You Will Need: A large roll of paper (2 to 3 ft. wide and perhaps as long as the classroom); marking pens of different colors; a yard or meter stick; string; scissors; glue; and magazines that may be cut up.

How to Do It:

1. To begin roll out several feet of the paper on a flat surface. Have the students use the pens and yard stick to draw several vertical number lines about a foot apart (see Example below). On the first number line have them determine and mark in the fractions that they are familiar with; at this juncture cut a piece of string the length of the number line and have the students fold it in half to help locate and mark the ½ position, in fourths to determine ¼, ²⁄₄, ¾, etc. Though it may get a bit "cluttered," have the students position and mark on the number line as many fractions as possible. Also, be certain to discuss the meaning of each fraction and its relative position; deal especially with queries such as why ⅝ is between ½ and ¾ on the number line.

2. On the second number line have the "division meaning" for each of the listed fractions written directly across from it. For example, ¾ can be read as 3 divided by 4 and written as $4\overline{)3}$. Then, on the third number line, have the students compute (a calculator might be used) and list the related "division meaning" which is, of course, the corresponding decimal.

3. The fourth number line might be used to make comparisons to cents (¢) in a dollar. Using ¾ as an example again, ¾ of a dollar can be written as $.75 (except for the $ sign, this is the "division meaning" or decimal). In relation to the fifth number line ask, "How many ¢ are there in one dollar? If ¾ of a dollar is 75¢, how might this be written in terms of 100¢?" The response, of course, should be recorded as 75/100. This leads naturally to a sixth number line where percent (meaning per 100) can be derived; as such, the 75/100 translates easily to 75%.

4. A seventh number line might deal with practical applications as the fraction or decimal or % of some whole thing. For example, a picture of ¾ pizza, or .75 pizza, or 75% of a pizza might be cut out of a magazine and pasted onto the number line. An eighth number line might portray a fraction or decimal or percentage of a group situation. To illustrate, if a picture of 8 elephants were pictured, the students might draw a fence around 6 of them to show ¾ or .75 or 75% of the elephant herd.

5. Subsequent number lines should be drawn and marked based on student interests and/or the need to develop concepts further. Of course, each of the number lines should, in time, be fully marked in to correspond with each of the fractions listed. As such, this may be a project that continues for some time. In fact, if "new" information becomes available to the students, they should be allowed to add it to existing number lines or to insert more of them. As such, it is suggested that the resulting Fraction/Decimal/Percent/Applications Chart (plus some blank space for additions) be taped to the wall to allow for continued work. (*Note:* These charts have often been placed above chalk- or bulletin boards and the students have been allowed to use a step ladder to add items, mark in new findings, etc.)

Example: These students are working cooperatively to mark in portions of their FRACTION/
DECIMAL/PERCENT/APPLICATIONS CHART. Often comments, like those the students have made
above, are very helpful in determining their "true" levels of understanding.

NUMBER POWER WALKS

Grades 4–8

☒ total group activity   ☒ concrete/manipulative
☒ cooperative activity   ☒ visual/pictorial
☐ independent activity   ☒ abstract procedure

Why Do It: To physically act out and conceptualize the powers of numbers.

You Will Need: No equipment is required, unless precise measurements are desired; then measuring devices such as yard (or meter) sticks, long tapes and/or trundle wheels plus chalk can be utilized.

How to Do It:

1. Be certain that the players understand that a *power* of a number is the product obtained by multiplying the number by itself a given number of times. For example, to *square* a number such as 3 (also called raising a number to its *second power*) means to treat it as 3^2 or 3×3 which yields 9. Likewise, 3^3 (read as 3 to the *third power* or 3 *cubed*) yields $3 \times 3 \times 3 = 27$; etc. As soon as the players have a basic grasp of these mathematical ideas, they are ready to act them out.

2. Have the players stand, perhaps in groups of 4, behind a starting line. Note that for the first round they will "walk off" number power distances for the number 2. The first participant from each group will walk forward 2^1 paces, the next individual 2^2 steps, the third person 2^3, and the fourth group member 2^4 paces; the individuals will have walked forward 2, 4, 8, and 16 steps respectively. Then ask, "How far would someone going 2^5 steps need to travel?" When the players agree on an answer, select someone to walk it off. Then, what about 2^6 or 2^7, etc.?

3. At some point the number of necessary steps will become too great to walk off in a straight line and still remain on the school grounds. Then have the players discuss and agree on an estimate of where several more powers for that number would place an individual. Next try another number, perhaps 4, and this time "hop off" the number power distances. Vary the physical activity for each new *Number Power Walk* and, if greater precision is desired, make use of trundle wheels, long tapes, and/or other measurement tools. After completing several such walks, the players will have gained a firm understanding of the powers of numbers, plus they will have enjoyed the experience.

Example: In the illustration shown on page 54, the players have made *Number Power Walks* of 2^1, 2^2, 2^3, and 2^4 paces.

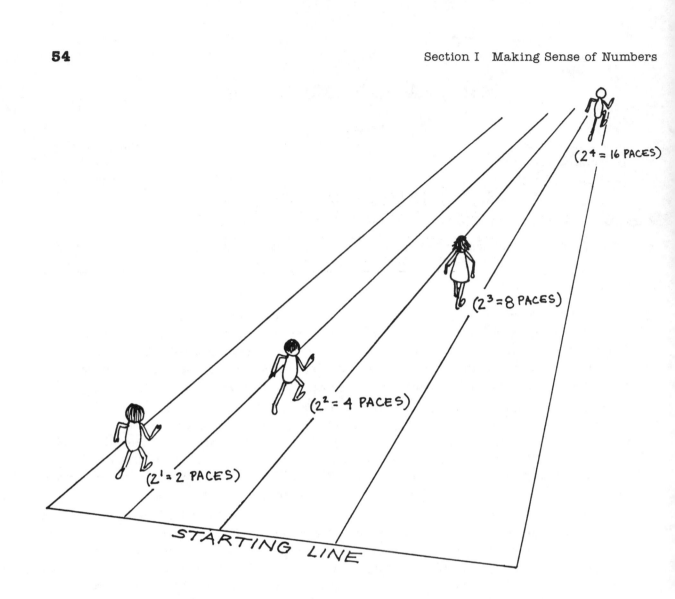

Extensions:

1. Try a situation where the powers remain constant, but the numbers sequentially increase in size. For example, what will result when you cube a series of numbers such as 2^3, 3^3, 4^3, 5^3, etc.? ·

2. When dealing with large numbers such as 10^2, 10^3, etc., or 50^3, 50^4, etc., it quickly becomes impractical to try to act out the results. In such cases, have students mentally estimate and discuss where they might end up if they actually took such *Number Power Walks*.

SECTION II

COMPUTATION CONNECTIONS

The activities and investigations in this section will help students to understand more than just how to "do" addition, subtraction, multiplication, and division. These learners will also have direct hands-on and visual experiences that clarify how and why computation procedures work. As such they will develop conceptual understandings and/or practice computation in ways that are meaningful to them. An added bonus is that the included tasks can be characterized as informative, interesting, and even fun.

Selected activities from other portions of this book might also be utilized to help reinforce computation understandings. Some of these are *Beans and Beansticks, Post-it*™ *Mental Math, Fraction Multiplication and Division Diagrams,* and others from Section I; *Verbal Problems* and *Student-Devised Word Problems* in Section III, plus *Dart Board Logic* and *Calculator Solution Logic* from Section IV.

PUNCHY MATH

Grades K–6

⊠   total group activity   ⊠   concrete/manipulative
⊠   cooperative activity   ⊠   visual/pictorial
⊠   independent activity   ⊠   abstract procedure

Why Do It: To understand and concretely "prove" number computation results.

How to Do It: You will use a paper punch, scrap paper and a pencil or crayons to work out math problems as shown below.

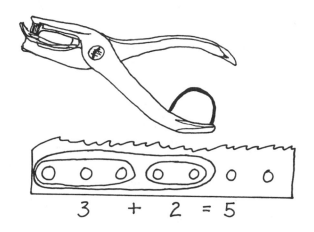

Example 1: For 3 + 2 punch 3 holes along one edge of the paper and use your pencil to loop and label them. Next punch, loop and label 2 more holes above the 3. Then draw a large loop around all of the punched holes and count the total. Finally, write the problem using numbers beside the punchy problem.

Example 2: For 3 × 7 fold your paper into 3 layers and punch 7 holes. Open the paper, loop, and label to show 7 + 7 + 7 or 3 × 7 = 21.

By turning the same punched paper sideways and drawing loops in the other direction, you can also show 3 + 3 + 3 + 3 + 3 + 3 + 3 or 7 × 3 = 21.

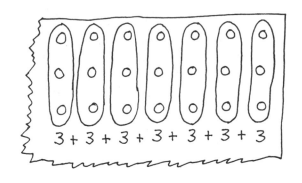

Extensions: Punch, loop, and label the following problems. Explain how you did each problem and how you can be certain of the correct outcome.

1. 3 + 5	2. 4 + 7	3. 2 + 2 + 2 + 2	4. 4 × 2	5. 2 × 4
6. 4 × 6	7. 5 × 8	8. 6 × 6	9. 4 × 9	10. 3 × 12

11. Choose any other problem that you wish. Then punch, loop and label it, and "prove" that your outcome is correct.

ARM LOCK COMPUTATION

Grades K–6

☒   total group activity   ☒   concrete/manipulative
☒   cooperative activity   ☒   visual/pictorial
☐   independent activity   ☒   abstract procedure

Why Do It: To bring about greater understanding of mathematical computations by physically acting out solutions.

How to Do It: *Arm Lock Computations* are acted out by player groups of different sizes; generally the solutions will involve up to the number of students in a class (approximately 30). Note the solutions for the examples that follow, and then go on to solve similar problems. Finally, if ready, the players might solve more complex problems (those requiring more than 30 students) by following procedures outlined in the Extensions section.

Example 1: In the situation shown below, young students were asked to "lock arms" with 3 in the first group and then with 2 in another group. They were next to figure out the total number of players with locked arms; that is, they were to "add" the 3 students and the 2 students (if they wished they might also have "arm locked" the two groups together). Notice also that the related equations for $3 + 2$ were written on the chalkboard.

Example 2: The following setting called for 9 students and asked them to get into groups of 4. They discovered that they could form 2 groups of 4 players with 1 player left over; that is, they found 9 "divided by" 4 to yield 2 groups with a remainder of 1 player. Furthermore, the numerical equations for $9 - 4$ have been recorded for everyone to see. (*Note:* The example just completed denotes Measurement Division; for comparison, the players might also utilize the same numbers in a Partitive Division problem where the outcome would instead be 4 groups with 2 players in each plus a remainder of 1 player.)

Extensions: Try some of the following procedures. Then create problems of your own or solve some from your math book using the arm lock method.

1. For subtraction begin with the total number of students in arm lock position and ask those to be "subtracted" to sit down or to move out of sight. The remaining students will comprise the answer. (*Note:* The situation above calls for Take Away Subtraction; the players might also use the same numbers in a Comparative Subtraction situation where the groups line up side by side and compare to see "what the difference is.")

2. Multiplication will call for the players to get into groups with the same number of players in each. For $3 \times 4 = \underline{\ ?\ }$ they should organize as 3 groups with 4 players arm locked in each group.

3. Computation with larger numbers (when 1-to-1 correspondence is still desired) can be accomplished by bringing several classes together. A problem like 56 divided by 7 might be done by first having the players line up and lock arms to 56. Then have them start over and count to 7, with the 7th person unlocking from her neighbor. Continue and count to 7 again with that person also unlocking from his neighbor. Repeat the process until finished, at which time the arm locked groups with 7 players each are counted to show that 8 groups of 7 yield 56 players.

4. For players who are ready to move beyond 1-to-1 correspondence, problems might be solved with the help of place value cards. That is, several players could hold up large cards reading 10 or 100 or 1000, etc. As such, a problem like $123 \times 4 = \underline{\ ?\ }$ would call for 4 groups each with a player holding a 100 card, 2 players with 10's cards and 3 individual players. The combined groups would total 4 players with 100's cards, 8 with 10's cards and 12 single players or $400 + 80 + 12$. Then, after "trading" 10 of the individual players for 1 with a 10 card, the product is shown to be $400 + 90 + 2 = 492$.

PAPER CLIP ADDITION CARDS

Grades K–6

☐ total group activity   ☒ concrete/manipulative
☒ cooperative activity   ☒ visual/pictorial
☒ independent activity   ☒ abstract procedure

Why Do It: To provide concrete, visual and abstract practice with addition (and subtraction) number facts.

How to Do It: Use paper clips and index cards to solve basic addition problems and keep a record of the combinations found on separate paper. Try the problems in the Extensions; also make up some problems of your own and share them with another player.

Example: The combinations for the number 5 are shown with paper clips and recorded below.

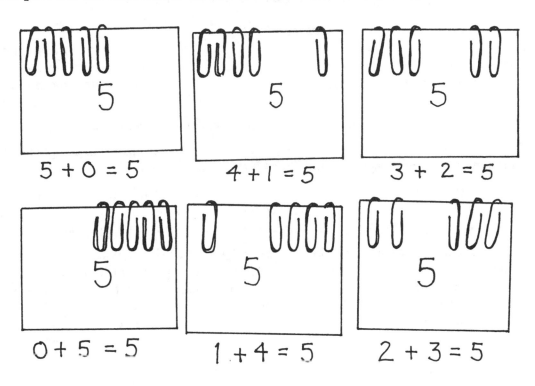

5 + 0 = 5

4 + 1 = 5

3 + 2 = 5

0 + 5 = 5

1 + 4 = 5

2 + 3 = 5

Extensions: Use paper clips on number cards to show your work. Record your answers in number sentences.

1. Use paper clips to find all of the combinations for 4.
2. Show and record the combinations for 7; for 10; and for 14.
3. Sometimes you will need to record number combinations in tens and ones. Can you show 23 in this way? How many groups of ten did you find? How many ones?
4. Explain how these paper clip number cards also show the related subtraction combinations.

BOUNCE IT

Grades K–6

☒ total group activity   ☒ concrete/manipulative
☒ cooperative activity   ☒ visual/pictorial
☐ independent activity   ☒ abstract procedure

Why Do It: To practice varied computation, mental math, and decision-making skills.

You Will Need: A ball that will bounce works best. Use a permanent marker to divide the ball into ten or more sections and write a single numeral from 0 to 9 in each section.

How to Do It: A leader tosses the ball to any player and when caught states which fingers designate the numerals to be used. The leader also notes what computation is to be performed and whether the player is to bounce or tell aloud the answer. If desired, individual or team scores may be kept.

Example 1: A young player catches the ball as shown below and the leader calls out "tell and bounce" what is under your right thumb. The player must then call out 4 and bounce the ball exactly 4 times. Also, the other players must agree.

Example 2: During another game a player is told to use the index and little fingers. Then subtract the smaller number from the larger and bounce the answer. Since $9 - 2 = 7$, the ball should be bounced 7 times.

Example 3: At a more advanced level the leader might call for the use of several numbers and more than one computation operation. For the situation below, the player is directed to use the 5 numerals touched and to multiply, divide, add, and subtract in any proper order to achieve the greatest result. In such an instance, pencil and paper or a calculator may be used and, if this is to be a team problem, the students may work together. (*Note:* Use the proper Order of Operations.)

Trials:

$6 \times 5 + 7 - 2 \div 4 = 36\frac{1}{2}$
$(6 \times 5) + (7 - 2) \div 4 = 31\frac{1}{4}$
$6 \times (5 + 7) - (2 \div 4) = 71\frac{1}{2}$

Extensions:

1. Attempt to get the lowest answer or one nearest a selected number (such as 100).

2. Dismiss individuals for lunch or recess with a bounced (or verbal) answer.

3. Practice *Order of Operations* with "Please Exercise My Dog And Snake" which translates to using in priority **P**arentheses, **E**xponents, **M**ultiplication or **D**ivision, and **A**ddition or **S**ubtraction in left to right order.

ZIPLOC™ DIVISION

Grades K–6

☐ total group activity   ☒ concrete/manipulative
☒ cooperative activity   ☒ visual/pictorial
☒ independent activity   ☒ abstract procedure

Why Do It: To enhance division concept understandings through manipulative, visual, and abstract experiences.

You Will Need: Several large Ziploc™ baggies; marbles of the same color (100 or more); masking tape; and a marking pen.

How to Do It: Place designated numbers of marbles (e.g., 10 or fewer for beginners and up to 100 for advanced players) in several Ziploc™ bags, squeeze the excess air out, and seal the baggies. On masking tape write separate division instructions for each marble set and tape them to the baggies. The players should then arrange the marbles (push them around without opening the baggies) into sets of the size called for. When finished manipulating, the players should record their findings either as sentences or division algorithms, and be ready to explain their outcomes. For further clarification, see the Examples below.

Example 1: The Ziploc™ bag shown below contains 10 marbles. The instructions, written on the masking tape, say, "Arrange the marbles in sets of 2. Then write a sentence that tells what happened."

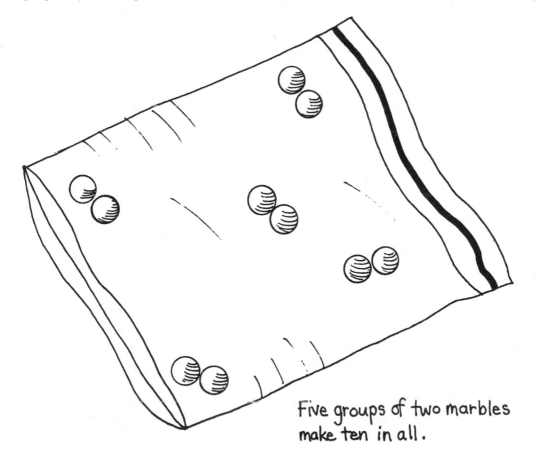

Five groups of two marbles
make ten in all.

Example 2: The directions on the masking tape state, "Place these marbles in groups of 6. Write your findings as a division problem. Then explain your work to another player."

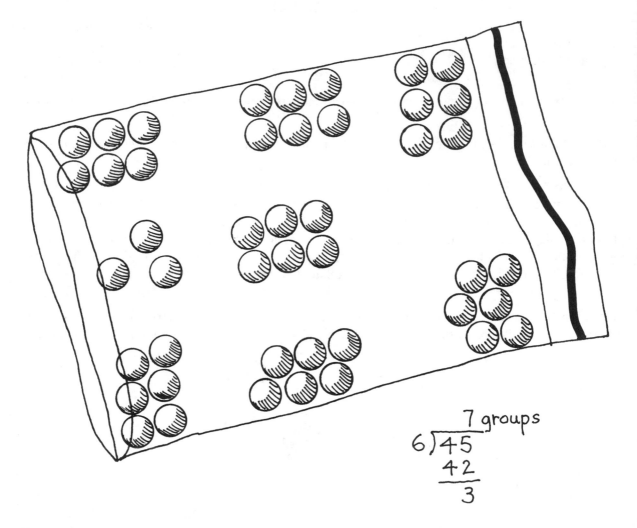

Extensions:

1. Beginning players should probably deal with division in an informal manner. That is, they should manipulate the marbles within the baggies and talk about how many groups of a certain size they were able to "divide" the entire set of marbles into. If ready, they might also keep records of their findings by writing simple sentences or numbers.

2. The examples noted above were both examples of Measurement Division (when you know the number in a set, but not the number of sets). Players should also experience Partitive Division (when you know the number of sets, but not the number in each set). As a partitive problem the first example above, with 10 marbles, might instead have the directions, "Arrange the marbles into 5 groups of the same size. How many marbles are there in each group?"

3. Advanced players might complete problems utilizing large numbers of marbles. A partitive division situation, for example, might require that 234 marbles be divided into 7 groups. As such, the 234 marbles might be distributed 1 at a time to each of 7 bags with the outcome showing 33 marbles per bag and 3 extras.

COMPUTER PAPER EDGE MATH

Grades K–6

☒ total group activity
☒ cooperative activity
☒ independent activity

☒ concrete/manipulative
☒ visual/pictorial
☒ abstract procedure

Why Do It: To construct diagrams that verify both the processes and the results for whole number computations.

You Will Need: A supply of computer paper edge strips; scissors; colored pens or crayons; glue; and colored paper.

How to Do It: Use the computer paper edge strips to show how your math problem results were arrived at. Cut some of the paper edges into strips with 10 holes showing (sometimes it is easier to see two 5's as a 10) and some into 1 hole segments. The examples below show how to begin. Finally, try the problems in the Extensions section below and/or some of your own.

Example 1: For 22 + 29 first lay out 22 as shown and color them (perhaps red) with a pen or crayon. Next color 29 another color and place these along side. Then rearrange the strips to make as many 10's as possible, with any 1's off to the side; when satisfied that the 10's and 1's are in the "best" position, glue them in place. Now showing are five sets of 10 and one 1. Thus, 22 + 29 = 51.

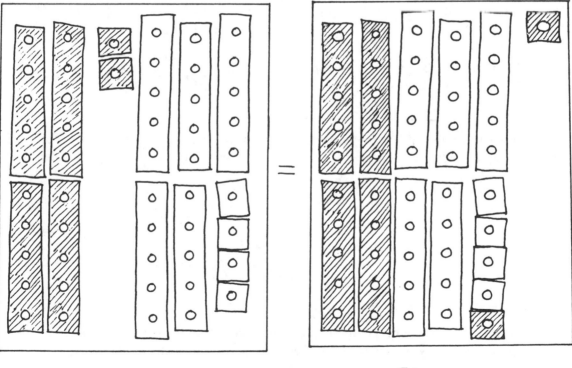

22 + 29   =   51

Example 2: The problem 100 − 32 can be shown by gluing ten strips of 10 to your paper. Begin at an edge and color 32 as three strips of 10's and two 1's. Those not colored are the answer. Thus, 100 − 32 = 68.

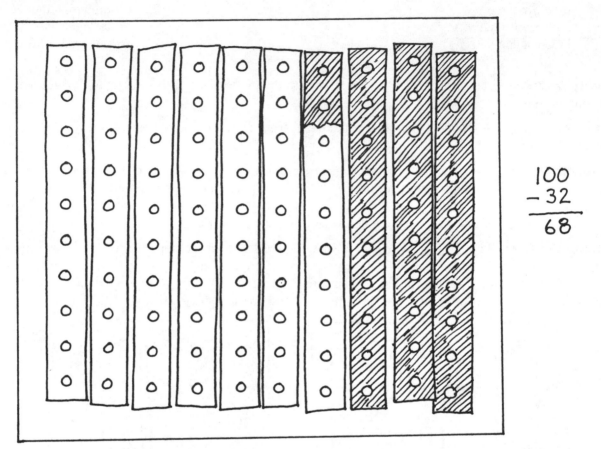

$$\begin{array}{r} 100 \\ -\ 32 \\ \hline 68 \end{array}$$

Extensions: Use computer paper edge strips to solve the following problems or some others that you need to work with. Label all portions of your paper strip diagrams and be ready to explain how you solved each problem.

1. $\begin{array}{r} 13 \\ +8 \\ \hline \end{array}$ 2. $\begin{array}{r} 37 \\ +54 \\ \hline \end{array}$ 3. $\begin{array}{r} 67 \\ -42 \\ \hline \end{array}$ 4. $\begin{array}{r} 112 \\ -37 \\ \hline \end{array}$

5. $\begin{array}{r} 8 \\ \times 6 \\ \hline \end{array}$ 6. $\begin{array}{r} 12 \\ \times 9 \\ \hline \end{array}$ 7. $7\overline{)44}$ 8. $30\overline{)127}$

9. Use the computer edge paper to create some picture problems of your own, but keep the numbers on separate paper. Then have someone else try to find the problem(s) and check with you to find out if they are correct.

MULTIPLICATION FACT FOLD-OUTS

Grades K–6

- ☐ total group activity
- ☒ cooperative activity
- ☒ independent activity

- ☐ concrete/manipulative
- ☒ visual/pictorial
- ☒ abstract procedure

Why Do It: To construct and use visual practice devices that will help individuals conceptualize and reinforce multiplication (and repeated addition) facts.

You Will Need: Several lightweight tagboard strips approximately 3″ by 24″ (may be cut from 18″ by 24″ stock) for each participant; marking pens; and a large supply of identical stickers (optional).

How to Do It:

1. To construct a *Fact Fold-Out,* begin by folding and creasing a lightweight tagboard strip. The first fold should equal 1 inch; each successive fold will "grow" a little larger. Make the next fold over the top of the first (e.g., like a toilet paper roll) and continue in this manner until the entire strip is folded and creased.

2. Next, use a marking pen to write sequential fact problems and to draw the associated visual images (or use stickers for the visuals). Do so by unrolling one segment of the fold-out and writing 1 × (*factor being studied*) = _____ on the "fat portion" and drawing the related visual image on the "flap." Unfold a second segment and on the "new fat portion" write 2 × (*factor being studied*) = and draw a repeat image on the newly exposed "flap segment." Continue in this manner until reaching 10 or 12 × (*factor being studied*) = _____ . Cut off any excess tagboard and the *Fact Fold-Out* is ready for use.

3. After the leader has constructed a *Fact Fold-Out* and demonstrated how to do so, each player should, over a period of time, construct several of his or her own. They should utilize the strips to practice the multiplication facts on their own, with other players, and with parents or other adults; notice that they are not only practicing facts, they are also "getting" a visual image of "how many-ness" each time they make use of the *Fact Fold-Outs.*

Example 1: The *Fact Fold-Out* below was constructed to provide both visual and abstract multiplication fact practice with the 3's. Utilizing both frog stickers and numbers, the *Fact Fold-Out* is unrolled first to show 1 × 3 = 3, then 2 × 3 = 6, and further 3 × 3 = 9.

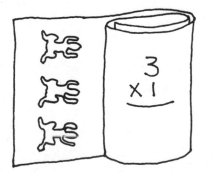 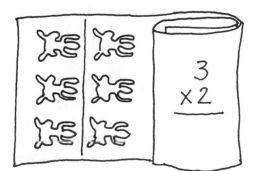

Example 2: This *Fact Fold-Out* is demonstrating 6 × 5 = _____ .

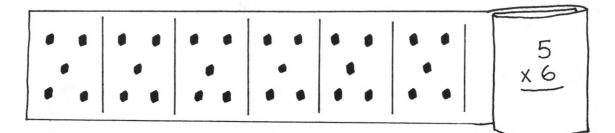

Extensions:

1. Young players might make use of similar *Fact Fold-Outs* to study repeated addition. As such, in the Example 1 above, the 2 × 3 might be related to as 3 + 3, the 3 × 3 as 3 + 3 + 3, etc.

2. Use calculators in conjunction with the fold-outs. For example, have the players press 3 + 3 = _____ , = _____ , = _____ , = _____ , = _____ , etc., and keep a record of the displayed answers. How do the calculator answers compare to those for multiplication (or repeated addition) on the fold-outs?

3. Make *Multiplication Fold-Outs* for any facts (up to 10 × 10 or 12 × 12) that need practice. Show how they can be used to "prove" whether or not an answer is correct.

DOT PAPER DIAGRAMS

Grades K–8

☒ total group activity   ☐ concrete/manipulative
☒ cooperative activity   ☒ visual/pictorial
☒ independent activity   ☒ abstract procedure

Why Do It: To enhance computation understandings and to emphasize mathematical connections.

You Will Need: Dot paper (masters with 50, 100, 1000+, and 10,000 dots are located on the following pages); colored markers; and a pencil.

How to Do It: Use dot paper to show the solutions for addition, subtraction, multiplication, or division problems. Look closely at the examples. Then try the problems in the Extensions below (or others that you need to work with) by looping or marking the number values on your dot paper. At times it helps to use markers of several different colors. Also show your numerical computation and answer for each problem.

Example 1: The problem $5 + 4$ might be shown by looping 5 in one color and 4 immediately following in another. Then a larger loop should be drawn around both so that $5 + 4 = 9$.

Example 2: Use a grid with more dots to figure out $27 - 9$. First 27 dots must be looped and then 9 marked out. Those remaining show the answer.

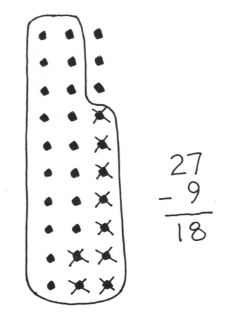

$$\begin{array}{r} 4 \\ + 5 \\ \hline 9 \end{array} \qquad \begin{array}{r} 27 \\ - 9 \\ \hline 18 \end{array}$$

Example 3: A multiplication fact like 5×9 might be shown in more than one way. An efficient method (so that you don't have to recount the dots) is to fill each row of 10.

Example 4: A division problem like $30\overline{)197}$ will require two 100-dot areas. First loop 197 dots and then subdivide these into groups of 30. The number of full groups of 30 is the whole number answer, plus the area with fewer than 30 dots is your remainder.

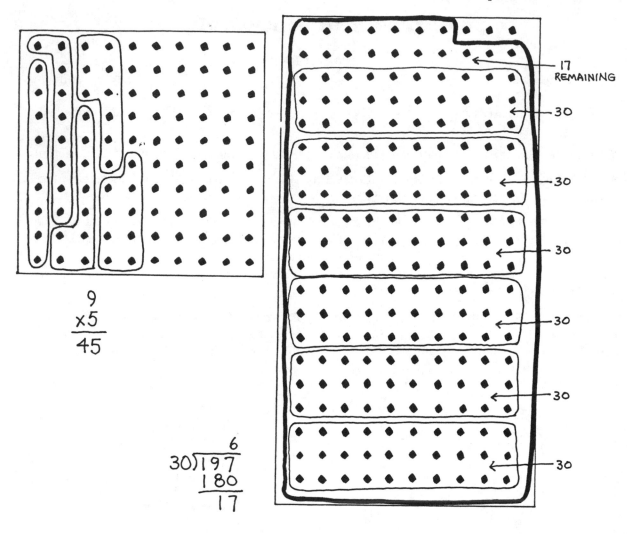

$$\begin{array}{r} 9 \\ \times 5 \\ \hline 45 \end{array}$$

$$\begin{array}{r} 6 \\ 30 \overline{)197} \\ 180 \\ \hline 17 \end{array}$$

Extensions: Use dot paper to solve as many of these problems as you can. Also show your numerical computation and answer for each problem.

1. $7 + 2 =$

2. $\begin{array}{r} 27 \\ +14 \\ \hline \end{array}$

3. $\begin{array}{r} 9 \\ -3 \\ \hline \end{array}$

4. $88 - 45 =$

5. $6 \times 7 =$

6. $\begin{array}{r} 23 \\ \times 4 \\ \hline \end{array}$

7. $\begin{array}{r} 179 \\ -87 \\ \hline \end{array}$

8. $9 \overline{)27}$

9. $155 \div 20$

10. Create three or four of your own problems. Share them with a friend.

100'S DOT PAPER

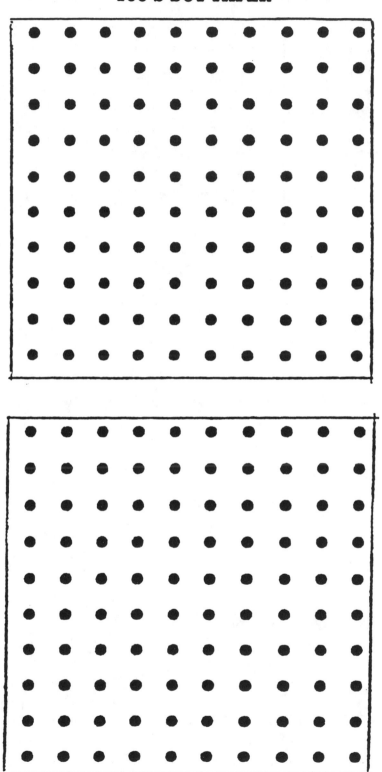

DOT PAPER FOR 1,000 AND MORE

10,000 DOTS

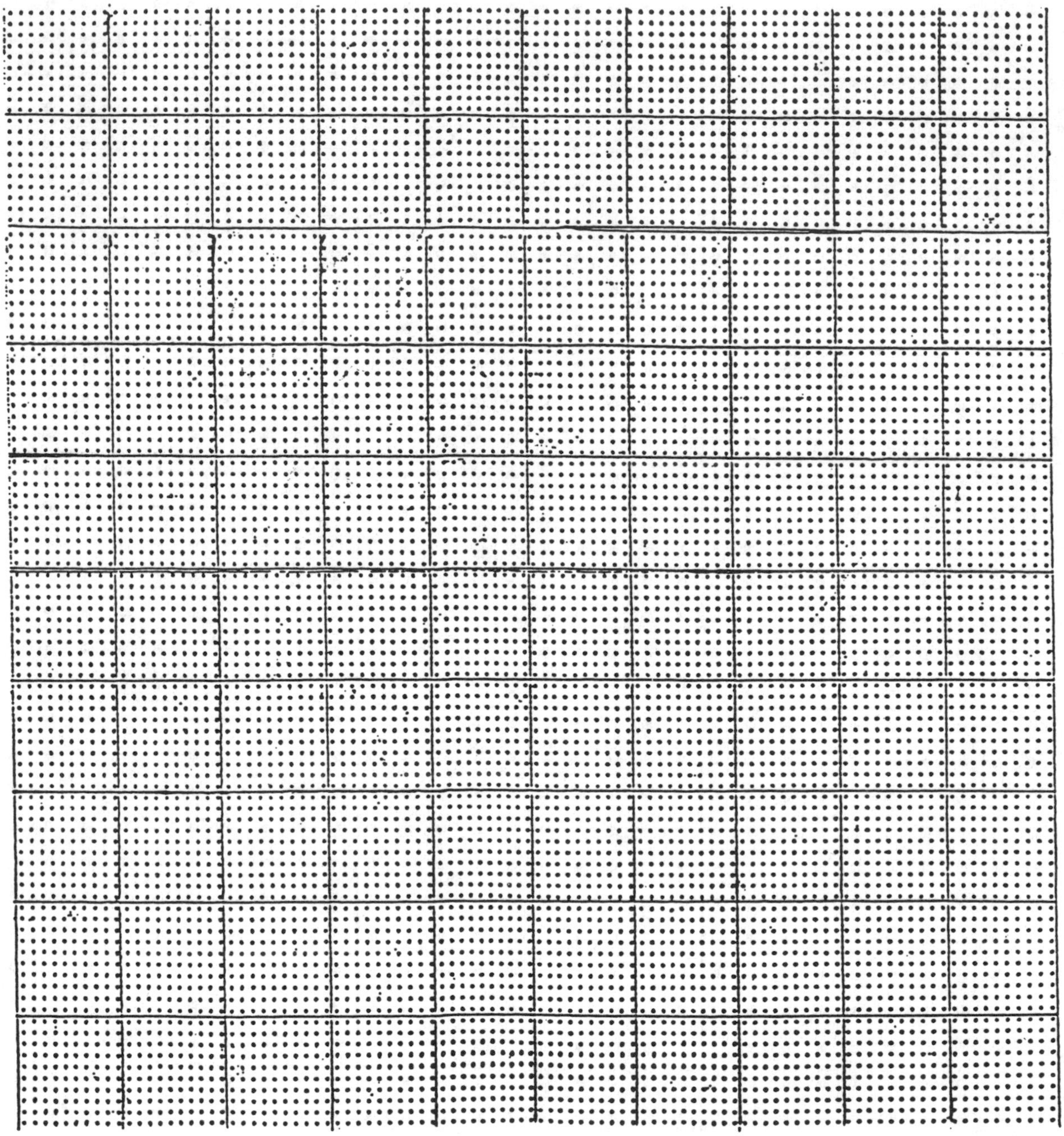

FLOOR NUMBER LINE ACTIONS

Grades K–8

☐ total group activity   ☒ concrete/manipulative
☒ cooperative activity   ☒ visual/pictorial
☐ independent activity   ☒ abstract procedure

Why Do It: To physically act out computation and mathematical problem-solving situations.

You Will Need: A walk-on number line that can be constructed by writing large numerals, about 1 foot apart, on the playground or floor with soft chalk. If the number line will be used more than once it can be made with number cards that are taped down, or it might be painted on the playground surface. Beginning problems will likely make use of the numerals 0–10, but as the work becomes more difficult the number line may be expanded to 100 or more; or if signed numbers are to be used, it should also be extended from 0 to −1, −2, −3, etc.

How to Do It: Solve math problems by using a number line that you can walk on. The examples below show how to begin. Once you understand the procedure, try some of the problems in the Extensions section and/or some of your own. Be ready to explain how you "walked out" each problem, and also be certain that you can use pencil and paper to show the same solution.

Example 1: For 4 + 3, begin at 0 and take four steps to 4. Then take 3 more forward steps and check the number you are now on; it should be 7. (See the solid → on the illustration below.) Finally, keep a record by writing 4 + 3 = 7 on your math paper.

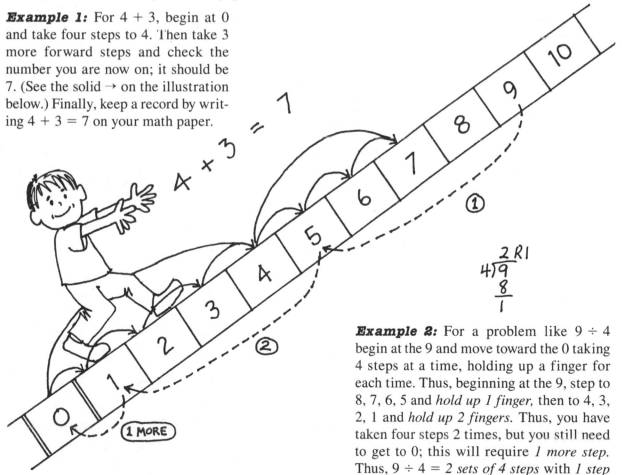

Example 2: For a problem like 9 ÷ 4 begin at the 9 and move toward the 0 taking 4 steps at a time, holding up a finger for each time. Thus, beginning at the 9, step to 8, 7, 6, 5 and *hold up 1 finger,* then to 4, 3, 2, 1 and *hold up 2 fingers.* Thus, you have taken four steps 2 times, but you still need to get to 0; this will require *1 more step.* Thus, 9 ÷ 4 = *2 sets of 4 steps* with *1 step remaining;* so 9 ÷ 4 = 2 remainder 1.

Extensions: Use the floor number line to help solve the following problems or some others that you need to work with. Also, make up several of your own problems and have your classmates use the number line to figure out the solutions.

1. 8 + 3   2. 7 − 4   3. 4 × 6   4. 20 ÷ 5   *5. −2 + −4   *6. −3 × −4

*(*Hint:* Face in the direction of the first signed number and then change direction for each negative number encountered.)

CHALKBOARD SPINNER GAMES

Grades K–8

☒ total group activity
☒ cooperative activity
☐ independent activity

☐ concrete/manipulative
☐ visual/pictorial
☒ abstract procedure

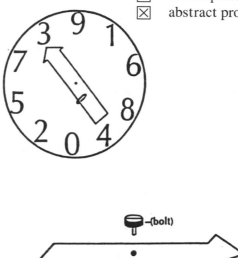

Why Do It: To provide skill practice with most number and operation concepts while also allowing an element of chance.

You Will Need: To construct your large spinner use a piece of heavy posterboard (approximately 3″ × 18″); a suction cup; a short bolt; and a large paper clip. Cut the posterboard into an arrow shape, punch a small hole in the arrow at the balance point, and insert the bolt through it into the suction cup. Suction the arrow to the chalkboard and spin it several times to check the balance; if it needs adjustment, attach the paper clip and move it until even spins result. Now write numerals in the circle around the spinner.

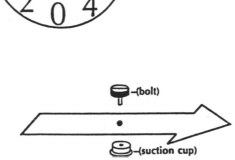

How to Do It: To begin play the leader indicates the type of problem to be dealt with and then has each player sketch the needed numeral blanks on his or her individual paper. (For instance, a place value problem in the 10,000's would require ___ ___ , ___ ___ ___ .) Then, for each spin of the spinner, a number must be written in one blank on each player's recording sheet. Once a number has been written it may not be moved. When all blanks are filled, all players with correct answers win that round.

Example 1: During a place value game the leader stated that the answer nearest to 3,000 would win the round. Four spins yielded the numbers 5, 8, 2, and 4. Three players got the answers shown below. Who won?

5, 2 4 8	2, 4 5 8	4, 2 5 8
(*Player 1*)	(*Player 2*)	(*Player 3*)

Example 2: The "least product" was called for during a multiplication game. Five spins gave the numbers 9, 4, 3, 1, and 7 in that order. Which player below won?

3 1 9	4 3 1	1 4 3
× 4 7	× 7 9	× 9 7
(*Player A*)	(*Player B*)	(*Player C*)

Extensions:

1. Young players might simply be asked to name the numeral that the spinner stopped at, or bounce a ball that many times, or display that number of objects.

2. Winning players might have the greatest, or least results, or those nearest a designated number.

3. Organize the numeral blanks for use with fraction or decimal problems.

4. Try some mixed practice problems such as ____ × ____ ÷ ____ + ____ − ____ = ____ .

5. Make use of some nonstandard situations. For instance, the winner might be the player who obtains the greatest remainder when dividing a 3-digit number by a 2-digit number.

FILE FOLDER ACTIVITIES

Grades K–8

☐ total group activity
☒ cooperative activity
☒ independent activity

☐ concrete/manipulative
☐ visual/pictorial
☒ abstract procedure

Why Do It: To provide practice with basic facts, computation, problem solving, etc. Also to encourage individualized or small group work plus self checking and/or an alternate means of testing.

You Will Need: Use manila file folders; glue; library pocket envelopes; 3″ × 5″ index cards; and marking pens to create a variety of math matching activities. Glue the library pockets inside the file folders as needed for the particular operation (sample folders are shown). Then with marking pens write problems on the pockets and the related answers on the index cards; a hidden answer key should also be placed in the answer pocket.

How to Do It: Prior to starting, put all of the index cards in the answer card pocket. To begin, a player must take all the answer cards and place them in the matching problem pockets. In some cases two players may wish to work together. If pencil and paper computation is necessary, it should be done on small pieces of scratch paper and placed in the same pocket as the answer card. The player's solutions should be checked against the answer key, or by another player (sometimes with a calculator).

Example 1: Using the file folder below, a player must match multiplication facts with corresponding answers.

Example 2: Telling time from a clock face is being practiced with this file folder. Digital times are being matched to those on "regular" clock faces.

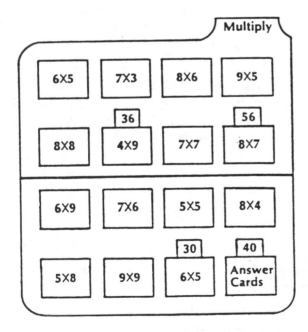

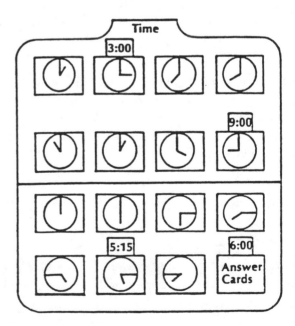

Extensions:

1. Devise file folders for any area in which practice is needed. After seeing how they are constructed, the players should construct a variety of folders for each other. These file folders can be made for matching numerals with pictured amounts, basic facts, fractions, decimals, measurement, geometric identification, time, money, short story problems, etc.

2. Older students can provide special help for younger learners when they construct and use such file folders to help them. Especially helpful are those dealing with numerals, number sense, place value, and basic math facts.

3. Two tactics may be utilized to increase the difficulty level, and thereby promote careful thinking. One is to include more than a single correct answer card for certain problems (for example, 36 might be answered with 4×9 and 6×6). Another tactic is to include a few answers that do not answer any of the folder problems. In fact, when making use of one or both of these tactics, a math quiz results.

BEAT THE CALCULATOR

Grades 1–8

☒ total group activity   ☐ concrete/manipulative
☒ cooperative activity   ☒ visual/pictorial
☐ independent activity   ☒ abstract procedure

Why Do It: To effectively practice basic facts and mental math with one or more calculators and two or more people.

You Will Need: At least one calculator will be needed. An overhead projector calculator is especially effective if *Beat the Calculator* is to be a large group or whole class activity. Alternately, if it is to be a small group activity, a calculator will be needed for each group.

How to Do It:

1. To play *Beat the Calculator* as a small group activity (as with one calculator and three people), the following procedure works well: Person #1 calls out a math fact, such as 6×7. Person #2 uses a calculator to solve and state the answer to the problem. At the same time Person #3 solves it mentally and says the answer. The first to give the correct answer (Person #2 or #3) wins. After a time the players' roles should be rotated. Finally, if competition is desired, the number of correct first responses may be tallied. (*Note:* The players will soon discover that, if they have practiced their basic facts, they will be able to "beat the calculator" nearly every time.)

2. *Beat the Calculator* may also be played as a whole class activity. When doing so the teacher or a leader operates the calculator (an overhead projector calculator is very effective), the players simultaneously do the mental math and call out answers, and a judge serves to call out the problems and determine the winner of each round. The object, once again, is to determine which way is faster; is using your mind or a calculator the more efficient method for obtaining the solutions to basic fact problems?

Example: In the small group situation on page 80 Sean has called out 5 × 9. Susan has been attempting to solve the problem with a calculator before Randy could do so mentally. However, since he had mastered his 5's multiplication facts, Randy was able to "beat the calculator."

Extensions:

1. Young students might try counting with a calculator. To do so enter a number (try 1), an operation (try +), and = = = = to make the calculator count by 1's. They might also start with any number, say 20, and enter 20 + 1= = = =. They might also try counting forward or backward (by subtracting) by any multiple; for example, enter 3 + 3 = = = = and see what happens. (*Note:* Use a calculator that has an automatic constant feature built in; most basic calculators do. To test, simply try the calculator; if it "counts" as noted above, it has the needed constant.)

2. Middle grade students might use a calculator that has an automatic constant (see note in #1 above) to individually practice basic multiplication facts. For example, to practice the 4's facts, enter 4 × =, which the calculator holds in its memory. Then any number entered will be multiplied by 4 when the = key is pressed. Thus, the student might enter 8, mentally think what the answer should be, press =, and 32 is displayed.

3. Advanced students might work in pairs with one player trying to "beat the calculator" with tasks such as 2 × 12 ÷ 8 + 3 − 5 = _____ or 7 + 32 ÷ 4 − 5 × 2 = _____ . (*Note:* In such cases be certain to have the players use the proper Order of Operations. The phrase Please Excuse My Dear Aunt Sally sometimes aids in remembering the order as Parentheses, Exponents, Multiply or Divide, and Add or Subtract from left to right. Students are frequently unclear about this concept, and only a few calculators have the Order of Operations as a built-in feature. Thus, in proper order, the final problem from above must be considered as 7 + (32 ÷ 4) − (5 × 2) = 5.)

SKUNK

Grades 3–8

☒ total group activity

☒ cooperative activity

☐ independent activity

☐ concrete/manipulative

☐ visual/pictorial

☒ abstract procedure

Why Do It: To play a highly motivational game that involves both chance and computation practice.

You Will Need: To participate in this group game each player must have a record keeping chart (master copies are provided or draw your own as shown below) and the leader needs a pair of random number generators (or dice).

How to Do It:

1. To begin the leader rolls both random number generators (dice) and all players mentally add the values together for a total that they record above the dotted line in their own **S** column. (Scores above the dotted line in any column are "temporarily safe.") Then the leader asks who wants to try for additional points in the **S** column; those who do raise their hands high, whereas any players wishing to stay out for the rest of the column lay pencils down and fold hands. (*Important Note:* Players trying for additional points do take the chance of getting SKUNKED which means losing all of his/her points in that column if a "1" or "single dot" appears on either of the thrown number generators.) Play continues in the **S** column until no player is brave enough to try for additional points (players may drop out after any "safe" roll, but then cannot return to the game until play in the next column is started), or until a SKUNK occurs. At this time each player totals her/his score and records it at the bottom of the **S** column; of course those who got SKUNKED get zero points. Other players add their totals to the point where they stopped.

2. Play continues in the same manner for the remaining columns. A final rule, which affects scoring beginning with the second column, is the DOUBLE SKUNK rule; it notes that if you are trying for additional points (below a dotted line) in any column and "1's" (single dots) turn up on both number generators, you lose all of your scores up to that point. Finally, all the column scores are added together for a Grand Total; the player with the greatest Grand Total is the winner.

Example: Two players, during the first column of this game of *Skunk,* scored as shown below.

Player #1

S	K	U	N	K
8				
6				
(stop)				
14				

Numbers Rolled
and Scores

3 + 5 = 8

4 + 2 = 6

6 + 5 = 11

5 + 4 = 9

"1"+ 3 = SKUNK

Player #2

S	K	U	N	K
8				
6				
11				
9				
SKUNK				
0				

Extensions:

1. Paste blank stickers on the random number generators (or dice) and write two- or three-digit numbers on them; let numbers with repeating digits (like 77 or 333) be the SKUNK numbers. Play the game for addition.

2. Could you play *Subtraction Skunk?* (Perhaps you might subtract the smaller number from the larger and record differences on your score chart. The winner might be the player nearest an agreed-upon number.)

3. What about *Multiplication Skunk?* Or *Division Skunk?* (For division how might you deal with the remainders; perhaps you could add just the remainders and see who obtains the greatest, or least, Grand Total.)

4. Paste fraction (or decimal) stickers on your number generators (or dice), decide on the rules to be followed, and play *Fraction Skunk.*

S	K	U	N	K	
					Grand Total

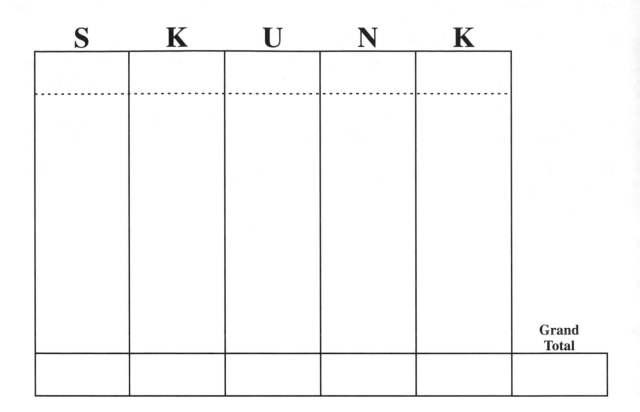

S	K	U	N	K	
					Grand Total

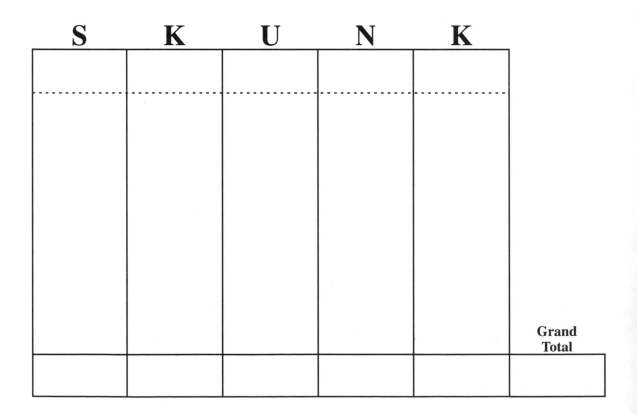

SUBTRACTION SQUARES

Grades 2–8

☒ total group activity
☒ cooperative activity
☒ independent activity

☐ concrete/manipulative
☐ visual/pictorial
☒ abstract procedure

Why Do It: To provide subtraction computation practice at any level (e.g., with single or multiple digits, including positive and negative numbers and zero) in a different and interesting format.

You Will Need: Only pencils and paper. However, for some students it might be advisable to have copies of blank Subtraction Squares available; a master copy is provided.

How to Do It:

1. The players complete the same Subtraction Square with pencil and paper that the leader demonstrates on the chalkboard or overhead projector. In Example 1 below, the players were asked to choose the four corner numbers to start; they selected 23, 16, 8, and 12 and placed them in the same corners. They then subtracted the smaller number along each side from the larger and wrote the difference in the answer circle between them (Step 1). Next, they connected those answers with diagonal lines, subtracted again, and inserted the new answers in the diagonal line answer circles (Step 2). They connected these new answers, vertically and horizontally, and subtracted again (Step 3). The players continued this process until no further subtracting could be done (Step 4).

2. After completing one or two such Subtraction Squares, the players will likely ask whether the result will always be zero and/or whether the number of "squares" or "steps" will always be the same. Suggest that they try several problems and then share what they found. *A word of caution:* It is advisable to have two or more students work the same Subtraction Square since, by doing so, they can easily compare and locate any discrepancies.

Example 1: The players selected corner numbers 23, 16, 8, and 12 for this Subtraction Square.

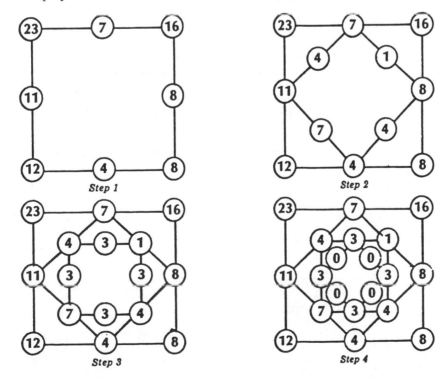

Example 2: The corner numbers were 16, 2, −11, and 0 for this Subtraction Square.

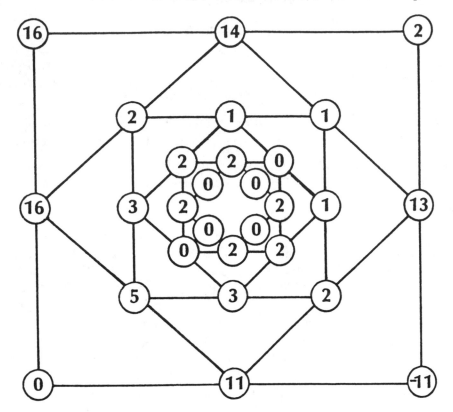

Extensions:

1. When appropriate, utilize *Subtraction Squares* as homework, instead of textbook practice assignments or duplicated workpages.

2. Young players will likely be most successful when using printed Subtraction Squares (see master copy) and single-digit numbers.

3. Players might attempt a variety of arrangements. For instance, try a single-digit number in one corner, a two-digit number in another, a three-digit number in a third corner, and a four-digit choice in the last.

4. *Subtraction Squares* utilizing fractions or decimals might be accomplished by able players.

5. Advanced players might try the process as *Division Squares*. Notice that the final answers will not be zero, and that it will sometimes be necessary to round-off the decimal portions of answers.

SUBTRACTION SQUARE

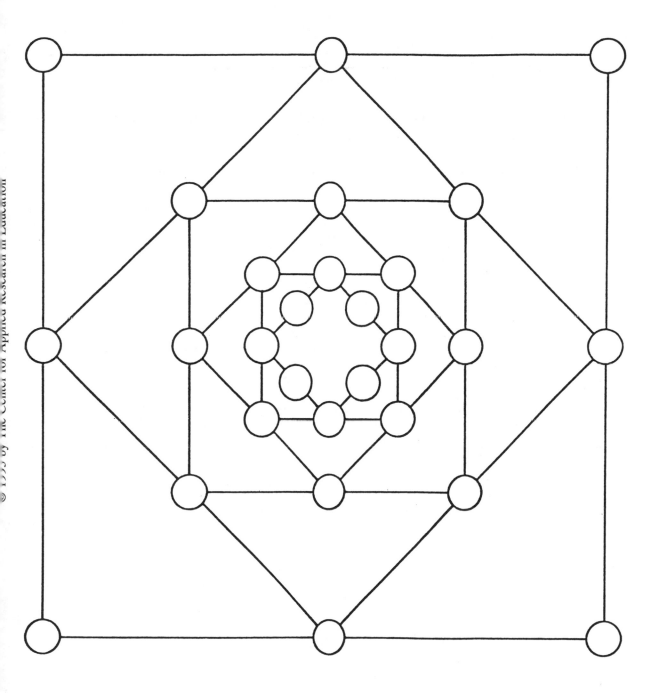

CROSS-LINE MULTIPLICATION

Grades 2–8

☒ total group activity   ☐ concrete/manipulative
☒ cooperative activity   ☒ visual/pictorial
☒ independent activity   ☒ abstract procedure

Why Do It: To visually enhance multiplication understandings.

How to Do It: Use your pencil to draw crossing lines that correspond to factors (numbers) in any given multiplication problem. Then count the number of intersections (line crossings) to find the answer to that specific problem. Follow the Example for clarification.

Example: For 6 × 2 you need to show 6 groups of 2. So draw 6 lines and cross them with 2 lines to get 6 × 2 = 12 crossings.

Also: By turning your drawing sideways the problem 2 × 6 or 2 groups of 6 can also be shown. Thus, 2 × 6 = 12.

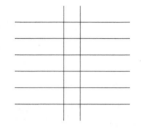

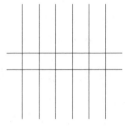

(shows 6 × 2 = 12)

(shows 2 × 6 = 12)

Extensions: Show your drawings for each problem.

1. Draw crossing lines to show 3 × 5. There are _____ line crossings.

   So 3 × 5 = _____

3. Show 4 × 15.

   4 × 15 = _____

2. Draw lines for 7 × 5. How many line crossings are there? _____

   So 7 × 5 = _____

4. Choose a multiplication problem. Draw the line crossings for it. Your problem is:

   _____ × _____ = _____

5. Use the back of this sheet to figure out more cross-line problems. Share them with the class.

HIGHLIGHTING MULTIPLICATION

Grades 2–8

☒   total group activity   ☐   concrete/manipulative
☒   cooperative activity   ☒   visual/pictorial
☒   independent activity   ☒   abstract procedure

Why Do It: To gain a visual perspective while practicing multiplication facts.

You Will Need: A supply of multiplication charts (master copies are provided) and highlighter pens or colored pencils.

How to Do It: Use a chart(s) and highlighter pens (or colored pencils) to shade areas that show the answers to multiplication facts. On a separate paper write the problems and the answers that your highlighted areas show.

10	10	20	30	40	50	60	70	80	90	100
9	9	18	27	36	45	54	63	72	81	90
8	8	16	24	32	40	48	56	64	72	80
7	7	14	21	28	35	42	49	56	63	70
6	6	12	18	24	30	36	42	48	54	60
5	5	10	15	20	25	30	35	40	45	50
4	4	8	12	16	20	24	28	32	36	40
3	3	6	9	12	15	18	21	24	27	30
2	2	4	6	8	10	12	14	16	18	20
1	1	2	3	4	5	6	7	8	9	10
×	1	2	3	4	5	6	7	8	9	10

Shows 3×5 (as 3 groups of 5) = 15. Or, viewed from the side, 5×3 (as 5 groups of 3) = 15.

Extensions: Try the following problems. Also try some of your own and share your findings with another player.

1. Shade in the area for 2×3. How many spaces did you highlight? Thus, $2 \times 3 =$ _?_. Explain how you have also shown the area for 3×2.

2. Highlight 3×5. Thus, $3 \times 5 =$ _?_ and $5 \times 3 =$ _?_.

3. Show 5×8. Thus, $5 \times 8 =$ _?_ and $8 \times 5 =$ _?_.

4. When you do 9×3 or 3×9, the area equals _?_.

5. 7×9 or $9 \times 7 =$ _?_. What do you notice, on the multiplication chart, about the location of the answer number?

6. Complete a series of highlighted charts and post them next to each other on a bulletin board. For example, do the 7's facts; that is, highlight 7×1 on the first chart, 7×2 on the second, 7×3 on the next, etc.

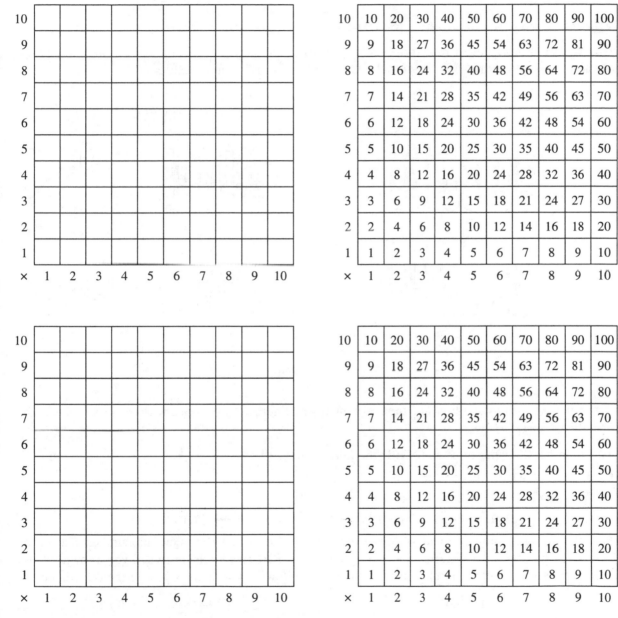

10										
9										
8										
7										
6										
5										
4										
3										
2										
1										
×	1	2	3	4	5	6	7	8	9	10

10	10	20	30	40	50	60	70	80	90	100
9	9	18	27	36	45	54	63	72	81	90
8	8	16	24	32	40	48	56	64	72	80
7	7	14	21	28	35	42	49	56	63	70
6	6	12	18	24	30	36	42	48	54	60
5	5	10	15	20	25	30	35	40	45	50
4	4	8	12	16	20	24	28	32	36	40
3	3	6	9	12	15	18	21	24	27	30
2	2	4	6	8	10	12	14	16	18	20
1	1	2	3	4	5	6	7	8	9	10
×	1	2	3	4	5	6	7	8	9	10

10										
9										
8										
7										
6										
5										
4										
3										
2										
1										
×	1	2	3	4	5	6	7	8	9	10

10	10	20	30	40	50	60	70	80	90	100
9	9	18	27	36	45	54	63	72	81	90
8	8	16	24	32	40	48	56	64	72	80
7	7	14	21	28	35	42	49	56	63	70
6	6	12	18	24	30	36	42	48	54	60
5	5	10	15	20	25	30	35	40	45	50
4	4	8	12	16	20	24	28	32	36	40
3	3	6	9	12	15	18	21	24	27	30
2	2	4	6	8	10	12	14	16	18	20
1	1	2	3	4	5	6	7	8	9	10
×	1	2	3	4	5	6	7	8	9	10

PAPER CLIP DIVISION

Grades 2–8

☒   total group activity   ☒   concrete/manipulative
☒   cooperative activity   ☒   visual/pictorial
☒   independent activity   ☒   abstract procedure

Why Do It: To provide concrete 1-to-1 experiences with division concepts.

How to Do It: Use one or more boxes of paper clips to show your division work. Follow the Examples below as you begin. Also use pencil and paper to record the same results.

Example 1: For $2\overline{)12}$ use 12 paper clips and divide them into 6 groups of 2.

Example 2: For $7\overline{)44}$ use 44 clips and put them into groups of 7. You will get 6 groups of 7 plus 2 extra paper clips.

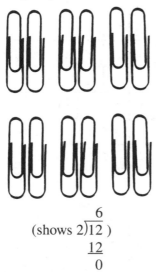

(shows $2\overline{)12}$)
$$\begin{array}{r} 6 \\ \underline{12} \\ 0 \end{array}$$

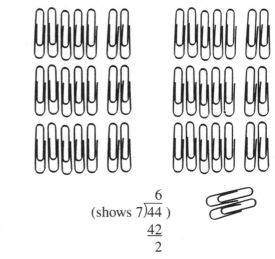

(shows $7\overline{)44}$)
$$\begin{array}{r} 6 \\ \underline{42} \\ 2 \end{array}$$

Extensions: Work with clips and then with numbers. Share your findings with the group, the leader, or another player.

1. Count out 25 paper clips and divide them into groups of 5. ⟶ $5\overline{)25}$

2. Show $6\overline{)21}$ with clips. ⟶ $6\overline{)21}$

3. Show $9\overline{)63}$. ⟶ $9\overline{)63}$

4. Use 2 boxes of paper clips to show 198 divided by 37. ⟶ $37\overline{)198}$

5. The Examples above were all of Measurement Division (when you know the number in a set, but not the number of sets). Also try some problems of Partitive Division (when you know the number of sets, but not the number in each set). The following problems illustrate the difference.

$$\begin{array}{r} 6 \text{ people get apples} \\ 2 \text{ each }\overline{)12} \text{ apples} \\ \underline{12} \\ 0 \end{array}$$

$$\begin{array}{r} 6 \text{ apples per person} \\ 2 \text{ people }\overline{)12} \text{ apples} \\ \underline{12} \\ 0 \end{array}$$

(Measurement Division)   *(Partitive Division)*

6. Make up some paper clip problems of your own and share them with the class.

SQUARE SCORES

Grades 2–8

☐ total group activity   ☐ concrete/manipulative
☒ cooperative activity   ☒ visual/pictorial
☐ independent activity   ☒ abstract procedure

Why Do It: To provide practice with addition, subtraction, multiplication, or division facts; and to utilize logical thinking strategies in a game setting.

You Will Need: When first playing this activity use a prepared Square Score Grid (see the Example or those provided on the following pages). Once familiar with the activity, the players might also devise Square Score Grids for each other (see Extensions).

How to Do It: *Square Scores* is usually played by two students on one grid. Each uses a pencil or pen of a different color and at her/his turn draws a vertical or horizontal line between any two adjacent dots. Play continues in this manner until a line is drawn that closes a square. The player who draws that line must attempt to answer the problem within. If the problem is answered correctly that player is allowed to claim the square and to shade or mark it. If an incorrect answer is given, the square is marked X and no credit is allowed. (Answers might be checked with a calculator or by utilizing an answer sheet.) When all squares are closed, the players may count the boxes claimed to see how many facts they knew.

Example: Each of the players pictured below are practicing their multiplication facts for 6's while also attempting to capture as many squares as possible. Thus far, Juanita has captured and marked the three squares marked \\\\\ and Jose has claimed the two facts marked /////.

Extensions:

1. If practice is needed with a certain operation, such as subtraction without renaming, then the Square Scores Grid should utilize only those types of problems. However, if mixed practice is desirable, a different Square Scores Grid might include $+$, $-$, $\times$, and/or $\div$ problems, or even fractions or decimals.

2. *Square Scores* also work well as a team game when played on the overhead projector. In such a setting the team members are allowed a strategy conference (for two minutes) and then the team leader draws the line for that turn. Play continues in this manner until all squares on the overhead transparency are surrounded and marked. The winning team is the one that has captured the most squares.

3. Players can easily devise their own Square Scores Grids. This is done by having them write equations designated for practice on blank grids (see model provided) or by utilizing one inch or larger graph paper in the same manner. (*Note:* The grid designer should also create an answer key.) Furthermore, the designed Square Scores Grid might be duplicated on a photocopy machine and tried by several other players.

4. Advanced levels of the game might include having three, four, or more players competing on the same Square Scores Grid and/or the inclusion of "bonus" squares (including problems more difficult than typical for the grade or age level; such as 9×12 when most students are only working on problems to 10×10, etc.)

SQUARE SCORE ADDITION AND SUBTRACTION

. . . . . .

2+3   5+1   6-2   4-4   3+7   1+4

. . . . . .

5+5   6-4   2+2   8+2   6-3   3+3

. . . . . .

7-4   5+6   4+4   7-5   3+6   4+2

. . . . . .

2+5   9-5   6+6   5+5   3+8   9-2

. . . . . .

SQUARE SCORE MULTIPLICATION AND DIVISION

5x5	15÷3	4x6	12÷3	7x4	6x2
2x7	5x8	27÷9	6x6	18÷2	9x7
45÷9	7x8	35÷7	36÷4	6x9	24÷8
9÷3	9x7	6x8	60÷10	3x8	9x2

CREATE YOUR OWN SQUARE SCORE GRID

I HAVE _____ , WHO HAS _____?

Grades 3–8

☒ total group activity   ☐ concrete/manipulative
☒ cooperative activity   ☐ visual/pictorial
☐ independent activity   ☒ abstract procedure

Why Do It: To enhance mental math computation abilities, to provide focused reviews of math facts, and to utilize logical thinking skills.

How to Do It: A sequential set of *I Have _____ , Who Has _____?* playing cards, with one card per player, needs to be prepared in advance. (Provided on the following pages are: (1) a sample for 30 students, which includes a variety of question types, and (2) a blank form for creating your own.) The cards should be well mixed and then randomly distributed. A leader is designated and that player starts the activity by calling out the WHO HAS _____ (question) from his/her card. All the other players then look at the I HAVE _____ (answer) portions of their cards to see whether they might have the correct response. The player with the proper answer then calls out I HAVE _____ (correct answer) and, if all agree, then reads aloud the WHO HAS _____ (new question) portion of her/his card. Play continues in this manner until each player has both correctly answered a question (assistance may be provided) and has asked a question of the other players. (*Note:* If there are exactly the same number of playing cards and players, the final answer will be on the designated leader's card.)

Example: In the situation shown below (for just 4 players) John, as the designated leader, called out WHO HAS_8 + 9_? Sara responded I HAVE_17_, and, after a pause to determine if all agreed, read aloud WHO HAS_the number of wheels on 4 tricycles_? In turn, Amber responded I HAVE_12_, paused, and then called out WHO HAS_6 × 4 − 5_? Jose said I HAVE_19_, paused, and then said WHO HAS_the number of ears on 8 students_? John stated I HAVE 16_. This completed the game since John, as the leader, had asked the first question and now has answered the final question.

Extension: The following *I Have _____ , Who Has _____?* activity has been set up with relatively easy problems. Cut out the cards, distribute them one to a player (if fewer than 30 players, some may need to hold more than one card), and allow the students to play and enjoy this sample game while also learning the procedure. Next, make copies of the "blank" game cards, fill in appropriate questions and responses. (*Note:* If the students are able, challenge them to create their own *I Have _____ , Who Has _____?* activities), and enjoy playing while also enhancing mental math and logical-thinking skills.

I HAVE _____ , WHO HAS _____ ?

I HAVE 100. WHO HAS 2 + 2?	I HAVE 3. WHO HAS 30 − 4?	I HAVE 27. WHO HAS the number of ears on 8 students?
I HAVE 30. WHO HAS 15 − 5?	I HAVE 11. WHO HAS 6 + 6?	I HAVE 21. WHO HAS 11 + 11?
I HAVE 8. WHO HAS the number of legs on 5 dogs?	I HAVE 15. WHO HAS 4 × 7?	I HAVE 29. WHO HAS 10 + 10 + 3?
I HAVE 24. WHO HAS the number of sides on a hexagon?	I HAVE 14. WHO HAS 5 + 5 + 3?	I HAVE 18. WHO HAS 20 − 3?
I HAVE 1. WHO HAS 30 − 28?	I HAVE 7. WHO HAS 5 × 5?	I HAVE 9. WHO HAS 20 − 1?
I HAVE 2. WHO HAS 3 + 4?	I HAVE 25. WHO HAS 3 + 3 + 3?	I HAVE 19. WHO HAS 10 × 10?
I HAVE 6. WHO HAS 7 + 7?	I HAVE 13. WHO HAS 20 − 2?	I HAVE 17. WHO HAS 100 − 99?
I HAVE 20. WHO HAS the number of wheels on 5 tricycles?	I HAVE 28. WHO HAS 30 − 1?	I HAVE 23. WHO HAS 8 + 8 + 8?
I HAVE 10. WHO HAS 5 + 6?	I HAVE 12. WHO HAS 30 − 9?	I HAVE 22. WHO HAS 5 + 3?
I HAVE 4. WHO HAS the number of sides on a triangle?	I HAVE 26. WHO HAS 9 + 9 + 9?	I HAVE 16. WHO HAS 40 − 10?

© 1995 by The Center for Applied Research in Education

I HAVE _____ , WHO HAS _____ ?

Important: When creating your own game be certain (1) to cut out exactly one card per player, (2) that each problem has a different answer, and (3) that the WHO HAS question on the last card matches the I HAVE answer on the first card.

I HAVE	I HAVE	I HAVE
WHO HAS ?	WHO HAS ?	WHO HAS ?
I HAVE	I HAVE	I HAVE
WHO HAS ?	WHO HAS ?	WHO HAS ?
I HAVE	I HAVE	I HAVE
WHO HAS ?	WHO HAS ?	WHO HAS ?
I HAVE	I HAVE	I HAVE
WHO HAS ?	WHO HAS ?	WHO HAS ?
I HAVE	I HAVE	I HAVE
WHO HAS ?	WHO HAS ?	WHO HAS ?
I HAVE	I HAVE	I HAVE
WHO HAS ?	WHO HAS ?	WHO HAS ?
I HAVE	I HAVE	I HAVE
WHO HAS ?	WHO HAS ?	WHO HAS ?
I HAVE	I HAVE	I HAVE
WHO HAS ?	WHO HAS ?	WHO HAS ?
I HAVE	I HAVE	I HAVE
WHO HAS ?	WHO HAS ?	WHO HAS ?
I HAVE	I HAVE	I HAVE
WHO HAS ?	WHO HAS ?	WHO HAS ?

MATH CONCENTRATION

Grades 2–8

☒ total group activity   ☐ concrete/manipulative
☒ cooperative activity   ☒ visual/pictorial
☐ independent activity   ☒ abstract procedure

Why Do It: To cite mathematical connections and to provide practice with number concepts and basic facts.

You Will Need: Small cards (as 3″ × 5″ index cards) and marking pens will be needed.

How to Do It: Each player selects a math fact or concept, and on either two or four of their cards will represent it in different ways. When all the players' cards are ready they are shuffled together and placed face down in rows and columns. A player then turns up 2 cards; if the player can "prove" a match she gets to keep them and try again. If not, the cards are returned to their spots and *Math Concentration* continues with the next player. The player holding the most cards at the end of the game wins.

Example 1: These concentration cards match the two concepts *perpendicular* and *intersecting* with a drawing.

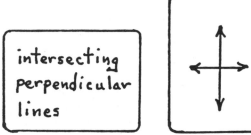

Example 2: A dot diagram, an addition problem, a multiplication fact, and the numeral have been utilized as four ways to represent 20 for the *Math Concentration* game noted below.

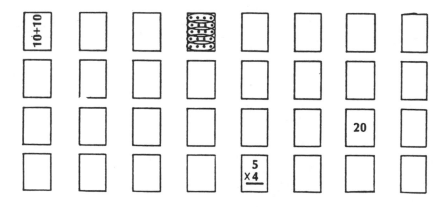

Extensions:

1. Match equivalent fractions, fractions with decimals, either fractions or decimals with percentages, etc.

2. Together with either English or metric rulers, match measurements with pictures or drawings of corresponding lengths (as 2″ with a circle of that diameter).

3. Match simple word problems and solutions. "Tricky" problems, such as the following, can be fun too. (How much dirt can be taken from a hole 6′ long by 2′ wide by 1 foot deep? *Answer:* NONE! *Reason:* It is a hole and, as such, the dirt is already gone.)

NUMBER GRIDS

Grades 3–8

☒   total group activity
☒   cooperative activity
☒   independent activity

☐   concrete/manipulative
☐   visual/pictorial
☒   abstract procedure

Why Do It: To provide practice with addition, subtraction, multiplication, and division facts; or to challenge players to locate equations that utilize more than one operation.

You Will Need: When first playing this activity use a prepared Number Grid (sample provided). Once familiar with the activity, the players might devise number grids for each other (see Extension #2 below).

How to Do It: On the number grid use a pencil or pen to loop and label as many correct equations as possible; use different colors if overlapping equations are allowed. The numerals for an equation must be in adjacent spaces. After a set time, discuss your findings. If desired, a leader might use an over-head transparency of the same number grid to "highlight" certain equations; if this is done, each player should contribute one or more "looped equations" to the display.

Example: Several equations are looped on the sample number grid below. Notice that some involve a single operation whereas others utilize several. Can you locate more equations that might be looped?

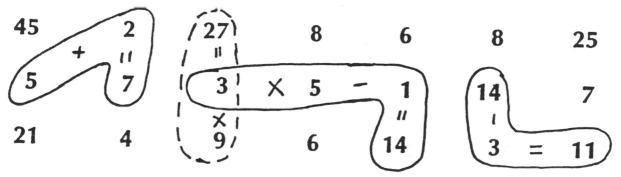

Extensions:

1. If practice is needed with a certain operation, such as multiplication, then each player should loop only multiplication equations.

2. Players can easily devise their own *Number Grids.* This is easily done by placing the numerals for selected equations in adjacent spaces on a blank grid (graph paper works well) and then filling the remaining spaces with likely numbers. Once completed a player's number grid might be duplicated on a photocopy machine and tried by several other players.

3. Advanced players might restrict themselves to finding equations that use at least three of the four basic operations.

4. A long-term game may run on for several days and involve having the players work on the number grid at home, and also allow help from friends, parents or anyone who wishes to contribute. In such a situation be certain to use different colored pens or pencils and also have the equations written on additional paper for easier verification. The players may wish to check each other's work. Calculators may be a help, but only a few of the most recent models operate using the proper order of operations. Be prepared to find more than 100 equations on most one-page number grids.

NUMBER GRID

45	6	81	42	7	6	19
5	2	27	8	6	8	25
9	7	3	5	1	14	7
21	4	9	6	14	3	11
56	7	28	2	15	2	9
3	18	2	3	10	8	3
36	9	14	2	28	42	7
4	5	7	56	9	6	4
20	4	2	70	3	14	24
80	1	28	35	17	22	6
4	19	7	35	29	2	16
15	0	5	1	10	11	2
60	19	12	69	5	22	8
67	34	24	105	79	57	32

SCRAMBLE

Grades 2–8

☒ total group activity
☒ cooperative activity
☐ independent activity

☐ concrete/manipulative
☐ visual/pictorial
☒ abstract procedure

Why Do It: To reinforce addition, subtraction, multiplication, and division facts and to practice mental and/or pencil-and-paper computation.

How to Do It: *Scramble* is usually played with two to four teams each having 10 people. Each team member holds a single colored card with a numeral from 0 to 9 on it; the cards for one team might be red, another team green, etc. (Card masters, that may be duplicated, are provided.) The leader calls out a number problem and the players from each team holding the correct answer numerals "Scramble" (walk or run) to the answer area for their team. Each team achieving a correct answer receives a point, plus the first team to do so is also given a bonus point. In the case of a tie more than one bonus point may be allowed. The team with the highest score wins.

Example: In the situation shown below, the leader called out 8 + 9. The Red team players with the 1 and the 7 scrambled to their answer location to show 17 as the proper answer; they received a point for the correct answer plus a bonus point for being first. The Green team has the correct numerals, but in the wrong order; if they reorder before the leader says "freeze" they might still get one point.

RED TEAM = WINNER   GREEN TEAM = WRONG ORDER

Extensions: If simple questions are called out it is quicker to do them "in your head." For more difficult ones, the teams may "talk them through," use pencil and paper to help find answers, or use calculators. Try some of the following problems. Make up problems of your own. You might ask your teacher to supply some questions, too!

1. Addition situations:

Basic facts	$3 + 4 =$ _____	$5 + 5 =$ _____	$7 + 8 =$ _____
No renaming	$12 + 12 =$ _____	$33 + 11 + 21 =$ _____	
Renaming	$8 + 13 =$ _____	$25 + 26 =$ _____	$98 + 103 =$ _____

2. Subtraction:

Basic facts	$7 - 2 =$ _____	$12 - 9 =$ _____	$13 - 5 =$ _____
No renaming	$24 - 12 =$ _____	$46 - 31 =$ _____	$147 - 22 =$ _____
Renaming	$33 - 24 =$ _____	$87 - 19 =$ _____	$312 - 215 =$ _____

3. Other:

Multiplication or Division	$7 \times 9 =$ _____ $96 \div 12 =$ _____
Mixed	$(5 \times 8) +$ (the days in a week) $- 13 =$ _____
Nontraditional	(Show the remainder only to $108 \div 12$)

SCRAMBLE CARDS

SPIN YOUR OWN HOMEWORK

Grades 2–8

☒ total group activity   ☐ concrete/manipulative
☒ cooperative activity   ☐ visual/pictorial
☒ independent activity   ☒ abstract procedure

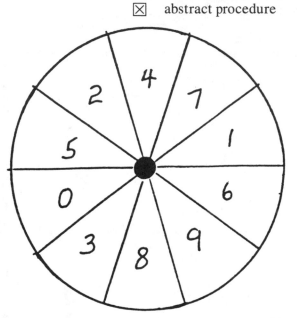

Why Do It: To encourage player ownership of homework problems.

You Will Need: This spinner chart together with a pencil and a paper clip may be used to *Spin Your Own Homework.*

How to Do It: Lay the paper clip so that one end overlaps the center point of the chart. Put your pencil through the end loop of the paper clip and hold it on the center point of the chart. Use your other hand to flip the paper clip. The paper clip spinner will randomly point to different numbers.

Example: The players were asked to get an answer near 2,500. The order in which the numbers were spun was 4, 1, 3, and 0. As such, the players were required to write each number in one of their blanks immediately after each spin; numbers were not allowed to be moved once they were written. Thus, after four spins, the answers they obtained are shown below. Which is the closest to 2,500?

3,014   1,304   1,340   1,430

(*Player 1*)   (*Player 2*)   (*Player 3*)   (*Player 4*)

Extensions:

1. Spin 6 numbers and place them in the blanks below and add to get the greatest possible answer.

2. Spin 5 numbers and place them to get the greatest difference.

3. Arrange 5 numbers in the blanks to get the least product.

— — —
× — —

4. Spin and arrange 5 numbers to get an answer as near 50 as possible.

5. Spin and write several more problems. You may want to use a calculator to check your answers (be careful when checking division with remainders). Be certain to record all of your work and be ready to share your findings.

PALINDROMIC ADDITION

Grades 2–8

☒ total group activity   ☐ concrete/manipulative
☒ cooperative activity   ☐ visual/pictorial
☒ independent activity   ☒ abstract procedure

Why Do It: To provide both a challenge and an interesting way to practice addition computation.

You Will Need: Pencil and paper. The *Guide to Palindromic Sums* for numbers less than 1,000 (on the next page) is not required, but will likely prove helpful.

How to Do It:

 1. To begin, the leader should select a number less than 1,000 that is not palindromic (reversible) and add the number to it that is obtained by reversing its digits (e.g., if 158 was the selected number, then add 851 to it). Continue this process until a palindromic sum (a sum that reads the same in either direction) is attained.

 2. As the players begin to work in small groups or individually, it is suggested that 3- or 4-step solution numbers be set forth (see the *Guide to Palindromic Sums*) for their initial attempts. Also, at least two students should work each problem; as such, they can compare and check their work. Players who are ready might then go on to try problems of 6 or 8 or 10 or even 24 steps!

Example 1: A palindromic (reversible) sum in 3 steps.

$$
\begin{array}{r}
158 \\
+851 \\
\hline
1009 \\
+9001 \\
\hline
10010 \\
+01001 \\
\hline
11011
\end{array}
$$

Example 2: Here 6 steps are necessary.

$$
\begin{array}{r}
79 \\
+97 \\
\hline
176 \\
+671 \\
\hline
847 \\
+748 \\
\hline
1595 \\
+5951 \\
\hline
7546 \\
+6457 \\
\hline
14003 \\
+30041 \\
\hline
44044
\end{array}
$$

Extensions:

 1. Young players, who are able to add, might work initially with numbers less than 20.

 2. Look also for words that are palindromes (e.g., mom, dad, level).

 3. Find out what happens when two palindromes are added together (e.g., 88 + 88 = 176 and 176 + 671 = 847, and 847 + 748 = _____ , etc.).

 4. Challenge the players to find a palindromic sum in exactly 7 steps; or with an answer of more than 13 digits (see 89 or 98 in the *Guide to Palindromic Sums*), etc.

5. Have the students determine color-coded patterns for the numbers from 1 to 100 on either 99's or 100's charts. Duplicate copies of the following charts, allow the players to select their own color scheme and, individually or in small groups, shade in the patterns on the charts as noted below:

Choose a color for each:

☐ already a palindrome	☐ 4-step palindrome
☐ 1-step palindrome	☐ 5-step palindrome
☐ 2-step palindrome	☐ 6-step palindrome
☐ 3-step palindrome	☐ more than 6 steps

0	1	2	3	4	5	6	7	8	9
10	11	12	13	14	15	16	17	18	19
20	21	22	23	24	25	26	27	28	29
30	31	32	33	34	35	36	37	38	39
40	41	42	43	44	45	46	47	48	49
50	51	52	53	54	55	56	57	58	59
60	61	62	63	64	65	66	67	68	69
70	71	72	73	74	75	76	77	78	79
80	81	82	83	84	85	86	87	88	89
90	91	92	93	94	95	96	97	98	99

Try a 99's Chart

1	2	3	4	5	6	7	8	9	10
11	12	13	14	15	16	17	18	19	20
21	22	23	24	25	26	27	28	29	30
31	32	33	34	35	36	37	38	39	40
41	42	43	44	45	46	47	48	49	50
51	52	53	54	55	56	57	58	59	60
61	62	63	64	65	66	67	68	69	70
71	72	73	74	75	76	77	78	79	80
81	82	83	84	85	86	87	88	89	90
91	92	93	94	95	96	97	98	99	100

Try a 100's Chart

GUIDE TO PALINDROMIC SUMS

3 steps

"sum"	*numbers*
11,011	158, 257, 356, 455, 544, 653, 752, 851, 950
13,431	168, 267, 366, 465, 564, 663, 762, 861, 960
15,851	178, 277, 376, 475, 574, 673, 772, 871, 970
3,113	199, 298, 397, 496, 694, 793, 892, 991
5,115	249, 348, 447, 546, 645, 744, 843, 942
5,335	299, 398, 497, 596, 695, 794, 893, 992
6,666	156, 255, 354, 453, 552, 651, 750
8,888	157, 256, 355, 553, 652, 751, 850
6,996	186, 285, 384, 483, 582, 681, 780
7,337	349, 448, 547, 745, 844, 943
7,117	389, 488, 587, 785, 884, 983
7,557	399, 498, 597, 795, 894, 993
9,119	439, 538, 637, 736, 835, 934
9,559	449, 548, 647, 746, 845, 944
9,339	489, 588, 687, 786, 885, 984
9,779	499, 598, 697, 796, 895, 994
4,444	155, 254, 452, 551, 650
2,662	164, 263, 362, 461, 560
4,884	165, 264, 462, 561, 660
2,552	184, 283, 382, 481, 580
4,774	185, 284, 482, 581, 680
2,992	194, 293, 392, 491, 590
1,111	59, 68, 86, 95
747	180

4 steps

5,115	174, 273, 372, 471, 570
9,559	175, 274, 472, 571, 670
9,339	195, 294, 492, 591, 690
4,884	69, 78, 87, 96
25,652	539, 638, 836, 935
23,232	579, 678, 876, 975
22,022	599, 698, 896, 995
45,254	629, 728, 827, 926
44,044	649, 748, 847, 946
47,674	679, 778, 877, 976
46,464	699, 798, 897, 996
13,431	183, 381, 480
6,996	192, 291, 390
69,696	729, 927
68,486	749, 947
67,276	769, 967
66,066	789, 987
89,298	819, 918
88,088	839, 938
2,662	280
2,552	290

5 steps

"sum"	*numbers*
79,497	198, 297, 396, 495, 594, 693, 792, 891, 990
45,254	166, 265, 364, 463, 562, 661, 760
44,044	176, 275, 374, 473, 572, 671, 770
59,895	549, 648, 846, 945
99,099	639, 738, 837, 936

6 steps

45,254	182, 281, 380
44,044	79, 97
475,574	779, 977
449,944	799, 997
881,188	889, 988

7 steps

233,332	188, 287, 386, 485, 584, 683, 782, 881, 980
881,188	197, 296, 395, 593, 692, 791, 890
45,254	190

8 steps

1,136,311	589, 688, 886, 985
233,332	193, 391, 490

10 steps

88,555,588	829, 928

11 steps

88,555,588	167, 266, 365, 563, 662, 761, 860

14 steps

8,836,886,388	849, 948

15 steps

8,836,886,388	177, 276, 375, 573, 672, 771, 870

17 steps

5,233,333,325	739, 937
133,697,796,331	899, 998

22 steps

8,813,200,023,188	869, 968

23 steps

8,813,200,023,188	187, 286, 385, 583, 682, 781, 880
8,802,236,322,088	879, 978

24 steps

8,813,200,023,188	89, 98

HERE I AM

Grades 3–8

☒   total group activity
☒   cooperative activity
☐   independent activity

☐   concrete/manipulative
☐   visual/pictorial
☒   abstract procedure

Why Do It: To reinforce multiplication facts, to stimulate logical thinking, and to enhance coordinate graphing skills.

You Will Need: A "master" multiplication gameboard with answers, and several players' gameboards without answers (see reproducible copies). Lettered discs for the message HERE I AM (or another selected short message) should also be made up. Furthermore, the leader may wish to cover his/her gameboard (and possibly the student boards as well) with a plastic lamination or clear self-stick vinyl so that it may be written on with water-soluble marking pens or grease pencils.

How to Do It:

1. The leader tells the players what the hidden message will be (HERE I AM in this example) and places the lettered discs on the master gameboard, being careful to keep their locations secret. The discs may be placed in horizontal, vertical, or diagonal fashion, but the letters of each word must be in adjacent spaces and there may be only one space between words.

2. The game begins when one player calls out a pair of multiplication factors and suggests an answer. If agreed that the stated answer is correct, each player writes it on his/her own grid in the proper position (e.g., if the player notes that $7 \times 3 = 21$, the answer must be written in the location 7 over and 3 up; that is +7 along the X-axis and then +3 on the Y-axis). Further, if the answer matches a lettered space on the master gameboard, the leader states "HERE I AM" and all players mark that location.

3. The game continues with players, in turn, calling out a new pair of factors and answers, and recording the products in the proper multiplication grid locations. At any turn, if a player "hits" a lettered location, the leader states "HERE I AM." When one or more players think they know the location of all the HERE I AM discs (or those for another specified message), they may ask to be "checked"; as such, they must call out all of the multiplication fact problems and answers that correctly indicate the disc locations. Any player to properly do so is a winner!

Example: The leader hid the HERE I AM discs as shown on the Master Gameboard. When the first player called out the fact that $7 \times 7 = 49$, the leader said, "Correct," and all the players wrote the answer on their own gameboards. The second player stated that $3 \times 4 = 12$ and the leader said, "Correct and HERE I AM!" As such, all the players wrote 12 on their gameboards and marked it with an "X" (to indicate that they had located one of the message letters). Subsequent players called $4 \times 4 = 16$, $7 \times 3 = 21$, and $3 \times 3 = 9$, and each time the leader responded, "Correct." Since the game is not finished, it will continue until the players place "X's" in locations where seven of their answers match the message letters and one or more players are able to identify both the multiplication fact problems and the correct letter locations. Any player to do so will be a winner!

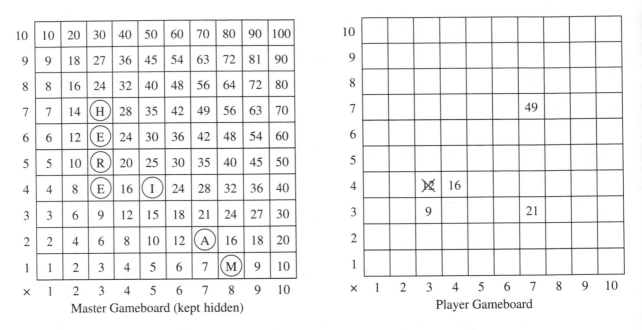

Master Gameboard (kept hidden)

Player Gameboard

Extensions:

1. At the onset, it is a good idea for the leader to use a large player-type gameboard (on the chalkboard or an overhead projector) to record the players' answers. This will further reinforce correct multiplication products and also help to clarify the written placement of the answers. (*Note:* The players are also informally learning about coordinate geometry.)

2. Change from HERE I AM to some other short message. If, for example, it is Dan's birthday, the message might be DAY FOR DAN. In another instance, the players might be told that they will spell the name of the smallest state (RHODE ISLAND), etc.

3. Logically analyze possible answer locations and the factors related to them. In the Example shown above, a "hit" was made at 3 × 4 = 12, but not at 4 × 4 or 3 × 3. Thus, what other locations could possibly contain a HERE I AM letter? (*Remember:* Words can be placed horizontally, vertically or diagonally, and there will be a single empty space between words.)

MASTER GAMEBOARD

×	1	2	3	4	5	6	7	8	9	10
10	10	20	30	40	50	60	70	80	90	100
9	9	18	27	36	45	54	63	72	81	90
8	8	16	24	32	40	48	56	64	72	80
7	7	14	21	28	35	42	49	56	63	70
6	6	12	18	24	30	36	42	48	54	60
5	5	10	15	20	25	30	35	40	45	50
4	4	8	12	16	20	24	28	32	36	40
3	3	6	9	12	15	18	21	24	27	30
2	2	4	6	8	10	12	14	16	18	20
1	1	2	3	4	5	6	7	8	9	10

PLAYER GAMEBOARDS

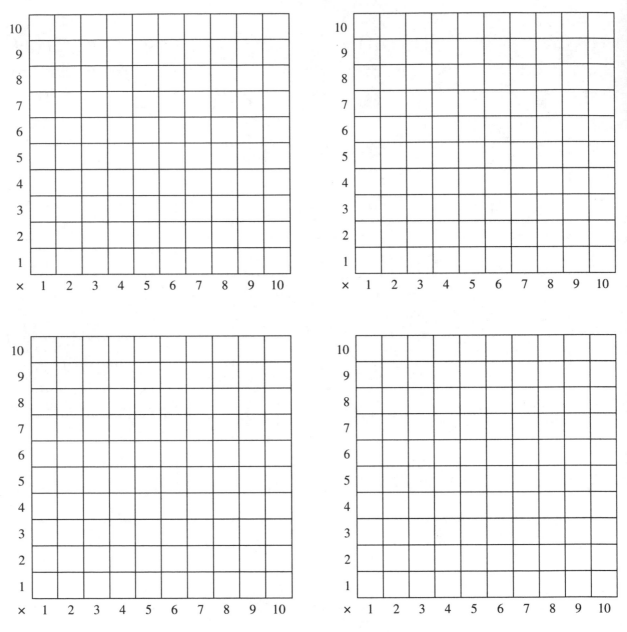

CHECKERBOARD MATH

Grades 4–8

☐ total group activity
☒ cooperative activity
☐ independent activity

☐ concrete/manipulative
☐ visual/pictorial
☒ abstract procedure

Why Do It: To provide practice with basic facts and to enhance mental math skills.

You Will Need: A checkerboard and checkers; masking tape; and a marking pen will be needed. Tear off 10 or more short pieces of masking tape, write basic fact or computation problems on them, and randomly stick them on the playing squares of the checkerboard.

How to Do It: *Checkerboard Math,* with one exception, is played with the same rules as a standard checkers game. The difference is that a player cannot move to a problem square until the fact or problem is answered correctly.

Example: The checkerboard below is set up so that selected multiplication facts might be practiced.

Extensions:

1. Play the game for mixed practice by including addition, subtraction, multiplication, and/or division facts on the tape strips. Check answers with a calculator.

2. Reverse the process by having answers taped to the checkerboard and the related basic fact, computation, or short story problems on index cards. Each player must identify the matching problem before he or she is allowed to move to the game square in question.

3. Advanced players might play chess in any of the ways noted above.

CHECKERBOARD MATH

EQUATION MATCH-UP

Grades 4–8

☒ total group activity
☒ cooperative activity
☐ independent activity

☐ concrete/manipulative
☐ visual/pictorial
☒ abstract procedure

Why Do It: To provide either mental math or pencil-and-paper practice with basic facts, computation, and/or problem-solving situations.

You Will Need: Each player must prepare an *Equation Match-Up* playing card by dividing a sheet of paper into a designated number of square areas, such as those shown in the Example below. Each player will also need a small supply of markers such as plastic discs or corn kernels.

How to Do It:

1. As a series of number facts, computations, and/or problem situations are discussed, the players record the equations for them, plus a "free" space, at random positions on their own cards. At the same time the leader is preparing matching answer cards, plus a few that do not match any of the equations discussed.

2. To begin play the leader mixes the answer cards and places them face down in a pile. The top card is turned over, and if a player believes she has a match, a marker is placed on top of that equation. The first player(s) to fill a line vertically, horizontally or diagonally wins; however, he or she must verify each result by calling out the equations and their proper answers.

Example: Notice that the match-up cards for the two players contain the same equations, but in different positions.

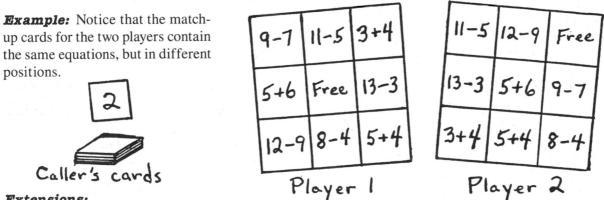

Extensions:

1. Young players might begin by coloring dots to match numerals in each of the areas on their match-up game cards. Then, to play they would place a marker on each dot diagram that matches an answer numeral.

2. *Equation Match-Up* can also be played in much the same manner as a *Bingo* game where each column is designated by a letter. To do so another pile of cards, with the letters B-I-N-G-O (repeated several times), is also needed. A letter card and an answer card are to be turned over at the same time and the player must have an equation to match in the designated letter column. For example, N-3 would mean that the player must have an equation with the answer of 3 under the N column.

3. Use several types of match-ups such as Fractions and Pizzas (for example, ⅓ and a picture or drawing of ⅓ pizza); Geometric Vocabulary and Drawings (pentagon and a drawing of a pentagon); simple Word Problems and Solutions, etc.

SILENT MATH

Grades 4–8

☒ total group activity
☒ cooperative activity
☐ independent activity

☐ concrete/manipulative
☒ visual/pictorial
☒ abstract procedure

Why Do It: To require players to think logically, find patterns, construct related diagrams, and practice basic facts.

How to Do It: In this game no talking is allowed. The leader puts diagrams, like those shown below, on the chalkboard. When the diagram contains all of the needed symbols and numbers the leader will indicate this by nodding yes. If some of the information is missing, and some player needs to provide it, the leader will make a questioning gesture. Players who think they know how to complete the diagram will raise their hands, and the leader will point to someone to finish the diagram. If the player completes the diagram correctly the leader shakes his or her hand. Play continues in this way until the leader is quite sure everyone has a good idea of what is happening. The "no talking" rule is then removed and the players discuss their strategies. During a follow-up session each player might be expected to contribute one or two partial diagrams to be solved by the other players.

Examples and Extensions: The samples A through T below are sequenced from easy to more complex. The leader should place them on the board, one at a time, and either nod yes, or make a questioning motion and appoint players to attempt solutions. Items A, B, E, F, and O are completed examples that will help the players understand how to proceed. (Solutions to the unfinished problems are provided at the end of this *Silent Math* description, but should be utilized only if the players are truly "stuck.")

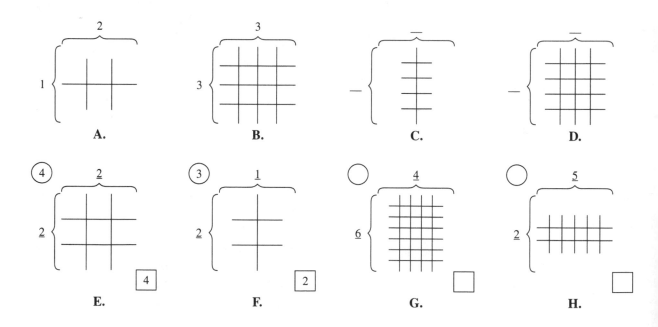

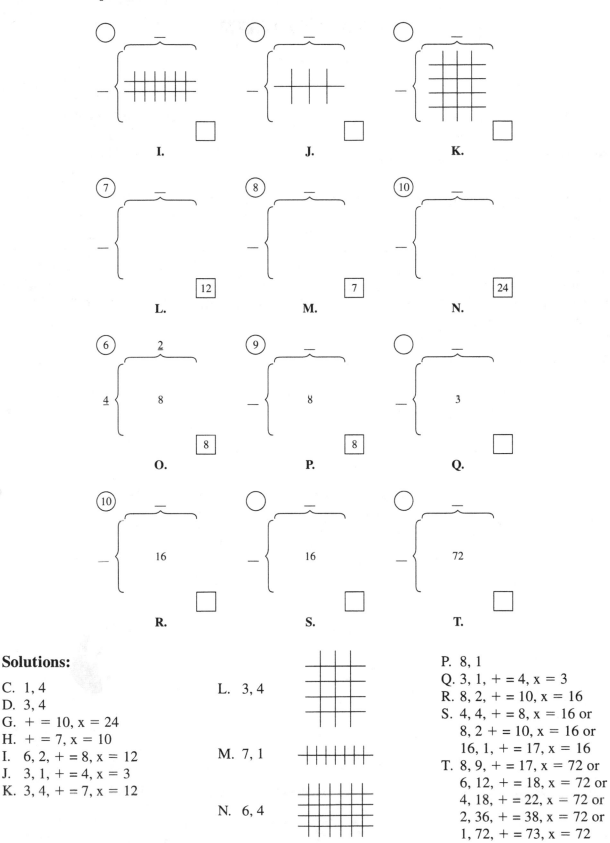

Solutions:

C. 1, 4

D. 3, 4

G. + = 10, x = 24

H. + = 7, x = 10

I.   6, 2, + = 8, x = 12

J.   3, 1, + = 4, x = 3

K. 3, 4, + = 7, x = 12

L. 3, 4

M. 7, 1

N. 6, 4

P. 8, 1

Q. 3, 1, + = 4, x = 3

R. 8, 2, + = 10, x = 16

S. 4, 4, + = 8, x = 16 or
    8, 2 + = 10, x = 16 or
    16, 1, + = 17, x = 16

T. 8, 9, + = 17, x = 72 or
    6, 12, + = 18, x = 72 or
    4, 18, + = 22, x = 72 or
    2, 36, + = 38, x = 72 or
    1, 72, + = 73, x = 72

RAPID CHECKING

Grades 4–8

☒ total group activity
☒ cooperative activity
☒ independent activity

☐ concrete/manipulative
☐ visual/pictorial
☒ abstract procedure

Why Do It: To provide learners with a quick way to check addition, subtraction, multiplication, and division answers.

How to Do It: To quickly check any computation problem, add the digits together (repeatedly if needed) for each of the initial problem numbers until a single-digit "representative number" is reached. Redo the problem process (add, subtract, multiply, or divide) with the representative numbers, and then add those digits to get a single-digit representative answer. Next, go to the original answer you determined and add those digits together until you get another single-digit representative answer. Finally, compare your two representative answers; if they are the same, your answer checks. IT IS ACTUALLY EASIER TO FOLLOW THE PROCEDURE IN THE EXAMPLES THAT FOLLOW! (*Note:* Please read the "tips for checking subtraction and division" in the examples below. Also, an error possibility is cited in the Extensions section.)

Example 1: Remember to add digits to obtain single-digit "representative numbers" as you follow the rapid checking of this problem.

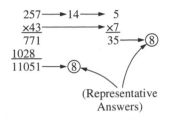

(Representative Answers)

Example 2: Now let us try the same process with a column addition problem.

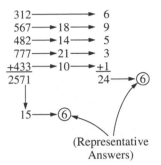

(Representative Answers)

Example 3: When rapidly checking a division problem, it often helps to think of it in terms of multiplication. Also, be sure to include any remainder.

Think:

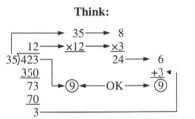

Example 4: Subtraction computations are most readily checked when thought of in terms of addition.

Think:

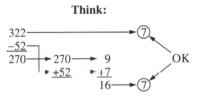

Extensions:

1. See if the rapid check works for relatively easy problems such as 12 ┃ 45 or 8 × 9.

2. How about using it with decimals like .97 + .42 + .38 or .4321 + .5 + .892?

3. Be careful that you don't switch the digits around in your original answer; if you should do so, the rapid check would say OK, but your answer would not be correct! For example, in the addition problem (Example 2) the true answer is 2571, but if you mix the digits to read 2517 the representative outcome would be 6 in either case. (Such offsetting errors happen infrequently. Thus, most answers rapidly checked will be correct. In addition, the rapid checking process tends to captivate user interest!)

SECTION III

INVESTIGATIONS AND PROBLEM SOLVING

Educators cannot prepare learners for every problem they will encounter throughout life. They can, however, expose them to a wide variety of situations warranting investigation and equip them with problem-solving strategies. As such, the activities in this section stem from a variety of real-life situations and include both written and verbal word problems, a problem-solving plan, and problems with multiple answers, plus investigations involving spatial thinking, statistics and probability, measurement, scheduling, etc. Furthermore, because many of the tasks are hands-on and nearly all call for direct participation, the learners will find themselves becoming interested and likely having fun.

Activities from other parts of this book might also be utilized to help learners develop problem-solving understandings. Some of these are *Everyday Things Numberbooks, Celebrate 100 Days,* and *A Million or More,* from Section I; *Computer Paper Edge Math, Dot Paper Diagrams,* and *Silent Math,* in Section II; plus *Mystery Object Guess, Problem Puzzlers,* and *String Triangle Geometry,* from Section IV.

SHOE GRAPHS

Grades K–3

☒	total group activity		☒	concrete/manipulative
☒	cooperative activity		☒	visual/pictorial
☐	independent activity		☒	abstract procedure

Why Do It: To investigate everyday applications of mathematics and to organize the information into "real" graphs.

You Will Need: One shoe from each student; a yard stick; a marking pen; and masking tape.

How to Do It: Use the masking tape to mark out a floor grid of 3 or 4 columns by 10 to 12 rows (the grid spaces should each measure about 1 square foot). Label each column according to the type of shoe that may be placed in it: (1) slip-ons, (2) tie shoes, (3) Velcro fasteners, and (4) other types. Have the students, beginning at the base line, each place 1 of their shoes in a labeled column that matches. The leader should then initiate a discussion based on questions such as, "How many people were wearing slip-on shoes? How many more people were wearing slip-ons than shoes with Velcro fasteners?" During such discussions the yard stick may be used as a marker; it might be placed at the top of one shoe column (as in the example below) such that the number of additional shoes of a select type can be easily viewed and counted. For able students, continue the analysis with questions as, "We counted 8 tie shoes in that column. So, if 8 people are wearing tie shoes, and each needs 2 shoes, how can we find out the total number of shoes those 8 people must have?" (*Note:* Most adults would, of course, say 8 × 2 = 16, but many young students will not yet have acquired multiplication skills. Such beginners might be helped to count the occupied column spaces by 2's.)

Example: In the situation shown above, the students have each placed one of their shoes in a column that matches. The teacher is now asking one of a series of questions that will help the learners to analyze their "real" graph data.

Extensions: Following initial experiences, where the students have considered how many total, how many more or less, etc., they might be asked to consider some of the following possibilities.

1. What color hair do most people have? Have them stand in columns on the floor graph according to hair color (blonde, brown, black . . .). If there are 9 people with blonde hair in this class, and there are 8 classes at this school, how many blonde people might there be in the whole school? Allow the students to work in small groups as they attempt to find an answer. When they think they have a solution, ask them to explain their thinking. Probe further and ask whether there is a single answer to the problem, or whether their solution is an estimate. (*Note:* Construct similar graphs for color of eyes, type or color of shirt being worn, etc.)

2. The use of personal photos of the students when building graphs is a very effective technique. (*Note:* Since a number of pictures of each student will be needed, photocopy the class photograph to help reduce costs.) When a supply of individual photos are available various types of data can be considered, such as favorite flavors of ice cream, number of pets each family has, preferred physical education activity, favorite thing to do on weekends, etc. Once such data has been collected, representative graphs can be made by pasting the student's individual photos in the appropriate columns. The graphed data should, of course, be analyzed by the learners in as many ways as are feasible.

SUGAR CUBE BUILDINGS

Grades 1–8

☒ total group activity   ☒ concrete/manipulative
☒ cooperative activity   ☒ visual/pictorial
☒ independent activity   ☒ abstract procedure

Why Do It: To utilize logical-thinking skills in the investigation of an applied geometry problem.

You Will Need: Initially each student will need four sugar cubes; at more advanced stages, each group, or each learner, may wish to work with as many as 10 sugar cubes at a time. For the most advanced investigations each group may need to work with 36 or 48 or 100 sugar (or other) cubes. Furthermore, the students will need graph paper to keep records of their findings (see *Number Cutouts* for graph paper that may be photocopied), and those completing further investigations might also need "3-D Drawing Paper" (see reproducible page) and pencils.

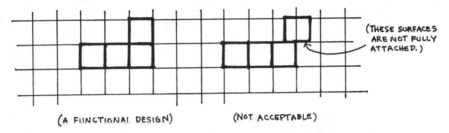

(A FUNCTIONAL DESIGN)   (NOT ACCEPTABLE)

How to Do It:

1. When first introducing *Sugar Cube Buildings* each student should be given four sugar cubes and told that several "jobs" need to be accomplished. Their first job is to design and build—with the requirement that each cube be fully attached to the side of at least one other cube (see examples below)—as many single-story buildings as possible. As workable arrangements are found, the designs should be recorded, as top views, on graph paper. When finished the learners should be allowed time to discuss, compare, and contrast their findings. Also, if desired, permanent models of the building designs can easily be constructed by moistening selected surfaces of the sugar cubes, placing them tightly together in an approved design, and allowing them to dry.

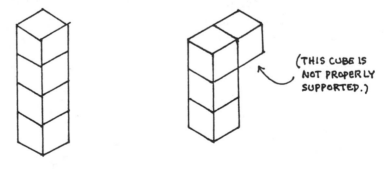

(A FULLY SUPPORTED DESIGN)   (NOT ALLOWABLE)

2. The learner's second job, again using four sugar cubes, is to design as many multiple-level buildings as possible. An additional requirement is that all cubes, except those on ground level, must be fully supported (see examples above). Findings should be recorded, as side views, on graph paper or the learners may do so using the "3-D Drawing Paper." Again, if desired, models can be made by moistening the sides of the sugar cubes and sticking them together.

3. A third job might involve giving the learners more cubes, perhaps eight, and asking them to design all possible buildings of 1-story, 2-stories, 3-stories . . . 8 stories. A few of the possible designs are shown (on 3-D drawing paper) in the Example.

Example: Shown below are some of the student designs for *Sugar Cube Buildings* when working with eight sugar cubes.

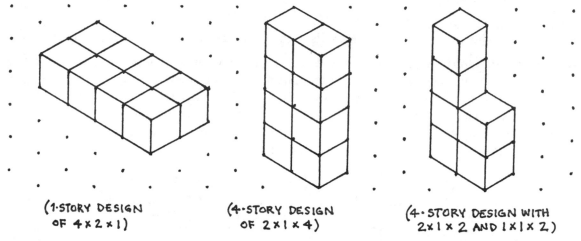

(1·STORY DESIGN   (4·STORY DESIGN   (4·STORY DESIGN WITH
OF 4×2×1)   OF 2×1×4)   2×1×2 AND 1×1×2)

Extensions:

1. Challenge the students to use a large number of sugar cubes, perhaps 36 (or 48 or 100), for their next job. With the specified number of cubes they are to create all possible buildings that are rectangular solids (they might think of them as solid box shapes with no openings). The learners should, of course, record, discuss, compare and contrast their findings. In particular, they should note any patterns discovered.

2. For advanced learners, assign costs per square unit and have them determine the total price for different building designs that utilize the same number of sugar cubes. For example, using the prices listed below, determine the costs for all the different four-cube buildings. The same may be done with buildings utilizing more, or fewer, sugar cubes.

Costs: Roof   = $5,000 per square unit
            Floor (or land) = $10,000 per square unit
            Outside Walls   = $3,000 per square unit

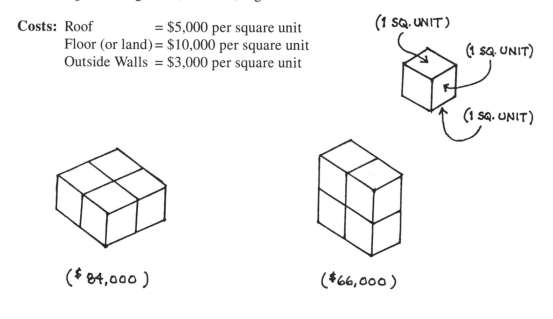

($84,000)   ($66,000)

3-D DRAWING PAPER

A CHOCOLATE CHIP HUNT

Grades 1–8

☒ total group activity	☒ concrete/manipulative
☒ cooperative activity	☒ visual/pictorial
☒ independent activity	☒ abstract procedure

Why Do It: To utilize estimation, data gathering, information organization, and logical-thinking skills while investigating a real-life application of mathematics.

You Will Need: Several packages of commercially baked chocolate chip cookies; napkins; pencils; and a "Chocolate Chip Records" page.

How to Do It:

1. Begin by asking who would like to have a chocolate chip cookie? As most will respond positively, suggest that they wash their hands, because their next math activity uses chocolate chip cookies and, if they wish, they will be able to eat them when finished.

2. Pass out a "Chocolate Chip Records" page, napkins and one cookie (use the same brand for everyone) to each participant. Their first math job is to estimate how many chocolate chips they think are in their cookie, and to write their estimate on the records page. Their next job is to break the cookie into small pieces in order to locate and count all of the chocolate chips in it; the number found should also be recorded. (If the learners wish, the cookie portions may now be eaten.) At this point, the teacher, or a leader, should begin to solicit and organize the individual findings on the chalkboard (or on butcher paper or an overhead transparency). Following a discussion about this data, the students might cooperatively develop a bar graph portraying the information gathered.

3. The learners might next be asked, "If I give you another cookie of the same brand, how many chocolate chips will this new cookie have? Will it have the same number of chips as your first cookie? On your recording sheet, write down your estimates and tell why you think as you do." Allow the learners to have a second cookie and to complete this new math job. Again the teacher should solicit the chocolate chip information and, with the learner's help, organize it on the chalkboard. A bar graph should also be developed, and the information compared and contrasted with that from the first trial.

4. A third math job might involve the use of different brands of chocolate chip cookies. As such, the learners should estimate, record their estimates, break up the cookies and count the actual chips, record and organize this information, graph it, and compare, contrast and discuss their findings. They may also, if they wish, eat the data! Their comparisons of the numbers of chocolate chips in the different brands should be most revealing.

Example: In the situation pictured below, the learners are comparing two different brands of cookies to find out which is the "chocolate chippiest"!

I'VE EATEN 3 COOKIES FROM THIS BOX. SO FAR I FOUND 9, 13, AND 12 CHIPS. I DON'T THINK THIS BRAND IS VERY "CHOCOLATE CHIPPY".

HEY, THAT'S 19, 16, 18 AND 17 CHIPS IN MY BRAND OF COOKIES SO FAR. THAT'S AN AVERAGE OF 17½ CHOCOLATE CHIPS PER COOKIE. THAT'S PRETTY GOOD!

Extensions:

1. The activities for young learners might include estimating, counting, tallying, and graphing the chocolate chips, as well as doing some comparing and contrasting. Middle-grade and older students should also make brand comparisons of price versus value received.

2. Able students should also compare the chocolate chip cookie data in terms of means, medians, and modes. If done, for instance, in terms of the number of chips in one brand of cookies, the learners might find the chocolate chip *range* (lowest to highest number), the chip *mean* (the average number of chips), the *median* (the "middle" number of chips), and/or the chocolate chip *mode* (the number found most frequently).

CHOCOLATE CHIP RECORDS

What I found when checking for chocolate chips in one brand of cookies was:

	1st Cookie	2nd Cookie	3rd Cookie
Estimated number of chips			
Actual number of chips			

What the whole group found when checking one brand of cookies for chips was:

Class Chocolate Chip Graph for _____ Brand of Cookies

People who found this number of chocolate chips	10	
	9	
	8	
	7	
	6	
	5	
	4	
	3	
	2	
	1	

Numbers of Chocolate Chips per Cookie

What we found when checking several brands of cookies for chocolate chips was:

Class Chocolate Chip Graph for Several Brands of Cookies

Brands of Cookies

Numbers of Chocolate Chips per Cookie

FLEXAGON CREATIONS

Grades 1–8

☒ total group activity
☒ cooperative activity
☒ independent activity

☒ concrete/manipulative
☒ visual/pictorial
☒ abstract procedure

Why Do It: To physically investigate and analyze the attributes of geometric 3-dimensional figures.

You Will Need: Flexagon patterns (as shown below); a supply of card stock (discarded file folders work well); rubber bands; pencils; scissors; and the "Can You Create a Flexagon?" workpage. A math dictionary and/or math textbooks with good glossaries may also prove helpful.

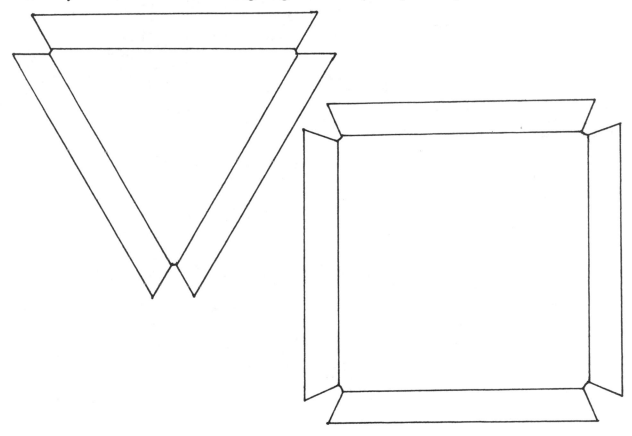

How to Do It: Have the learners trace the triangle and square flexagon patterns on card stock, cut them out, and fold the tabs in both directions. Approximately ten of each pattern will be needed for each group, or each individual. Next, provide rubber bands and allow the students to explore what happens when the tabs of the flexagons are banded to each other. The learners will soon make findings such as 4 triangles rubber banded together make a closed figure (a triangular based pyramid), 6 squares banded together can make a cube, etc. Now distribute the "Can You Create a Flexagon?" workpage and have the students predict whether they will be able to build the suggested geometric configurations. They should then attempt to construct them using flexagons and rubber bands and discuss whether they were able to do so and why. The learners might also wish to know the names for each figure; various reference sources may help, but a mathematics dictionary and/or math textbooks containing good glossaries will likely be the most helpful.

Example: Shown below are some student-designed flexagons. Student #1 has used a square and 4 triangles to create a square-based pyramid and Student #2 utilized 10 squares to build the framework for a rectangular solid.

(STUDENT #1)   (STUDENT #2)

Extensions:

1. Challenge the learners to create geometric shapes other than those built when completing the "Can You Create a Flexagon?" workpage. They may use as many triangle and square flexagon pieces as they wish.

2. Construct flexagon patterns with 5, 6, 7, 8, or more edges. Then build "new" flexagons and keep a record of the number of faces of each type, the number of edges, the number of vertices, and what the name for each figure is.

3. Slightly different frameworks can be built with plastic straws (of the same lengths) and paper clips. To do so insert a paper clip into each end of a straw, but leave loops of about ⅛ inch extending. Into each loop hook another paper clip. Insert these "new" paper clips into "new" straws and continue the process until the desired framework has been constructed.

4. A fun extension, once the plastic straw and paper clip frameworks have been built (see Extension 3 above), is to dip them in soap film and make note of the bubble configurations that result. The learners, and maybe the teacher too, will be surprised. (*Note:* The soap film is of the same type used in children's bubble-blowing sets. You may make your own with a bucket of water and dishwashing liquid soap; mix it fairly strong.)

CAN YOU CREATE A FLEXAGON?

Can you make a closed figure with:	Prediction: (Yes) (No)	Build it if you can. Were you able to?	What is the mathematical name for this flexagon?
3 triangles?			
4 triangles?			
5 triangles?			
6 triangles?			
3 squares and 1 triangle?			
3 squares and 2 triangles?			
5 squares and 4 triangles?			
6 squares and 2 triangles?			
1 square and 4 triangles?			
1 square and 5 triangles?			
4 squares?			
6 squares?			
8 squares?			
10 squares?			

Use triangles and/or squares and try to create some more flexagons. In the spaces below list any that you found.

What did this investigation show? Describe it with a simple statement.

WATERMELON MATH

Grades K–8

☒ total group activity
☒ cooperative activity
☐ independent activity

☒ concrete/manipulative
☒ visual/pictorial
☒ abstract procedure

Why Do It: To have the learners experience a hands-on mathematical investigation using a watermelon (or other fruit or vegetable). When doing so they will utilize estimation, counting, place value, computation, and graphing skills.

You Will Need: String; scissors; weights (or use 1 pound of butter, etc., as cited below); a weight scale; graph paper; plastic or paper cups; napkins; a large knife; paper; and pencils.

How to Do It:

1. Begin by secretly bringing the watermelon to class in a box. The learners should try to find out about the contents of the box by asking attribute questions that can be answered yes or no. (They may ask questions as, "Is it spherical (or round shaped)," but not, "Is it a soccer ball?") When they are quite certain they know what it is, a last "Is it a (specific item)" question is allowed. Then hold the watermelon up for everyone to see.

2. Continue by providing each participant with a piece of string. Ask them, "How big around (the girth) is the watermelon?" Then have each person estimate and cut off a piece of string that they think is the proper length. Wrap a new piece of string around the watermelon and cut it off to equal exactly the girth. Then make a string graph with the categories TOO SHORT, JUST RIGHT, and TOO LONG by suspending all of the strings from the top of a bulletin board in ascending order. Discuss the students' findings and how they might make closer estimates in the future.

3. The learners might next deal with the weight of the watermelon. To do so, they might lift and compare it with pound (or metric) weights (or if not available use 1 pound of butter, 5 pounds of sugar, and a 10-pound sack of flour), and then estimate how many pounds they think the watermelon weighs. The melon should then be weighed using a scale, and a graph indicating TOO LIGHT, JUST RIGHT, and TOO HEAVY should be developed and discussed.

4. Ask the participants to wash up because next they get to eat watermelon, but they must save all the seeds. Before eating, however, they must estimate how many seeds will be in the watermelon. Also, have them help decide how to divide the melon into pieces that are about equal, tell what fraction each piece will be, cut it into pieces, and eat the watermelon. When finished eating, provide small cups (clear plastic are best) and have them place 10 seeds in each cup. Together count all the seeds: 10, 20, 30 . . . to the total. (*Note:* Pile each 10 cups together to equal 100's. When doing so be certain to help the students see the place value connections.) Furthermore, another graph may be constructed to note and discuss TOO FEW, JUST RIGHT, and TOO MANY.

5. A further activity to determine how much of the watermelon was rind and how much was edible might be examined. This can be done, of course, by weighing all of the leftover rind pieces together and subtracting from the total weight of the melon, which had been determined earlier.

Example: In the illustration below, the learners are counting the watermelon seeds, putting 10 in each clear plastic cup, and stacking 10 cups together to make 100's.

Extension: Use other fruits and vegetables for similar investigations. Apples or oranges work especially well when students are working individually. Pumpkins or squash will also work well for large-group investigations. Even peanuts can be investigated as to the number in each shell, how many it takes to equal a pound, how much space they take up in versus out of the shells, etc.

RESTAURANT MENU MATH

Grades K–8

☒ total group activity
☒ cooperative activity
☒ independent activity

☐ concrete/manipulative
☒ visual/pictorial
☒ abstract procedure

Why Do It: To investigate real-life math application problems students are interested in.

You Will Need: A supply of restaurant menus will be needed (if asked, many restaurants will provide old menus for free; or menus may be photocopied) plus pencils and paper.

How to Do It: Have the learners decide, for instance, who they might be going to breakfast with on Sunday morning. It then becomes their job to "take the orders" and determine the total cost including tax and tip. The learners might also check each other's bills for accuracy and/or work with money (real or facsimile) to make change for each.

Example: Shown below is the breakfast portion of a menu. A student and his mom and dad will be eating breakfast together. What items will each order, and what will the total cost be?

Breakfast Anytime

OUTRAGEOUS OMELETTES
Three egg omelettes are served with six golden hotcakes, or hashbrown potatoes and toast.
Biscuit and gravy may be substituted for toast. Bagels for toast - 55¢ extra

THREE CHEESE OMELETTE — American, Swiss and Cheddar cheese	3.95	LINGUICA — Filled with diced linguica and cheese	4.65
HAM AND CHEESE — Tender diced ham and melted cheese	4.75	BARN BURNER OMELETTE — Topped with chili beans and cheese	3.95
WESTERN OMELETTE — Fresh bell peppers, onions and diced ham	4.75	COUNTRY FARM — Diced sausage blended in the omelette & covered with country gravy	4.75
PARTY OMELETTE — Filled with ham, bacon, green peppers, mushrooms, onions and tomatoes, covered with delicious cheese sauce	5.25	VEGETARIAN OMELETTE — Filled with bell peppers, mushrooms, onions, tomatoes, & cheese	4.75
GIANT CAMPUS OMELETTE — Four eggs with ham, bacon, sausage, Swiss, Cheddar, and Armstein cheese	5.65	CALIFORNIA OMELETTE — Filled with mushrooms and tomatoes, topped with Swiss cheese and guacamole	4.95

Breakfast Combinations
Served with six golden hotcakes, or hashbrown potatoes and toast.
Biscuit and gravy may be substituted for toast. Bagels for toast - 55¢ extra
(Egg substitute scrambled available - no extra charge)

SAMPLER BREAKFAST — Two eggs, 2 slices of bacon, 2 link sausages, 1 small slice of ham, hashbrowns and 1 biscuit topped with country gravy	3.95	LINGUICA AND EGGS — Two eggs and linguica sausage	4.65
TWO EGGS, ANY STYLE	2.95	GIANT CHICKEN FRIED STEAK — Homemade chicken fried steak, smothered in country gravy, served with 2 eggs, hashbrowns and toast	4.95
BACON AND TWO EGGS — Cooked any style with four bacon strips	3.95	CORNED BEEF HASH AND EGGS	4.45
SAUSAGE AND EGGS — Two eggs with sausage patty or three large links	3.95	NEW YORK STEAK AND EGGS — Breakfast-sized steak and two ranch eggs	5.85
DICED HAM AND SCRAMBLED EGGS — Savory pieces of ham	3.85		
GIANT HAM AND EGGS — Savory smoked ham slice and two eggs	4.35		

JACK'S "CLASSIC" BREAKFAST
SPECIAL....3.45
One egg, choice of two strips of bacon or two
sausage links with six golden hotcakes, or hash
brown potatoes and toast.
Your choice of juice add 75¢

Juices & Fruit

ORANGE JUICE, TOMATO JUICE, GRAPEFRUIT JUICE, APPLE JUICE	...Reg. 1.10 ...Large 1.25	GRAPEFRUIT OR MELON (IN SEASON)	1.35
		FRESH FRUIT	1.65

More Breakfasts
Available anytime

Country Fixin's

ROBERT E. LEE — Fluffy buttermilk biscuits & creamy country gravy, choice of ham or country sausage, served with fruit or hashbrowns	4.45
COUNTRY BREAKFAST — Biscuits topped with country gravy and two bacon strips or sausage links	2.65
COUNTRY BREAKFAST BENEDICT — English muffin, chicken fried steak, country gravy with scrambled eggs and hashbrowns	4.95

Waffles
(served from 5 AM to 2 PM daily)

PLAIN WAFFLE	2.25
WAFFLE SANDWICH — 2 strips of bacon and one egg as you like it	3.45
STRAWBERRY WAFFLE — With lots of whipped cream	3.25
BELGIAN SUPER WAFFLE	2.65
BELGIAN WAFFLE SANDWICH — With 2 strips of bacon & 1 egg as you like it	3.75
STRAWBERRY BELGIAN WAFFLE — With lots of whipped cream	3.45
FRENCH TOAST SPECIAL — 2 wedges, 2 strips of bacon & 1 egg	2.95

Hotcakes

STACK (6) — Short Stack (4) ...2.25	2.45
STRAWBERRY HOTCAKES — Topped with whipped cream or dusted with powdered sugar	2.85
WHOLE WHEAT STACK (6) — Short Stack (4) ...2.45	2.65
HOTCAKE SANDWICH — 3 hotcakes stacked with 2 strips of bacon and 1 egg on top	3.25

Hungry Jack's
All Hungry Jacks Breakfasts are served with 3 eggs and
six golden hotcakes, or hashbrown potatoes & toast.
Biscuit and gravy may be substituted for toast

BIG LUMBER 'JACK' BREAKFAST — Three eggs, 4 strips bacon, 3 sausages, hashbrowns, toast and 6 hotcakes	5.95
NEW YORK CUT STEAK & EGGS	6.95
LARGE HAMBURGER STEAK & EGGS	4.35

Cereals -

Cold cereal, Oatmeal, or Cream of Wheat — with bananas...1.65	1.35
FRENCH TOAST	2.65
4 thick wedges, 4 strips of bacon or 3 sausage...	3.95

Side Dishes

SAUSAGE (3 Large Links or 1 patty)	1.95	BAGEL (with cream cheese or butter)	1.45
BACON (4 strips)	1.95	HOT BISCUITS & JELLY	.95
HAM (Giant Size)	2.25	HOT BISCUITS WITH GRAVY	1.75
LINGUICA	2.45	SWEET ROLL	1.25
1 EGG	.85	FRENCH FRIES (regular)	.95
2 SLICES OF TOAST	.85	FRENCH FRIES JUMBO (with gravy)	1.95
2 EGG SUBSTITUTE SCRAMBLED	1.60	COTTAGE CHEESE or POTATO SALAD	.85
BLUEBERRY OR BRAN MUFFIN	.95	HASHBROWNS	.95
ENGLISH MUFFIN	.95	with gravy...1.25	

Extensions:

1. The menus for young children might be made easier by pricing all items as $1, $2, $3, etc. (To do so place blank stickers over the original prices and write in the nearest even dollar amount.)

2. Meals from different restaurants might be compared. The learners might select a typical meal, do some menu research, and then discuss such items as quantity, variety (is a salad included?), cost, and perhaps even atmosphere. They might, further, wish to determine what the same meal would cost to prepare at home.

PEEK BOX PROBABILITY

Grades K–8

☒	total group activity	☒	concrete/manipulative
☒	cooperative activity	☒	visual/pictorial
☒	independent activity	☒	abstract procedure

Why Do It: To gain experience with sampling techniques for purposes of collecting, organizing, and interpreting data.

You Will Need: A small box for each group, or each individual, with a corner cut off (checkbook boxes work well), and at least 10 marbles per box. The marbles need to be of 2 colors and will be secretly placed in the boxes in selected ratios (as 6 red and 4 blue, etc.). Also, provide copies of the Peek Box Record Sheets for purposes of keeping tallies and analyzing outcomes.

How to Do It: Tell the learners that each of their boxes contain 10 marbles, some of which are red and some blue. (*Note:* Don't tell the students, but for the first trial all boxes should contain the same ratio of marbles, perhaps 6 red and 4 blue.) It is their job to shake the boxes 10 times each and keep a record, on the Peek Box Record Sheet, of how many reds and how many blues they see. When finished, discuss what their tallies were, what numbers of red and blue marbles they think are in the Peek Boxes and why. Then open the boxes and let them see that all were the same and allow further discussion. Repeat the process several times with different ratios of marbles in the boxes; be sure to allow time to discuss the "whys" and to clarify their thinking.

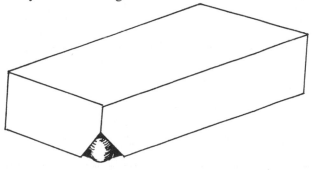

Example: The Peek Box above has 10 marbles in it that are either red or blue in color. Only 1 marble may be viewed at a time through the cut off corner. The box has been shaken and a marble viewed for 10 tries with a tally of 2 red and 8 blue recorded. How many marbles of each color do you think are in the box? Why do you think that is so? If your first answer isn't the correct one, how many of each color marbles do you think could be in the box and why? When all have had a turn discussing their predictions and reasons, open the box and count the actual number of marbles of each color.

Extensions:

1. As students are ready, try Peek Boxes with 20 marbles in them. Tell the learners that there are 20 marbles, but that they will only be allowed 10 shakes. Have them do their 10 shakes and tallies, make their predictions, and then discuss their tentative conclusions. (*Note:* Many times, when populations to be surveyed are very large, only a limited portion of the entire number can be sampled. Predictions as to totals or outcomes are often based on such probability samples.)

2. For advanced students, try Peek Boxes that contain marbles of 3 or 4 different colors and/or perhaps as many as 100 marbles. Again (as in Extension #1) allow only a limited sampling.

PEEK BOX RECORDS

	(Tallies)
Total Number of Marbles = _____	
Marble Color #1 = _____ . I got this color _____ times.	
Marble Color #2 = _____ . I got this color _____ times.	
So, I think there are _____ _____ marbles and _____ _____ marbles in the box.	
But, there could also be _____ _____ marbles and _____ _____ marbles in the box.	

PEEK BOX RECORDS

	(Tallies)
Total Number of Marbles = _____	
Marble Color #1 = _____ . I got this color _____ times.	
Marble Color #2 = _____ . I got this color _____ times.	
Marble Color #3 = _____ . I got this color _____ times.	
Marble Color #4 = _____ . I got this color _____ times.	

So, I think there are _____ _____ marbles and _____ _____ marbles in the box.

But, there could also be _____ _____ marbles and _____ _____ marbles in the box
or
there could even be _____ _____ marbles and _____ _____ marbles in the box.

A PROBLEM-SOLVING PLAN

Grades K–8

☒ total group activity   ☒ concrete/manipulative
☒ cooperative activity   ☒ visual/pictorial
☒ independent activity   ☒ abstract procedure

Why Do It: To provide a method that will help learners to analyze and solve both word problems and other problem situations.

You Will Need: A copy of "A Problem-Solving Plan" should be utilized initially.

How to Do It:

1. At the onset, the leader should utilize the problem-solving plan to work and **talk through** several examples with the participants. Then, after being oriented to the plan, the learners should be expected to utilize the step-by-step procedure each time they encounter difficulty with a word problem or another problem-solving situation.

2. In general, do not expect the participants to work every step of the problem-solving plan for every problem they encounter. They should, however, use it as a means for getting started and working through the "tough spots" in problems. In addition, the problem-solving plan can serve as a diagnostic tool in that it may be utilized to isolate the step(s) where an individual frequently gets "stuck."

3. Of particular importance is the step titled *Select a Strategy.* At this step, each participant must decide whether it might be helpful to try one or more of the following strategies:

   - Build a Physical Model   • Take a Sample
   - Act It Out   • Do a Simpler but Similar Problem
   - Draw a Picture or Diagram   • Work Backward
   - Make a Graph   • Guess and Check
   - Make a Table   • Use Logical Reasoning
   - Find a Pattern   • Use a Formula
   - Classify   • Write an Equation
   - Make a List   • Verify Your Work

4. Finally, the participants should be encouraged to **share and talk about** the "different" procedures and reasoning each may have used. Such sharing should include not only their answers, but especially **their thinking.**

Example: Six people were playing darts. Each threw 4 darts, and every dart hit the target shown. After adding their own point totals, they reported their scores as follows:

Jose = 19   Lisa = 28   Julie = 21
Dan = 30   April = 12   Jerry = 37

Dan said, "Some of these scores are not possible." Was Dan right or wrong? Which scores are possible and which are not? Explain why this is true.

A Problem-Solving Plan

MAIN IDEA (in your own words)

Some people are playing darts.

QUESTION(S)

Are some of the scores, or all of them, or none of them possible? How can we "prove" this?

IMPORTANT FACTS

- Each person threw 4 darts.
- All of the darts hit the target.
- Scores on the target = 1, 3, 5, 7, or 9.
- The players claimed totals of 12, 19, 21, 28, 30, and 37.

SELECT A STRATEGY

We might:
- Guess and Check
- Act It Out
- Find a Pattern

SOLVE IT

By Guessing and Checking we found that 12, 28, and 30 would work. Also, 37 was too large (since 4 darts × 9 points = 36 points). Then we noticed that all of the totals that worked were even numbers, so we decided to try to Find a Pattern. We found a pattern!

ANSWER SENTENCE

The scores 12, 28, and 30 are possible, but 19, 21, and 37 are not.

EXPLAIN WHY

We found the following Pattern:

Odd Numbers	(Target Scores)
× Even Numbers	(4 darts per player)
Even Numbers	(Final Score)

Extensions: Explain what happens when the following changes are made.

1. The same target is used, but an odd number of darts are thrown.

2. The target scores are all changed to even amounts and even numbers of darts are thrown.

3. Some of the target scores are even and some are odd. Explain what final scores will result.

A PROBLEM-SOLVING PLAN

MAIN IDEA (in your own words)

QUESTION(S)

IMPORTANT FACTS

SELECT A STRATEGY

SOLVE IT

ANSWER SENTENCE

EXPLAIN WHY

VERBAL PROBLEMS

Grades 1–8

☒ total group activity
☒ cooperative activity
☒ independent activity

☐ concrete/manipulative
☐ visual/pictorial
☒ abstract procedure

Why Do It: To cause learners to quickly analyze important problem information and to deal with problem solving in a manner that is typical of out-of-school situations.

You Will Need: A selection of verbal problems that are appropriate for your particular students. A listing of possible problems for Young Learners, Middle Grade Learners, and Older Learners follows.

Directions and Problems for Young Learners:

Directions:

• This is an exercise in listening as well as in working with numbers.

• I will read to you five questions.

• No grades will be taken on these questions. You will check your own answers.

• These are nonpaper and nonpencil questions; that is, you listen to the question, think of the answer, and write only the answer on your paper.

• Number your paper from one to five.

Problems:

1. Karen has 2 dolls. Cheryl has 1 more doll than Karen has. How many dolls does Cheryl have? *(3 dolls)*

2. David has 4 toy cars. Michael has 3 toy cars. How many toy cars do both boys have? *(7 cars)*

3. John has 5 pieces of gum. Steven has 6 pieces of gum. Which boy has more pieces of gum? *(Steven)*

4. Nancy is 43 inches tall. Susan is 40 inches tall. Which one is taller? *(Nancy)*

5. Larry went to the store and bought 5 apples. On the way home Jim gave Larry 1 apple. How many apples did Larry have when he got home? *(6 apples)*

6. Mary has 5 crayons in her box. Later the teacher gave her a yellow, an orange, and a purple crayon. How many crayons does she have now? *(8 crayons)*

7. John was asked to sharpen 10 pencils. Bill was asked to sharpen 6 pencils. Which boy has to sharpen more pencils? *(John)*

8. Ann has 3 cookies. Her mother gave her 2 more cookies. How many cookies does Ann have? *(5 cookies)*

9. Mark has a stick that is 7 inches long. Jim has a stick that is 9 inches long. Which boy has the longer stick? *(Jim)*

10. Sally brought 4 dolls to the tea party, and Jane brought 3 dolls. How many dolls did they have at the party? *(7 dolls)*

11. Tom had 25 marbles, and he gave 10 to his brother. How many did Tom have left? *(15 marbles)*

12. Mrs. Jones needs 100 napkins. If she already has 70, how many more does she need? *(30 napkins)*

13. Mary has 2 birds and 11 fish. How many pets does she have? *(13 pets)*

14. There are 20 students in our class. If ½ of them are absent, how many are present? *(10 students)*

15. Spark can bark 10 times without stopping. Larky can bark 8 times without stopping. How many more times can Spark bark than Larky can bark without stopping? *(2 more barks)*

16. If Ann brings 20 cookies and Kathy brings 10 cookies, how many cookies will they be bringing together? *(30 cookies)*

17. Joe has 2 pieces of cake and Bob has 4 pieces of cake. How many pieces do they have altogether? *(6 pieces of cake)*

18. Jackie had 11 marbles and gave 3 to her little brother. How many marbles does Jackie have left? *(8 marbles)*
19. Linda has 5 dolls and Mary has 6 dolls. How many dolls do they have altogether? *(11 dolls)*
20. Ken had 2 marbles. He won 5 more and then lost 3. How many marbles did he end up with? *(4 marbles)*

21. Sally's mother baked 12 cupcakes. Sally and her friends ate 7 of them. How many cupcakes are left? *(5 cupcakes)*
22. Paul wants to buy a pencil that costs 15¢. He has 8¢. How much more money does Paul need? *(7¢)*
23. Karen has 3 pieces of candy, Sue has 2 pieces of candy, and John has 5 pieces of candy. How many pieces of candy do they have altogether? *(10 pieces of candy)*
24. George has 2 dimes, 3 nickels, and 1 penny in his pocket. How much money does he have? *(36¢)*
25. Sam has 2 dogs, 3 goldfish, and 1 cat. How many animals does he have? *(6 animals)*

26. Mike threw the ball 9 feet and Ken threw the ball 14 feet. How much farther did Ken throw the ball than Mike? *(5 feet)*
27. Bill made 12 model airplanes. He gave 3 to John. How many did Bill have left? *(9 model airplanes)*
28. Sue put 12 balloons into groups of 4 each. How many groups of balloons did Sue have? *(3 groups)*
29. Jim bought one hot dog which cost 25¢. He paid the man with a one-dollar bill. How much change did Jim get back? *(75¢)*
30. Tom had 12 red cars and 8 blue cars. How many more red cars than blue cars did Tom have? *(4 more red cars)*

31. It is 8:00 A.M. and Tom must be at school in 25 minutes. At what time will Tom have to be at school? *(8:25 A.M.)*
32. Mr. Smith had 5 bowls, 4 plates, and 4 saucers. How many dishes did he have in all? *(13 dishes)*

33. Mr. Brown has 4 rows of tulips with 3 tulips in each row. How many tulips does he have in all? *(12 tulips)*
34. Mrs. Jones paid 80¢ for 4 greeting cards. How much did each card cost? *(20¢ each)*
35. If Johnny has a bag with 10 gum drops and if he stops at the store and buys 6 more and then he eats 2 on the way home, how many gum drops will Johnny have left? *(14 gum drops)*
36. Mrs. Davis is having 12 guests for dinner. If she has a loaf of bread with 24 slices, how many slices can Mrs. Davis serve each guest? *(2 slices)*
37. Farmer Brown has 4 chickens and each chicken lays 2 eggs each day. How many eggs does Farmer Brown collect in one day? *(8 eggs)*
38. The elevator man went up 7 floors and down 3. What floor was he on if he started on the 1st floor? *(5th floor)*
39. Bill weighs 85 pounds. When he goes to camp for the summer, he loses 7 pounds at camp. How much does Bill weigh when he goes back to school? *(78 pounds)*
40. If Sally has 5 dolls and she loses 2 dolls but later finds 1, how many dolls are still missing? *(1 doll)*

41. A mother hen has 4 black chicks and 5 yellow chicks. How many chicks does she have in all? *(9 chicks)*
42. There are 3 goldfish in our aquarium. How many more do we need to buy so we will have 10 fish? *(7 fish)*
43. The mother bird raised two families this spring. In one family there were 3 babies. In the second family there were only 2. How many babies did the mother bird raise? *(5 baby birds)*
44. We are going to have company for dinner tonight. There will be 5 guests and our family of 6. How many plates will we need? *(11 plates)*
45. Marcia and John are gathering eggs. They have 7 eggs in their basket. How many more will they need to find to have a dozen eggs? *(5 eggs)*

46. If Tom was to take 10 books and put them into 2 even piles, how many books would be in each pile? *(5 books)*
47. Roger weighs 7½ pounds while Bill weighs 2½ pounds less. How much does Bill weigh? *(5 pounds)*
48. In one of our reading groups we have 10 children. We have only 7 workbooks. How many more do we need so everyone has one? *(3 books)*
49. Tom worked 12 arithmetic problems. If 8 of them were hard, how many were easy? *(4 problems)*
50. Mother hen has 7 chicks, and 5 of these chicks are black. The others are yellow. How many chicks are yellow? *(2 chicks)*

Directions and Problems for Middle Grade Learners:

Directions:

- This is an exercise in listening as well as in arithmetic problem-solving skills.
- I will read to you ten questions. Odd-numbered questions such as 1, 3, 5, etc., are easier than the even-numbered questions. You may do only the odd- or even-numbered questions. You may do both if you wish.
- No grades will be taken on these questions. You will check your own answers.
- These are nonpaper and nonpencil questions; that is, you listen to the question, think of the answer, and write only the answer on your paper.
- Number your paper from one to ten. Remember you may choose to do only odd (easier) or even (harder) questions.
- The questions will be read only once. Listen carefully.

Problems:

1. Mother made one dozen cookies. If Paul ate 9, how many would be left? *(3 cookies)*
2. Three boys went to the store to buy bubble gum. Andy bought 8 pieces, Willy bought 15 pieces, and Jane bought 12 pieces. How many pieces did they buy altogether? *(35 pieces of gum)*
3. Robert had 23 marbles. He won 9 more in a game. How many did he have altogether? *(32 marbles)*
4. There are 33 students in one third-grade class, and 29 in another. How many students are there in both classes? *(62 students)*
5. Sally had 15 apples. She ate 2 and gave 6 away. How many did she have left? *(7 apples)*
6. There are 29 children in Mrs. Brown's third-grade class. If 16 are boys, how many are girls? *(13 girls)*
7. Bill and Jim went to the rodeo Saturday. They saw 8 white horses and 3 black horses. How many more white horses did they see than black horses? *(5 more white horses)*
8. Jane brought 2 pints of lemonade to the Thanksgiving party, and Susan brought 1 pint of lemonade. Each pint contains 2 cups. How many cups of lemonade could they serve at the party? *(6 cups)*
9. Mary went to the grocery store for her mother. She bought 3 boxes of cookies. There were 8 cookies to the box. How many cookies did she buy? *(24 cookies)*
10. At the end of the sixth inning, the score at the baseball game was 8 for the Redsocks and 5 for the Tigers. In the last inning the Redsocks made 4 runs, and the Tigers made 6 runs. Which team won the game? By how many runs? *(Redsocks by 1 run)*
11. John went to Mr. Lang's orchard to pick apples. If one bushel of apples weighed 50 pounds, how many would 4 bushels weigh? *(200 pounds)*
12. Mary has 3 skirts and 4 blouses. How many outfits can she make by using different blouses with each skirt? *(12 outfits)*
13. A pint is ⅛ of a gallon. How many gallons is 10 pints? *(1¼ gallons)* 24 pints? *(3 gallons)* 33 pints? *(4⅛ gallons)*
14. Mrs. Rivera went shopping and bought $12.48 worth of groceries. If she bought 12 items, what was the average cost of each item? *($1.04 each)*

15. The distance from Stockton to Lodi is 22½ miles. How many miles is the round trip? *(45 miles)*

16. If you saved 7¢ of every 20¢ that you earned, how much money would you have saved after you had earned 60¢? *(21¢)*

17. Ted and John bought a Christmas tree for their parents. Ted wanted to buy a 3 foot, 7 inch tree. John wanted to buy a 4 foot, 6 inch tree. They decided to buy the tree John had picked out. How many inches taller than Ted's tree is John's tree? *(11 inches)*

18. Mary wanted to buy some ribbon for her new dress. She liked a yellow ribbon that was 21 inches long. She also liked a green ribbon that was 2 feet long. If she bought the longer one, which one did she buy? *(green ribbon)*

19. There are 12 apples on the table. Three girls want to share the apples equally. How many apples will each girl eat? *(4 apples)*

20. Three boys went fishing and they caught 21 fish. Bob caught 7 fish. Jerry caught 8 fish. How many fish did Kim catch? *(6 fish)*

21. Claudia bought 2 yards of material. How many inches of material did Claudia buy? *(72 inches)*

22. The bus left Stockton at 8:25 A.M. It arrives in Sacramento 1 hour and 25 minutes later. What time will it arrive in Sacramento? *(9:50 A.M.)*

23. Mary had 4 pies that she wants to cut into pieces so 12 people can have equal shares. How much will each person get? *(⅓ of a pie)*

24. When Charlie took a trip, it took him ½ hour one way and ⅔ hour on the way back. How many minutes did his trip take? *(70 minutes)*

25. John has 7 cookies and Stan has 8. They wanted to divide them into 5 groups for their friends. How many cookies did each friend get? *(3 cookies)*

26. A rug is 4 feet wide and 12 feet long. What is its area? *(48 square feet)*

27. Harry walked 3¾ miles in the morning and 2¼ miles in the afternoon. How far did he walk altogether? *(6 miles)*

28. Jim has 59¢. How many stamps at 5¢ each can he buy? *(11 stamps with 4¢ left)*

29. Six classrooms are to share equally in a shipment of 42 new kickballs received at Terry School. How many kickballs will each classroom receive? *(7 kickballs)*

30. Karen has 54 photographs taken at Bass Lake last summer. She can put 6 photos on a page in her photo album. How many pages will she fill with the 54 photographs? *(9 pages)*

31. Jim practiced on his trumpet for 25 minutes on Tuesday and 15 minutes on Wednesday. How many total minutes did he practice? *(40 minutes)*

32. Janice spent 35¢ for lunch each day. How much did it cost her for 5 days? *($1.75)*

33. Betty must ride a bus to school. She walks ¾ of a mile to the bus stop. When she gets on the bus, she rides another 2¼ miles to school. How far does Betty live from school? *(3 miles)*

34. Dennis has 44 boxes all alike in a wagon. The total weight of all the boxes is 132 pounds. How much does each box weigh? *(3 pounds)*

35. Each person in Ms. Wilson's class will get 5 pieces of paper. If there are 30 children in the class, how many pieces of paper will Ms. Wilson need? *(150 papers)*

36. If a box of apples costs $2.50, how much will 4 boxes cost? *($10)*

37. Mr. Smith had 800 peaches to pack in boxes. If he puts 20 peaches in each box, how many boxes will he need? *(40 boxes)*

38. Sandra had 22 pieces of candy and received 5 more. She then gave 17 pieces away. How many pieces of candy did Sandra have left? *(10 candies)*

39. How much change will Mary receive from her 25 cents after she buys a pencil for 5¢, paper for 6¢, and candies for 5¢? *(9¢)*

40. At a Halloween party, 35 children were grouped in 3's to play a game. How many complete groups of 3 were there? *(11 complete groups)*

41. Mary has 28 paper dolls. How many will she give away if she gives her sister half of them? *(14 paper dolls)*

42. Mike placed 16 chairs in each row in the music room. How many chairs did he place in 3 rows? *(48 chairs)*

43. Ann bought a pair of mittens for 39¢. She gave the clerk 50¢. How much change did she receive? *(11¢)*

44. The Smiths are traveling 300 miles from the lake to their home. They have gone 248 miles of this journey. How many miles have they still to go? *(52 miles)*

45. In the number 8,621 what is the value of 2? *(2 tens or 20)*

46. Two quarts equals how many pints. *(4 pints)*

47. Which is smaller, ⅛ or ¹⁄₁₆? *(¹⁄₁₆)*

48. A pie is cut into 8 equal parts and John eats two of them. What fractional part of the pie is left? *(¾ or 75%)*

49. A baseball team needs 9 players. How many baseball teams can be made up from 27 players? *(3 teams)*

50. George has 88 pennies, which he wants to exchange for nickels. How many nickels can he get for them? *(17 nickels plus 3 pennies or 17.6 nickels)*

Directions and Problems for Older Learners:

Directions:

• This is an exercise in listening as well as in arithmetic problem-solving skills.

• I will read to you ten questions. Odd-numbered questions such as 1, 3, 5, etc., are easier than the even-numbered questions. You may do only the odd- or even-numbered questions. You may do both if you wish.

• No grades will be taken on these questions. You will check your own answers.

• These are nonpaper and nonpencil questions. That is, you listen to the question, think of the answer, and write only the answer on your paper.

• Number your paper from one to ten. Remember, you may choose to do only odd (easier) or even (harder) questions.

• The questions will be read only once. Listen carefully.

Problems:

1. Jack paid 90¢ for 3 special stamps. How much did each stamp cost? *(30¢)*

2. Mr. Brown's horse is 15 hands high. A hand is 4 inches. How many feet high is the horse? *(5 feet)*

3. Tom had 25 marbles, Tim had 50, and Joe had 100 marbles. How many more marbles did Joe have than Tom? *(75 marbles)*

4. A special super express train in Japan travels 320 miles between Tokyo and Osaka at 160 miles an hour. How many hours does the trip take? *(2 hours)*

5. If 36 children are grouped into teams of 9 each, how many teams will there be? *(4 teams)*

6. A company of soldiers marched 40 miles in five days. The first day they marched 9 miles; the second day, 10 miles; the third day, 6 miles; the fourth day, 8 miles. How many miles did they march on the fifth day? *(7 miles)*

7. Ned had 24 papers to sell. He sold 9 of them. How many papers has he left to sell? *(15 papers)*

8. One gallon of gasoline weighs 5.876 pounds. What will 10 gallons of gasoline weigh? *(58.76 pounds)*

9. Texas has an area of approximately 260,000 square miles and California has an area of approximately 160,000 square miles. How much larger is Texas than California? *(100,000 square miles)*

10. Jan bought a blouse for $5.25 and a scarf for $1.50. She gave the clerk a ten-dollar bill. How much change did she receive? *($3.25)*

11. Bob saved $15.98. He spent all but $1.98 of it for Christmas gifts. How much did he spend on Christmas gifts? *($14)*

12. A restaurant owner paid $12.50 for a turkey priced at 50¢ per pound. What was the weight of the turkey? *(25 pounds)*

13. A small town has 200 parking meters. The average weekly collection from each meter is $2. What would be the total weekly collection? *($400)*

14. At the equator the Earth's surface moves about 1,000 miles per hour as the Earth revolves on its axis. If you lived at the equator, how far would you be carried in a complete day? *(24,000 miles)*

15. Janet's father earned $120 for a 40-hour work week. What was his hourly rate of pay? *($3.00)*

16. The 5,000-mile trip from Seattle to Tokyo required 20 hours of flying time. What was the average speed in miles per hour? *(250 mph)*

17. Jack's father drives a bus. He has made 150 trips of 100 miles each. How many miles has he driven? *(15,000 miles)*

18. At 35 miles per hour, how long will it take to drive an automobile a distance of 210 miles? *(6 hours)*

19. The manager of a school store sold 100 dozen pencils. How many pencils did she sell? *(1,200 pencils)*

20. A traffic court showed that 615 cars passed a certain point in an hour. At this rate, how many cars would pass in 6 hours? *(3,690 cars)*

21. About $36,000 is spent each year for paint used on the Golden Gate Bridge. What is the average cost per month? *($3,000)*

22. John delivers an average of 200 newspapers a week. At this rate, how many newspapers will he deliver in a year? *(10,400 newspapers)*

23. A pound of sugar will fill 2¼ cups. How many cups can be filled from a 2-pound package? *(4½ cups)*

24. A paper company owns 4,000 acres of timber land. In order to increase its landholdings to 400%, how many additional acres must the company buy? *(12,000 acres)*

25. John and David want to share the cost of a model car kit that costs $3.00. How much will each boy have to pay? *($1.50)*

26. A pilot estimating the gasoline needed for a flight allowed a margin of 25% of the total gas needs for safety. If the trip required 200 gallons of gas, how many gallons were put into the tanks? *(250 gallons)*

27. Kathy wants to go horseback riding, which costs $1.50 for one hour. She can earn 50¢ an hour by babysitting. In how many hours of babysitting can she earn enough for one hour of riding? *(3 hours)*

28. The enrollment of a small college dropped 5% from a high of 1,000 students. What was the enrollment then? *(950 students)*

29. Ms. Garfolo and Ms. Bartell had 64 pupils between them. Ms. Garfolo had 40 pupils and Ms. Bartell had 24. In order for the teachers each to have the same number of pupils in her room, how many should each have? *(32 pupils)*

30. Bob's father can get a $200 outboard motor at a reduction of $20. What percent is the reduction of the regular price? *(10%)*

31. Jerry's team scored the following scores in kickball this week: Monday, 3 runs; Tuesday, 4 runs; Wednesday, 0 runs; Thursday, 2 runs; Friday, 1 run. How many runs did Jerry's team score altogether? *(10 runs)*

32. George's baby brother must be given his bottle every 4 hours. If the baby was last fed at 11:30 A.M., what time will the baby need his next bottle? *(3:30 P.M.)*

33. David's dog eats a can of dog food a day and the food costs 20¢ per can. How much does it cost to feed the dog per week? *($1.40)*

34. Ranger VIII took about 4,000 pictures of the moon during the last 10 minutes of flight. How many pictures a minute did the Ranger camera take? *(400 pictures)*

35. In arithmetic this week, Candy missed the following number of problems: 3, 4, 5, 1, 2. How many problems did she miss this week? *(15 problems)*

36. The astronaut, John Glenn, orbited the earth every 1½ hours. How many orbits did he make in 4½ hours? *(3 orbits)*

37. It takes Jim 5 minutes to walk to school. He also goes home for lunch each day. How much time does Jim spend each day in walking back and forth to school? *(20 minutes)*

38. Fire records showed that about 60 out of the last 150 fires were caused by sparks from other fires. What fraction of the fires were caused by such sparks? *(²⁄₅)*

39. Mary Ann's mother told her to be home at 4:00 P.M. Mary Ann didn't get home until 5:10 P.M. How late was she? *(1 hour, 10 minutes)*

40. John's class picture costs $1.50 for the large picture. The individual pictures cost 10¢ each if he buys 12 of them. How much should John's mother make the check for if he keeps them all? *($2.70)*

41. Kathy's mother told her to bake a double recipe of cookies. This means that Kathy must double all of the measurements. The recipe calls for 1 cup of milk. Will Kathy need a pint or a quart of milk for her cookies? *(1 pint)*

42. At a market, a sign for apples read: 4 pounds for 20¢. If Mary bought 5 pounds of apples, how much would she have had to pay? *(25¢)*

43. Jane bought a *Mad* magazine for 60¢ and a *Seventeen* magazine for 80¢. How much did Jane have left out of her $2 allowance? *(60¢)*

44. If Susan was 9 years old in 1984, how old was she in 1990? *(15 years old)*

45. How many hours is a school day that begins at 9:00 A.M. and ends at 3:30 P.M. with an hour out for lunch? *(5½ hours)*

46. Sam and Jerry were playing marbles. Sam began with 10 marbles and Jerry began with 12. At the end of the game Jerry had lost 3 of his marbles to Sam. Then how many marbles did Sam have? *(13 marbles)*

47. John wants a driving permit when he is 15½ years. He is now 11½ years. How long must he wait before he applies? *(4 years)*

48. If in 3 nights Mary slept 10, 6, and 8 hours respectively, what was the average amount of sleep she got per night? *(8 hours)*

49. In basketball Cincinnati had 30 wins and 12 losses. How many more wins than losses did Cincinnati have? *(18 wins)*

50. Four boys together bought 2 dozen cookies. They saved half of the cookies, and divided the rest evenly among themselves. How many cookies did each boy get? *(3 cookies)*

FRACTION QUILT DESIGNS

Grades 1–8

☒ total group activity
☒ cooperative activity
☒ independent activity

☒ concrete/manipulative
☒ visual/pictorial
☒ abstract procedure

Why Do It: To utilize logical-thinking skills in the investigation of real-life geometry problems.

You Will Need: Construction paper of several different colors; 1-inch graph paper; a ruler; pencils; scissors; and glue.

(EACH OF THESE DESIGNS SPLITS A SQUARE INTO ½s.)

How to Do It:

1. The first job is to find as many ways to split a square into congruent halves as possible. The learners should actually cut their proposed solutions from construction paper (pieces of 1 square inch work well), match them to check for congruence, and glue them on a larger paper for display purposes. Be sure the students have opportunity to compare, contrast, and discuss the varied designs.

2. Their second job is to design a 2 by 2 quilt pattern with ½ being of one color and the other ½ of another. To do so the students will need a 2 × 2 inch piece of graph paper and two colors of construction paper. After planning and marking the colored paper, they will cut out and glue the pieces on the graph paper. When finished they should be asked to "prove" that each color covers exactly ½ of the quilt design. They should also analyze how much area individual pieces cover; such as ¼, ⅛, ¹⁄₁₆, etc. (*Note:* See the Example on page 152.)

3. Successive jobs will call on the learners to design 3 by 3 and 4 by 4 square quilt patterns. They might also complete rectangular quilt patterns such as 3 by 6 and 4 by 8. When working with any of these patterns the learners, depending on their readiness, should explore the many fractional amounts and equivalencies, the areas in square units, the many quilt patterns, the significance of quilts in society, etc.

Example: The 2 by 2 quilt design shown on page 151 portrays some interesting fraction concepts. The large triangles, with ducks in them, each make up ⅛ of the entire quilt. Since there are 4 such areas they equal ⁴⁄₈ or ½ of the total quilt. The striped triangles each comprise ¹⁄₁₆ of the total quilt; thus, the 4 of them equal ⁴⁄₁₆ or ¼ of the total quilt area (or half as much as the duck triangles). The smallest size triangles, some of which are solid black and some dotted, are each ¹⁄₃₂ of the total quilt area. (*Note:* A number of additional questions might be asked. How many of the smallest size triangles would it take to make up ½ the quilt area? If the smallest size triangles were cut in ½, what fraction would name these new size pieces, etc.?)

Extensions:

1. Create a class quilt design on large size butcher paper. Each student might be responsible for making a 1 square foot block. Use several colors and a variety of design patterns. Post the finished quilt design on a large bulletin board or wall and spend time discussing the fractional amounts, areas occupied by the different segments, the significance of included logos, etc.

2. Read some books about quilt making and/or do some research about the significance of quilts in society. The following are potential sources:

> Bishop, Robert C. *Hands All Around: Quilts from Many Nations.* New York: E. P. Dutton Co., 1982.
> Duke, Dennis. *America's Glorious Quilts.* New York: H. L. Levin (distributed by Macmillan), 1989.
> Liddell, Jill. *The Changing Seasons: Quilt Patterns from Japan.* New York: Dutton Books, 1991.
> Linsley, Leslie. *A Quilter's Country Christmas.* New York: St. Martin's Press, 1990.

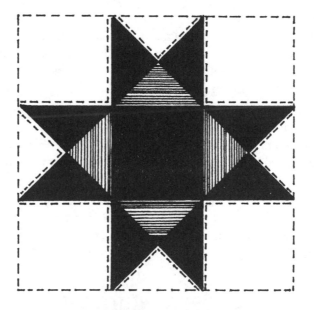

3. Interesting fraction questions might be asked about the above 3 by 3 quilt block such as: What fraction of the total block is the central square? When all of the white portions are combined, what fraction of the total quilt area do they make up? etc.

SCHEDULING

Grades 3–8

☒ total group activity   ☐ concrete/manipulative
☒ cooperative activity   ☒ visual/pictorial
☒ independent activity   ☒ abstract procedure

Why Do It: To allow students to investigate their own weekly time schedule and to deal with the real-life problem-solving skill of getting organized.

You Will Need: Each learner will need at least one copy of "My Weekly Schedule" for planning purposes.

How to Do It:

1. Provide each learner with a copy of "My Weekly Schedule." Have them first fill in the chart space(s), for the upcoming week, those activities that have designated times. Then, for any un-filled time slots, have them pencil in desired activities. Allow them to share and discuss their schedules with each other. You might also have them analyze their schedules in terms of the "wise use of time." (For example, if we are going to have a math test on Friday, is it wise to spend all your unscheduled time on Thursday evening watching TV?)

2. Certain activities might be specified for learners of different ages. Young learners might, for instance, spend 30 minutes getting ready for school in the morning, leave for school at a set time, etc. Middle-grade students might help with family chores, earn spending money doing weekend jobs, etc. Older learners may have the greatest need to use their time wisely because they often have practices to attend, part time jobs, etc.

Example: The learners shown below are comparing and commenting on their personal schedules.

Extensions:

1. Have the learners develop a schedule for a week when they will not be in school. They might want to compare and contrast it with a school week schedule.

2. As teacher, you might share your weekly or monthly lesson plan schedule with the students. When you do so be certain to point out not only what will be studied, but also why it is important that certain things be learned in sequence.

3. Allow the students to do some long-term planning. Planning a month-long period can often be very revealing. You might also want them to see some examples of year-long plans (or even 5- or 10-year projections).

MY WEEKLY SCHEDULE

	Sunday	Monday	Tuesday	Wednesday	Thursday	Friday	Saturday
6:00 A.M.							
6:30 A.M.							
7:00 A.M.							
7:30 A.M.							
8:00 A.M.							
8:30 A.M.							
9:00 A.M.							
9:30 A.M.							
10:00 A.M.							
10:30 A.M.							
11:00 A.M.							
11:30 A.M.							
12:00 P.M.							
12:30 P.M.							
1:00 P.M.							
1:30 P.M.							
2:00 P.M.							
2:30 P.M.							
3:00 P.M.							
3:30 P.M.							
4:00 P.M.							
4:30 P.M.							
5:00 P.M.							
5:30 P.M.							
6:00 P.M.							
6:30 P.M.							
7:00 P.M.							
7:30 P.M.							
8:00 P.M.							
8:30 P.M.							
9:00 P.M.							
9:30 P.M.							
10:00 P.M.							
10:30 P.M.							
11:00 P.M.							
11:30 P.M.							

STUDENT-DEVISED WORD PROBLEMS

Grades 3–8

☒ total group activity   ☐ concrete/manipulative
☒ cooperative activity   ☐ visual/pictorial
☒ independent activity   ☒ abstract procedure

Why Do It: To help students create and use their own word problems based on everyday things that are of personal interest.

You Will Need: Select or devise 3 or 4 word problems that every learner in the group will be able to solve quite easily. In addition, a copy of "A Problem-Solving Plan" and a list of the Strategies for Problem Solving should be available (to be found, earlier in this chapter, in the activity titled *A Problem-Solving Plan*). The students will also need a supply of scratch paper; pencils; and some 5 × 8 inch index cards.

How to Do It: At the onset, the learners should be asked to discuss and solve a simple word problem; the discussion and solution process should include using the problem-solving plan and one or more of the Strategies. After solving the problem, have the learners rewrite it, but with them supplying selected "new" information; then allow them to solve it based on the "new" information. Have the learners write the problem a second time with them supplying further "new" information; again have them solve it. Continue this process of modifying and rewriting (see the Example below which shows one problem that has been completely redone) until the learners have, in fact, created an entire new problem. (Then see the Extensions for enhancement activities.)

Example: The word problem below has been modified several times until it has become a totally new problem; a word problem that, since they created it, the learners have a personal interest in.

Original Word Problem:

Doug has 8 marbles and Susan has 11 marbles. Who has more marbles?

Note:
The initial word problem should be easily solved by everyone in the group; obviously advanced students would start with a more difficult problem.

1st Rewrite:

_____ has _____ marbles and _____ has _____ marbles. Who has more marbles?

Note:
The names and amounts have been left blank so that the learner may fill in his/her name and that of a friend plus number amounts that she/he feels comfortable working with. Having done so, the learner should then solve the new problem.

2nd Rewrite:

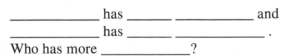

_____ has _____ _____ and
_____ has _____ _____ .
Who has more _____?

Note:
Now not only are the names and amounts to be changed, but the items being dealt with are also to be replaced.

3rd Rewrite:

_____ has _____ _____
and _____ has _____ _____ .
_____?

Note:
The learners have now also been required to change the question. (Typical questions as how many more? or how many less? or what is the total? should be discussed.) Point out to the learners that they have now created their own new word problem.

The learners will likely need to practice this word problem rewriting process, but once they have mastered it, they will begin to understand that all word problems have essentially the same components. As such, they will be ready to write word problems of their own with little or no assistance. Then, to enhance this procedure in interesting ways, have the learners try some of the Extensions noted below.

Extensions:

1. Once familiar with how to write their own word problems, the students might like to compose some of their own. Remind them that, as they write them, their problems must contain the elements listed on the problem-solving plan and they must be solvable. Then provide them with scratch paper and let them begin. On one piece of scratch paper they should write their proposed word problem and on another calculate the answer. When an individual thinks she/he has a problem completed, she/he must take the problem to another student and have it worked. If they both agree the problem is OK and get the same answer, it may be a "good" problem; but if something seems askew, the two of them must sit together and edit the problem until workable. Then, in turn, they must have a third student try the problem. If OK, it is shared with the teacher; if not, the three of them must edit it again.

    When finished writing and editing, the learner brings the problem to the teacher for a final check. If OK, the student is given a 5×8 index card and is directed to write the problem, in his/her best penmanship, on the front of the card. The front of the card must also say *Authored by (Student's Name),* and it may be decorated (as with a picture frame and/or with horse drawings, if that is what the problem is about, etc.) Finally, it must say *Solved by:* on the back of the card. One further point is that the answers remain only at the author's desk. Once each student has completed the writing of two or three such problems, allow a session where they attempt to solve each other's word problems. When an individual thinks he has the solution he must go to the author's desk to check whether the answer is correct; if so, he gets to write his name on back of the card where it says *Solved by.* Since these problems are personal, and about their friends, they will have a great time!

2. Have the students complete a similar word problem writing process (see Extension #1), but specify the numbers that must be included. "Easy" numbers to utilize are those that fit together easily, perhaps 3, 4, and 12. "Tough" numbers might include some like 2, 17, and 512. Whatever numbers are suggested, they may be included in the problem in a variety of formats including: (1) Seen Numbers—those that can be easily viewed when reading a problem; (2) Hidden Numbers—an answer might be considered as a hidden number; (3) Numbers as Words—as 3 written as three; (4) Important Information—as numbers necessary for the solution of the problem; (5) Extra Information— numbers not needed for solution, etc. Again, allow the students to create and use their own word problems based on everyday things that are of personal interest to them.

TIRED HANDS

Grades 2–8

☒	total group activity	☒	concrete/manipulative
☒	cooperative activity	☒	visual/pictorial
☐	independent activity	☒	abstract procedure

Why Do It: To participate in a physical exercise activity, keep endurance records, and then graph and analyze the outcomes.

You Will Need: A watch or clock that displays seconds; graph paper (and/or construct a group graph on the chalkboard or overhead projector); and pencils.

How to Do It:

1. Tell the participants that they will be taking turns exercising their hands for 90 seconds (1½ minutes) at a time. The exercise requires that one hand lay flat, palm up, with fingernails and wrist touching the table. The hand must then be clenched into a fist and opened, clenched and opened, etc. Allow them to practice this a few times; be sure to keep the back of the hand on the table.

Time in Seconds	Count for Each 15 Seconds
0–15	
16–30	
31–45	
46–60	
61–75	
76–90	

2. The players are to work in partners with one person doing the exercising and the other recording the number of hand closings at each 15-second interval. The exerciser is to count out loud 1, 2, 3, 4, . . . and the recorder must, when the teacher calls out RECORD, write down the total each 15 seconds (a chart similar to the one shown above may help). It also helps if the exerciser, without stopping hand movement, begins the count anew for each segment. Play continues in this manner for 90 seconds. The partners then change roles and the process is repeated.

> ... 31, 32; 1, 2 ...

3. When all have finished, each player should graph, analyze, and discuss the outcomes from his or her own hand exercise. The participants might also like to plot everyone's records on a group graph, such as the one displayed in the Example. The analyses of group graphs often show trends.

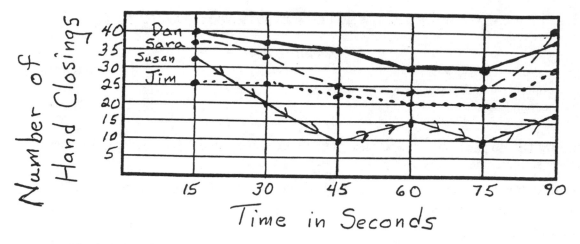

Example: The hand exercise group graph shown above indicates some interesting trends. For example, nearly all players started at a fast rate, then about midway seemed to become fatigued and slow down, but near the finish many made a last "sprint" to the end.

Extensions:

1. Suggest that the participants test their muscle recovery rates. To do so they should wait 30 seconds (after an initial 90-second test) and then exercise and keep records for another 30 seconds, then rest 30 seconds and exercise another 30 seconds, etc. Have them compare their own rates and discuss what happened.

2. Have the learners complete the hand exercise activity while using their nondominant hand. Then have them graph and compare the outcomes to those from their first experience.

3. Have the participants design a test to find the tiring and recovery rates for arm and/or leg muscles.

PAPER AIRPLANE MATHEMATICS

Grades 2–8

☒	total group activity		☒	concrete/manipulative
☒	cooperative activity		☒	visual/pictorial
☒	independent activity		☒	abstract procedure

Why Do It: To deal with problem solving, measurement, applied geometry and logical thinking in a situation that students will get excited about.

You Will Need: Typing paper; other paper of assorted types and weights; rulers (metric or English); yard or meter sticks; pencils; and scissors.

How to Do It:

1. Begin by having the students tell the "best ways" to make paper airplanes. Then supply each of them with several sheets of typing paper. Tell them that they may construct as many airplanes as they wish, but only two may be entered in the upcoming Paper Airplane Contest; one in Category A and one in Category B. Category A is for those planes attempting to fly the farthest. Category B airplanes will try to land on a target that is 10 yards (or meters) away. A further requirement (recommended for most students) is that before an airplane may be entered in the contest, a plan must be submitted. The plan must include:

- A sketch of the airplane
- Length of the plane
- Width at the tail
- Depth at the tail
- Area of the wing surfaces

- Notation of special features
- Distances flown during testing
- Flight test accuracy records
- Other important information

2. Allow the participants to begin designing, folding, cutting, and modifying their paper airplanes. Any folded shape is allowed, and extra material may be cut off, but nothing can be added. Also provide time for flight testing. At a designated time, hold the Paper Airplane Contest and have each student keep records (see the "Airplane Contest Records" sheet). Following the contest, encourage discussion about which paper airplanes went the farthest (Category A) and which were the most accurate (Category B) and why. If desired, the students may be allowed to design "better" airplanes, and a follow-up contest may be held. In either event, however, they should summarize their findings by answering the last questions on the "Airplane Contest Records."

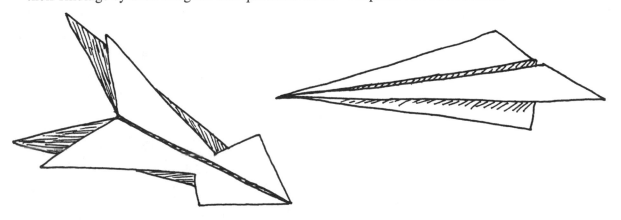

Example: The features of the paper airplanes shown on page 159 are quite different. Which do you think will fly the farther? Which will be more accurate? Which will stay aloft longer?

Extensions:

1. Which paper airplane will stay aloft the longest? This is a third category that might be added to the contest. If included, a stopwatch will be a needed piece of equipment.

2. Which airplane is capable of carrying the heaviest cargo over a specified distance? Paper clips might serve as the cargo.

3. Allow the learners to experiment with airplanes built using paper of different types and/or dimensions.

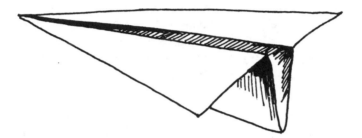

AIRPLANE CONTEST RECORDS

It is time for our Paper Airplane Contest. Get ready to tally the results. Keep a record of them on the following charts:

CATEGORY A: AIRPLANES FLYING THE FARTHEST

Name	Distance Flown	Features of the Plane

CATEGORY B: MOST ACCURATE AIRPLANES

Name	Distance from Target	Features of the Plane

Which of the paper airplanes flew the greatest distances? Did certain features seem to allow them to fly farther than other airplanes? If so, what features were they? Which airplanes were the most accurate in landing? Did they have features different from those flying long distances? If so, what were the differences?

_____

_____

_____

_____

_____

_____

_____

A DOG PEN PROBLEM

Grades 3–8

☒   total group activity   ☒   concrete/manipulative
☒   cooperative activity   ☒   visual/pictorial
☒   independent activity   ☒   abstract procedure

Why Do It: To discover perimeter and area relationships by mapping and physically creating fenced areas.

You Will Need: Several lengths of rope or string from 8 to 100 feet; a 1 square foot cardboard for each participant; chalk; tape; pencils; graph paper; and measuring devices as yards sticks, 1 foot rulers, and a measurement trundle wheel (optional).

How to Do It:

1. Help the participants review their understandings of terms like *square, rectangle, square foot, perimeter,* and *area.* Then use a rope or string, of perhaps 12 feet, to demonstrate the dog pen activity. Tape the rope to the floor or playground in a square and ask the students to determine the perimeter of the area. They should use yard sticks or foot rulers to measure the perimeter of this dog pen as $3' + 3' + 3' + 3' = 12$ feet. The students should next place as many of their cardboard square feet inside the roped off space as possible; they will find the area of this pen = 9 square feet. To summarize, the participants should use their graph paper to draw a map (see the Example) of this dog pen together with the measurements discerned.

2. Next allow the students to use the same length of rope to create other rectangular dog pen fence shapes. (*Note:* Initially, allow only measurements in increments of 1 foot.) They will soon discover that they can create a pen measuring $4' \times 2' \times 4' \times 2' = 12$ foot perimeter; using the cardboard squares they will also find the area = 8 square feet. They will also find, much to the surprise of some, that the same rope can be used to pen off $5' \times 1' \times 5' \times 1' = 12$ foot perimeter, but that this pen only has an area = 5 square feet. These findings should also be mapped on graph paper.

3. Ask the participants to explain, in their own words, what effect the shape of a dog pen has on perimeter and area. Next, organize the students into working groups and have them construct, measure, and record their findings for a variety of dog pens. (Good rope lengths to work with are 8', 16', 20', 24', 36', 40', 60', and 100'.) When finished, have them share their *Dog Pen Problem* understandings.

Example: The dog pen maps all have perimeters of 12 feet, but their areas are quite different.

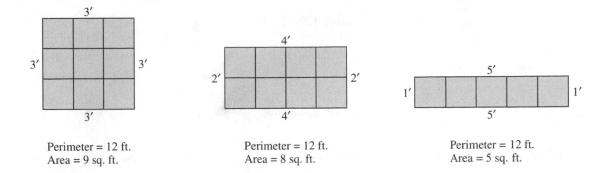

Perimeter = 12 ft.
Area = 9 sq. ft.

Perimeter = 12 ft.
Area = 8 sq. ft.

Perimeter = 12 ft.
Area = 5 sq. ft.

Extensions:

1. Challenge your advanced students to try shapes other than rectangles. They might try Dog Pens in the form of triangles or circles or ovals or . . . ? (*Note:* When doing so, it may be necessary to estimate and combine portions of square feet.)

2. Ask the learners to decide how the noted perimeter and area understandings apply to other everyday life activities. For instance, what shape room will it be the least expensive to purchase carpet for? (Carpet is usually sold by the square yard.) In another case, in what shape should a building be constructed to achieve the maximum inside area while utilizing the minimum of outside building materials?

BUILDING THE LARGEST CONTAINER

Grades 3–8

☒ total group activity
☒ cooperative activity
☒ independent activity

☒ concrete/manipulative
☒ visual/pictorial
☒ abstract procedure

Why Do It: To provide learners with a hands-on problem-solving experience that may be solved intuitively and/or logically.

You Will Need: A sheet of heavyweight paper or tagboard (file folder stiffness or thicker) for each student; scissors; rulers; masking tape; a bag of rice (or other dry material that may be poured and measured); and a volume measuring device (such as a large measuring cup for cooking or a scientific beaker).

How to Do It:

1. Provide each learner with an 8½ × 11 inch (or other standard size) sheet of tagboard. Explain that their job, using just one sheet of tagboard, is to construct the container that will hold the greatest volume of rice. They may measure, cut, bend, and/or tape the tagboard in any manner, but before doing so they should develop a plan (either cooperatively or individually) that they think will yield the largest container.

2. The teacher, or leader, might wish to complete one or two sample containers (as in the Example below) for initial comparisons. This may get the learners to begin to analyze some of the possibilities such as: (1) is a rectangular box-like figure the best shape, and, if so, should it have low or high sides? (2) what about a triangular shape? (3) would a cylinder be better?

3. Allow the learners to plan and experiment. When each container is completed fill it with rice and use the measuring device to determine its volume. Keep a record of the shapes and dimensions of the varying containers and encourage the learners to compare and contrast findings. Permit learners, who wish, to make two or three containers as they seek to improve their designs.

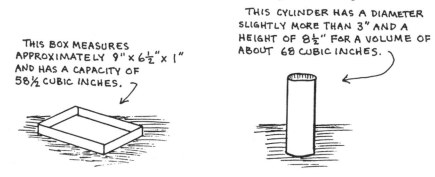

THIS BOX MEASURES APPROXIMATELY 9" × 6½" × 1" AND HAS A CAPACITY OF 58½ CUBIC INCHES.

THIS CYLINDER HAS A DIAMETER SLIGHTLY MORE THAN 3" AND A HEIGHT OF 8½" FOR A VOLUME OF ABOUT 68 CUBIC INCHES.

Example: The containers shown above have been built from 8½" × 11" tagboard, but the volume of rice that they will hold is quite different.

Extensions:

1. Younger learners will likely need to complete this task in an intuitive manner. However, do help them, by using examples, to begin to understand that shape does, in fact, affect volume.

2. Learners who are somewhat advanced should be expected to make use of volume formulas as they attempt to determine the "best" shape.

POST-IT™ STATISTICS

Grades 3–8

☒ total group activity
☒ cooperative activity
☐ independent activity

☒ concrete/manipulative
☒ visual/pictorial
☒ abstract procedure

Why Do It: To enhance understandings of statistical data gathering, related graphing techniques, and probability expectations.

You Will Need: Post-it™ Notes (or 2-inch paper squares and masking tape); a string of less than 12 inches; a ruler; and a pencil.

How to Do It: Begin by having someone in your group secretly cut a piece of string to a whole number measurement (less than 12 inches). Everyone should look at it, estimate the length of the string to the nearest inch, and write their estimated length on a Post-it™. Now, carefully measure the string and discuss whether your estimate was too long, too short, or just right. Continue by completing problems 1 and 2 in the Questions and Extensions section below.

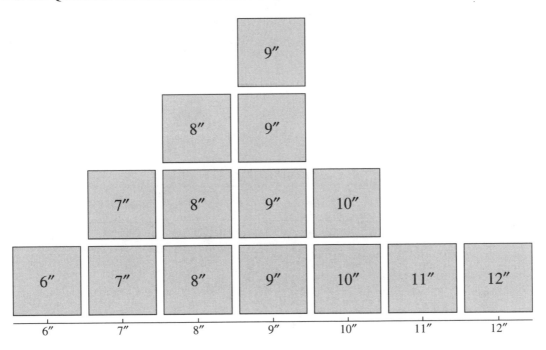

Questions and Extensions: Numbers 1 and 2 continue the string statistics activity started above; finish and discuss these first. Then try problems 3 and 4 which have to do with everyday statistics. Finally, problem 5 asks that each player pose statistical questions and suggest possible solutions.

1. On the chalkboard draw a number line labeled with inch measurements. Then have everyone put his or her Post-it™ above their estimated measurement. Does the graph that your group created look something like the one shown above? On your graph, which estimated measurement is the *mode* (with the greatest number of Post-its™)? What is the *range* (distance from the least to the greatest estimate) for your group?

2. Rearrange all of your Post-it™ estimates in a straight line from the smallest to the largest. Which measurement is your *median* (the estimate in the middle)? What is your *mean* or *average* (add all of the estimates together and divide by the number of Post-its™)?

3. If you had the following scores on 100-point tests, what would your *mean* or *average* be? Your *median?* Your *mode?* Your *range?*

89   96   78   81   96

4. It has been said that the average family has 2.5 children. Explain the meaning of this statistic.

5. What statistics would you like to know about? (For example, the range in prices for a certain type of new shirt, the typical number of puppies in a litter, the average cost for a new bicycle you'd like to have, etc.) Write your statistical question and then search out the needed data. Ask a variety of people for help. Share your findings.

A POSTAL PROBLEM

Grades 4–8

☒ total group activity
☒ cooperative activity
☒ independent activity

☒ concrete/manipulative
☒ visual/pictorial
☒ abstract procedure

Why Do It: To apply mathematical skills, including logical thinking, geometry, and computation with a calculator, to an everyday-life problem-solving situation.

You Will Need: Pencils; paper; and a calculator (recommended, but not required). Also, if some of the boxes are to be constructed, large pieces of cardboard or tagboard; scissors; and tape will be required.

How to Do It:

1. Share the following U.S. Post Office shipping requirement with the participants and ask how they might attempt to deal with it:

    U.S. Post Office regulations note that packages to be shipped must measure a maximum of 108 inches in length plus girth. What size rectangular box, with a square end, will allow you to send the greatest volume of goods?

2. After the students have shared various ideas, one or two proposed boxes should be diagrammed (or physically constructed with tagboard and tape) and their volumes determined. When calculating the volumes be certain that the learners understand how to relate the Length + Girth measurements to the formula Volume = Length × Width × Height (volume of a rectangular solid). To help do so, refer to the notes in the Example.

Box Dimensions	Length × Width × Height = Volume (in cubic inches)
108″ (total) −40″ (girth) 68″ (length)	68″ × 10″ × 10″ = 6,800 cu. in.
108″ (total) −48″ (girth) 60″ (length)	60″ × 12″ × 12″ = 8,640 cu. in.
108″ (total) −80″ (girth) 28″ (length)	28″ × 20″ × 20″ = 11,200 cu. in.

Example: Three boxes of different dimensions, but each totaling 108 inches in length plus girth, are shown above. Notice that the width and height measurements have, in each case, been derived from the initial girths (at the square ends of the boxes). Notice also that the computed volumes (a calculator is very helpful) for each are different. Is one of the examples shown the square-ended box which will yield the greatest volume, or will another be better? (*Hint:* The "best" arrangement is like two cubes piled one on top of the other.)

Extensions:

1. Some learners may need to physically compare the volumes. To do so boxes might be built of tagboard or cardboard to specified dimensions (such as those in the Example above). Then the volumes of the different shaped boxes can be compared by pouring the contents of one into another; Styrofoam packing chips work well when doing this comparison.

2. The United Parcel Service (U.P.S.) allows boxes up to 130 inches in length plus girth. What size rectangular box, with a square end, will allow you to send the greatest volume of goods via U.P.S.?

3. Considering either the 108-inch limit or the 130-inch limit, what shape box(es) will provide a greater volume than a square-ended rectangular box? Show your diagram(s) and calculations to "prove" your solution(s).

BUILD THE "BEST" DOG HOUSE

Grades 4–8

☒ total group activity   ☒ concrete/manipulative
☒ cooperative activity   ☒ visual/pictorial
☒ independent activity   ☒ abstract procedure

Why Do It: To provide a real-life investigation experience that may be solved in a variety of ways. The learners will draw plans and from them construct their own "best" dog houses.

You Will Need: A piece of 1-inch graph paper; a 4-inch by 8-inch piece of tagboard (old file folders may be cut up); tape; scissors; a ruler; and a pencil for each participant. A bag of rice, or other dry material, may be used when determining volume.

How to Do It:

1. Begin by posing the following problem:

> You have a new dog at home and it is your job to build a dog house. You have one 4-foot × 8-foot sheet of plywood and from it you want to build the largest dog house possible (having the greatest interior volume). You also decide that it will have a dirt floor, that any windows or doors must have closeable flaps, and that it will have a peaked roof (see drawing below). Prior to construction, you must first draw a plan showing how you will cut the pieces from the plywood, and you will also need to construct a dog house model using a 4-inch × 8-inch piece of tagboard.

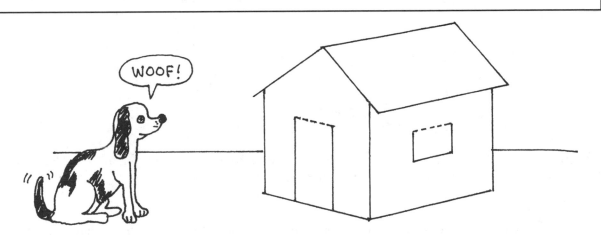

WOOF!

2. Provide each investigator with a piece of graph paper and have them use their rulers and pencils to mark a 4-inch × 8-inch border. Explain that this bordered area will represent (as a scaled version) the 4-foot × 8-foot sheet of plywood. Then provide time to investigate where "best" to draw the lines so that the cut-out pieces will allow them to create the largest dog house. Remind them that plywood does not bend and that all walls and the roof must be filled in. They may, however, splice together some sections of the dog house, but very small slivers are not allowable.

3. When investigators have finished their plans, provide each with a 4-inch × 8-inch piece of tagboard, scissors, and tape. Have them mark their tagboard, cut out the pieces, and tape them together to form a dog house model. (*Note:* Any material excess should be taped inside the dog house and their name should also be written inside.)

4. When a number of the investigators have finished, allow them to compare and contrast the dog house models that they built. Was it better to build a long dog house or a square one? Did a tall dog house provide more inside space (volume) than a short one, etc.? Advanced investigators may use mathematical formulas to determine the outcomes, but young learners may need to take a more direct approach as they decide which is the "best" (having the greatest volume) dog house. To do so simply tape any doors and windows shut, turn the dog house models upside down, fill one with rice (or other dry material), and pour from one to another until it is decided which model(s) holds the most. A follow-up discussion noting the attributes of the "best" dog house should, of course, follow.

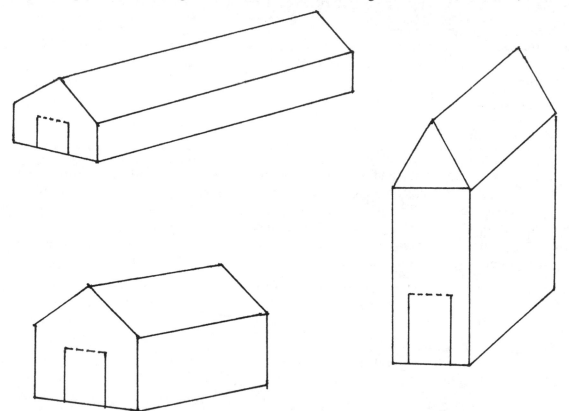

Example: The dog house models shown above have each been built from 4-inch × 8-inch pieces of tagboard, but their shapes and volumes are quite different.

Extensions:

1. Younger learners will likely need to complete this task in an intuitive manner; it may be helpful to relate it to the activity *Building the Largest Container* (found earlier in this Section). In any event, do help them to understand that shape does affect volume.

2. Learners who are somewhat advanced should be expected to make use of area and volume formulas as they attempt to determine the "best" shape for their dog houses.

3. Advanced learners might be challenged to discern the "best" dog house when allowed to use a 4-foot × 8-foot piece of bendable material, such as aluminum.

DOG RACES

Grades 4–8

☒ total group activity   ☒ concrete/manipulative
☒ cooperative activity   ☒ visual/pictorial
☐ independent activity   ☒ abstract procedure

Why Do It: To learn about probability while enjoying a "statistical" dog race game.

You Will Need: Dice; crayons or markers; and copies of the "Dog Race Chart."

How to Do It: Beginning at the top of the chart, number the dogs 1–13. Look closely and circle the dog that you think will win. At each turn, roll two Random Number Generators (or dice) and add the amounts together. Every time a number results, color in a square for that dog; continue until one dog wins the race. When finished, see if you can answer the questions below.

Extensions:

1. Did you pick the winner? How many times did the winning dog move forward? If this race was run again, would the outcome probably be the same? (Check by running the race again; run three or four races. Make extra copies of the "Dog Race Chart.")

2. Which dog, in this race lineup, is likely to win most often? Why?

3. Are there any dogs in this race that can never win? Why?

4. Make a chart and list the ways you can get each of the numbers 1 through 13 when using the Random Number Generators. What is the probability of dog #3 winning? Dog #7? Dog #11.

5. In a real dog race, which of these dogs would likely win? Which might come in second, third, etc.? (You might find out about the different breeds of dogs at your library or from an expert who raises dogs.)

DOG RACE CHART

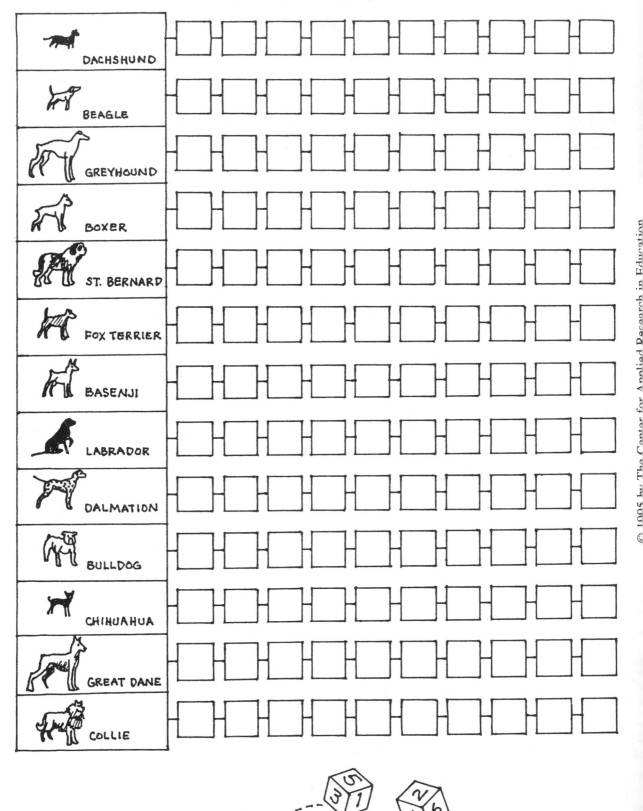

FOUR-COIN STATISTICS

Grades 4–8

☒ total group activity   ☒ concrete/manipulative
☒ cooperative activity   ☒ visual/pictorial
☐ independent activity   ☒ abstract procedure

Why Do It: To gain an understanding of statistical data-gathering processes and how such information can be used to make predictions.

You Will Need: Four coins per student; paper; and pencils.

How to Do It: Each person in class will be tossing or shaking four coins at a time and counting the number of heads and tails. However, before starting, predict the answers to Questions 1, 2, and 3 on page 174. Next, keep a record of your actual findings for 10 trials on a chart like the one shown here. How did your predictions compare with your actual findings? Finally, complete the remaining Questions and Extensions and discuss the outcomes.

4 Heads	3 Heads 1 Tail	2 Heads 2 Tails	3 Tails 1 Head	4 Tails

Questions and Extensions: Make a prediction for each question below, complete the task called for, compare your predictions with the actual outcomes, and discuss the findings with the leader and other players.

1. When tossing 4 coins at once, what combinations of heads and tails can you get? Show each of these possibilities with your own coins.

2. Use the chart on page 173 (or make your own) to keep a record for 10 tosses. Total your coin toss amounts for each column. Which column on your chart had the greatest total? The least?

3. Have everyone in your class record their findings on a large chart. What class totals were found for each column? How do the class statistics compare with your own totals?

4. Make a bar graph to show the class totals. Make a curved line graph to show the same set of statistics.

5. If your class repeats the experiment, will the results be exactly the same?

TUBE TAPING

Grades 4–8

☒ total group activity	☒ concrete/manipulative
☒ cooperative activity	☒ visual/pictorial
☒ independent activity	☒ abstract procedure

Why Do It: To investigate a real-life situation that has multiple-solution possibilities including hands-on experiences, visual mapping, and/or the utilization of formulas.

You Will Need: A collection of paper or plastic tubes of the same diameter (2-inch diameter tubes match the situation noted here, but another size will work if the story is modified); measuring tapes; rulers; pencils; paper; and circle drawing templates (optional).

How to Do It: Begin by posing the following problem.

In order to raise money for a field trip your class decided to operate a small business selling posters both on campus and by mail. When a mail order was received, the posters, which were already in tubes (of 2-inch diameters), were placed in a box which was taped shut, addressed, stamped, and sent.

One day Julie suggested that, since the posters were already in tubes, it wasn't necessary to also box them. A single tube could just be taped shut, addressed, stamped and sent; and the same for more than one tube to a single address, except that multiple tubes would need to be taped together. After some discussion, everyone agreed and they decided to use Julie's idea.

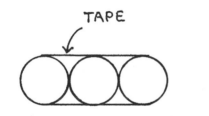

(SIDE BY SIDE WE NEED
15 3/8 INCHES OF TAPE.)

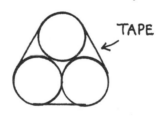

(AS A TRIANGLE WE NEED
13 3/8 INCHES OF TAPE.)

Soon, however, a couple of problems developed. Jose and Tony were taping together orders for 3 posters, but each did so differently; Jose placed his side by side and Tony organized his as a triangle. Susan didn't think the arrangement would make any difference, but Dan thought the triangle shape might take less tape. They decided to use a measuring tape to find out if there was a difference. What they found was that the tape needed for the side-by-side arrangement measured almost $14\frac{3}{8}$ inches + 1 inch overlap = $15\frac{3}{8}$ inches, whereas the triangle configuration was approximately $12\frac{3}{8}$ inches + 1 inch overlap = $13\frac{3}{8}$ inches.

Since most of the mail orders were for more than one poster, the class decided that they needed to know the "best" way(s) to arrange different numbers of tubes for taping. For instance, 4 tubes (see Example) might be arranged side by side, or as a square, or as a rhombus; which arrangement(s) will require the least tape? Since orders of up to 7 posters had been received, the class wanted to know the "best" arrangements for 1 to 7 tubes taped together.

Example: Shown below are possible arrangements for 4 to 7 tubes. In each situation, which is the "best" arrangement? (*Note:* See Extension #2 for a more in-depth explanation.)

4 TUBES

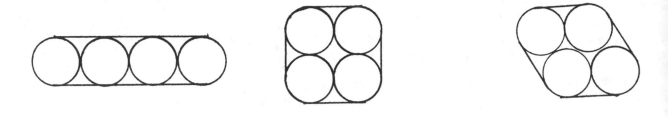

5 TUBES

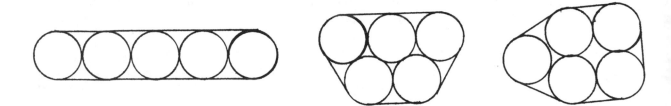

6 TUBES

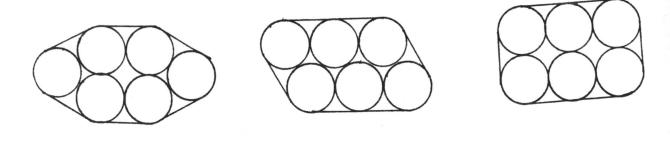

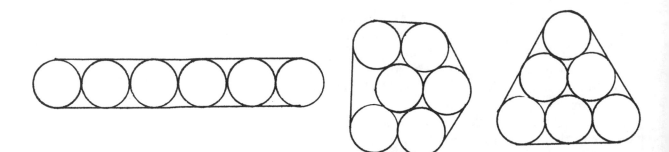

7 TUBES

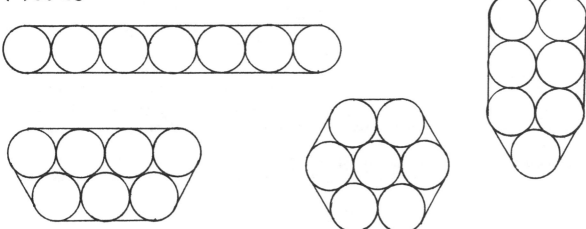

Extensions:

1. Younger learners will likely need to complete the designated task by physically taping tubes together and then measuring each configuration. In this manner they will gain intuitive understandings about the "best" organization patterns.

2. Students who have had some experience working with basic measurement and geometry diagrams and formulas should use them to come to mappings and generalizations like those noted below.

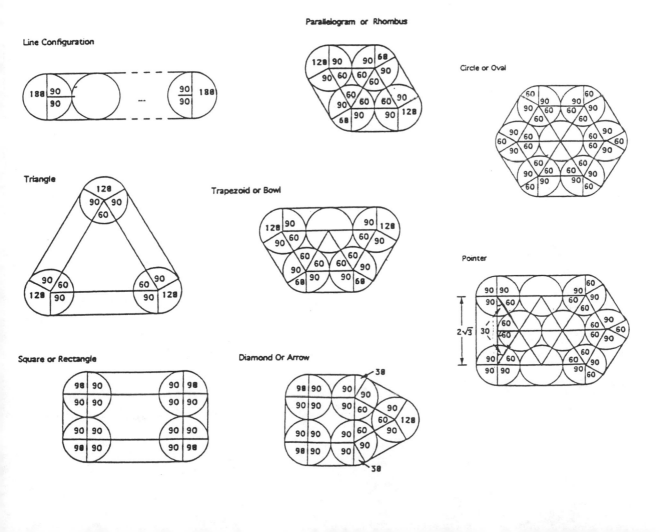

When considering tubes with 2-inch diameters, the participants should conclude:

- the tape will curve around the tubes and straighten out between the tubes
- no matter how the tubes are arranged, the curved part will always $= 2\pi$, the circumference of one tube
- the straight length of tape between any 2 tubes will always be the radius of 1 tube plus the radius of the other, which, in this situation, is 2 inches (the exception is the Pointer configuration)

3. Advanced learners might be challenged to consider costs in the same manner any small business should. Consider the potential cost just for the tape needed to ship 100 (or more) tubes with posters in them; as such, a variety of questions must be posed and tentatively answered. How many inches of strapping tape are on a roll and what does a roll cost; how many rolls will be needed? Are the tubes to be taped at 1 location or 2 or 3, and do the ends need to be taped shut? About how many tubes will be sent out taped in 2's, 3's, etc.? In addition, other concerns might be addressed as what will postage cost, how much must be charged to make a reasonable profit, etc.?

A BREAD PROBLEM

Grades 4–8

☒ total group activity   ☐ concrete/manipulative
☒ cooperative activity   ☐ visual/pictorial
☒ independent activity   ☒ abstract procedure

Why Do It: To experience real-life problem solving by collecting, organizing, and interpreting data about the bread eaten in our community.

You Will Need: Pencils; paper; and access to bread and the people who eat it.

How to Do It:

1. Ask the students what they know about bread. What types do they like best? How much bread do they eat during a day? Following such a discussion, tell them that their next math job involves bread and the following question. *How many loaves of bread do the people in our town eat in a year?* Then ask them what they will need to find out in order to solve this question. Specifically, help them to determine that they will need to know:

   • Approximately how many people live in our community?

   • How much bread does each person eat in a day?

   • How many slices are there in a loaf of bread?

   • What about thick and thin slices, and what about muffins and hamburger buns, etc.?

2. They might determine the town (or shopping area) population by contacting the Chamber of Commerce or the Mayor's Office or the City Library. To find out how much bread each person eats, it is likely that a number of people will need to be interviewed and their responses averaged. By counting through the clear plastic wrappers, the number of slices per loaf might be found and then averaged as a portion of the total. Finally, decisions must be made such as: a thick slice is equal to 2 regular slices; the top and bottom of a hamburger bun count as 2 slices; each ½ of an English muffin equals a slice of bread; etc.

Example: The students shown on page 179 have worked out their bread problem on the chalkboard. Their town has a population of about 70,000 and they decided that the average loaf contained 20 slices of bread.

Extensions:

1. Favorite types of bread might also be surveyed. Do more people prefer whole wheat bread, or sourdough, or cinnamon raisin, etc.? The learners could first survey the members of the class and graph those results. Then they should survey a broader population and compare preferences. The students might also translate their findings to fractional parts or percentages and/or represent them on circle graphs, etc.

2. The bread data might be discussed in terms of means, medians, and modes. If done, for instance, in terms of the cost of bread, the learners might find the *range* of prices (lowest to highest cost), the price *mean* (the arithmetical average), the *median* price (the "middle" price), and/or the price *mode* (the most frequently occurring).

PLAN A VACATION

Grades 4–8

☒ total group activity   ☐ concrete/manipulative
☒ cooperative activity   ☒ visual/pictorial
☒ independent activity   ☒ abstract procedure

Why Do It: To allow students to investigate both the mathematical and the social considerations necessary to plan a successful family vacation.

You Will Need: Each learner will need a wide variety of vacation-related materials and information (most of which they should obtain themselves) such as travel brochures, maps, time schedules, motel or hotel rates, campground information, menus, food prices, etc. A "Trip Itinerary" form, for detailed planning, is provided.

How to Do It:

1. Tell the learners that their next math job will be to plan a vacation and ask each of them to talk with their families about a vacation that they would like to take. They should note the type of transportation they would use, how long they plan to be away from home, where they will stay, what kinds of attractions they might visit, etc. Then hold a group discussion for the purpose of sharing vacation ideas and concerns and, while doing so, jointly develop a list of questions that all vacationers should have information about. Possible beginning questions might be:

 • Where would we like to go and what do we hope to see and do when there?

 • How will we travel, how much time will be spent traveling, and what will the cost be?

 • How will our pets be cared for and will there be other expenses at home?

 • What will it cost to see the attractions and do the other things we want?

- What will it cost to eat in restaurants and/or prepare our own food?
- What will hotels or motels or campgrounds cost?
- What other things do we need to consider and will there be costs for them?

2. Be sure that the learners understand that this math project is one where they must do most of the "digging" and that they will be working on it (sometimes after school hours) for at least a week! The teacher, or leader, will provide suggestions and minimal assistance, but the learners must take charge of their own vacation planning. If, for instance, they are to be traveling by car or motorhome, they must locate the needed road maps, determine the distances to be driven, the time needed, the cost for fuel, and perhaps even the cost to replace a ruined tire. If pets need to be cared for, will they stay with a friend or must they be boarded at a veterinarian and at what expense? In addition to the expenses planned for, what other costs might occur, etc.

3. Allow several days for the participants to gather information. They may need to determine airline prices, get bus schedules, go to a travel service, contact AAA or another road service, obtain restaurant menus, find out gasoline prices, get motel location and rate books, etc. When it appears that many of the needed materials and most of the information is available, the participants should each develop a day-by-day schedule (a "Trip Itinerary" form is provided) of their anticipated events and the related costs.

4. When planned as fully as possible, the students should share their vacation plans with the group. They may compare and contrast their findings. They will likely discover that some wished to take low-cost vacations and that others really wished to "live it up"; but in all cases they will have made plans that pertain to real life.

Example: Displayed below is the partial trip itinerary for one participant. It lists some interesting travel activities and the related expenses.

TRIP ITINERARY

Trip Destination: Yellowstone National Park

Persons: Mom, Dad, Sara and me

Method of Travel: our car   **Time Allowed:** 8 days

Advance Expenses: $167.50   **Total Expenses:**

Other: Our dog got sick so we had to leave him at the veterinarian.

Day 1			**Day 2**		
Activity:	*Time needed:*	*Cost:*	*Activity:*	*Time needed:*	*Cost:*
Traveling in car	3 hours	$9.96	Breakfast	1 hour	$17.25
Lunch at restaurant	1 hour	$18.87	Travel in car + snack	3 hours	$16.80
Traveling in car	3½ hours	$12.75	Flat tire + repair	1½ hours	$8.50
Stay at motel	all night	$56.85	Park entrance fee		$10.00
Dinner at restaurant	1 hour	$26.44	See sites in park	2 hours	
Swimming-motel pool	1 hour	0.00	Rent cabin	(for 3 days)	$140.00
		$124.87	Dinner at lodge	1 hour	$32.45
			Went to see buffalo		0.00
					$225.00

TRIP ITINERARY

Trip Destination: _____

Persons: _____

Method of Travel: _____   **Time Allowed:** _____

Advance Expenses: _____   **Total Expenses:** _____

Other: _____

DAY 1			DAY 2		
Activity:	*Time needed:*	*Cost:*	*Activity:*	*Time needed:*	*Cost:*
DAY 3			DAY 4		
Activity:	*Time needed:*	*Cost:*	*Activity:*	*Time needed:*	*Cost:*
DAY 5			DAY 6		
Activity:	*Time needed:*	*Cost:*	*Activity:*	*Time needed:*	*Cost:*

HEIGHT WITH A HYPSOMETER

Grades 4–8

☒ total group activity   ☐ concrete/manipulative
☒ cooperative activity   ☒ visual/pictorial
☒ independent activity   ☒ abstract procedure

Why Do It: To apply geometry and measurement concepts in a manner very similar to that used by surveyors.

You Will Need: The following supplies for each participant: one sheet of graph paper; a piece of stiff cardboard or tagboard about 10 by 12 inches; 20 inches of string; a heavy washer or other weight; a "fat" plastic straw; and tape and glue.

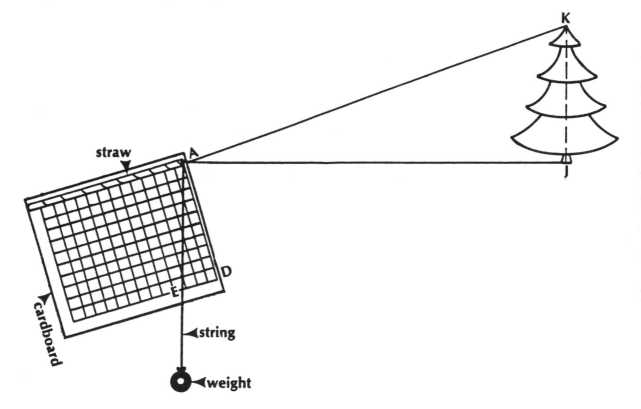

How to Do It:

1. Instruct the students to glue a sheet of grid paper on stiff cardboard. Next, tape a plastic straw along the upper edge of the cardboard and grid paper as shown in the illustration. Then they should also hang a weight on a piece of string from point A. They are now ready to measure the height of objects by utilizing similar right triangles.

2. Take the completed hypsometer outdoors and use it to determine the height of a tree (or building). To do so, measure (or pace off) the distance from the tree—perhaps 10 yards. Now hold the hypsometer and sight through the straw so that the weight string hangs perpendicular to it.

Then carefully tilt the device until you can site the top of the tree and clamp the string in place with your finger.

3. By sighting triangle AJK, and clamping the string in place with your finger, you automatically created a similar triangle ADE (as well as others) on your hypsometer grid paper. Now count off the appropriate number of grid spaces along AD to correlate with the measured distance from the base of the tree; in this case, 10 grid spaces to represent 10 yards. Then, count the number of spaces from point D to point E and this will represent the number of yards in height the tree is; in this case, 3 spaces to denote 3 yards. Also, be certain to add in your height, since you were likely standing and sighting from eye level when you took your hypsometer reading; thus, a person just over 2 yards (6 feet) tall would find the tree to be 3 yards + 2 yards = 5 yards tall.

4. The hypsometer arrangement of similar right triangles can also be indicated through ratios. Using the same illustration, we show that right triangle ADE is similar to right triangle AJK and as such:

$$\frac{AD}{DE} = \frac{AJ}{JK}$$

5. Then, as long as we add our sighting height to JK, we can be quite accurate in determining the height of the tree.

6. As soon as the students have grasped the concepts relating to measurement with similar right triangles, suggest that they try the procedure on objects where the heights can readily be determined. In this way they can check the accuracy of their sighting measurements. They might try the school flagpole—most can be lowered for maintenance—or a commercial building where the architect's plans can be reviewed, etc. In this manner the students will begin to understand applications for geometry in ways that surveyors, forest service personnel, and others utilize them.

Extension: Transits and levels (which are similar to the hypsometer) are frequently utilized when accurate land or architectural or other measurements are made. Invite someone who uses such devices, such as a highway department surveyor, an architect, a forest service timber cruiser, and/or others, to give a class demonstration.

BUILDING TOOTHPICK BRIDGES

Grades 4–8

☒   total group activity   ☒   concrete/manipulative
☒   cooperative activity   ☒   visual/pictorial
☒   independent activity   ☒   abstract procedure

Why Do It: To involve learners with a hands-on applied geometry problem-solving experience.

You Will Need: One box of wooden toothpicks for each group (or individual) and any type of fast drying glue. Spray paint and decorative items are optional.

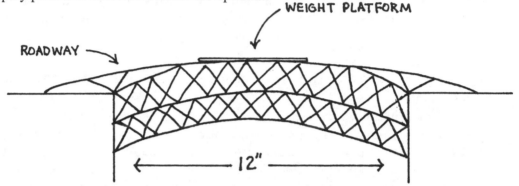

How to Do It: Let the participants know that their next math job requires them to apply geometry by building "strong" model bridges. Their bridges may be constructed of toothpicks and glue only, they must span a 12-inch space, and they must support at least 5 pounds. The bridges and related research work will be started during class time, but it will likely require some homework time too. The learners may work together in groups of up to 4 people, or they may work independently. The bridge-building rules and suggestions are as follows:

- Reference books and materials may be used to obtain information and illustrations of different types of bridges (arch, cantilever, suspension, etc.).

- Use a maximum of 1 box of wooden toothpicks (750 count) per bridge.

- Any kind of glue may be used, but only on the joints. There must be a non-glue area completely around each toothpick.

- The bridge must be functional. (There must be space to drive a toy car across it.)

- The support structure may be built above and/or below the roadway, but may not touch the floor or ceiling.

- The bridge must be at least 2 toothpicks wide.

- The length of the bridge must be exactly 12 inches between the supports, but the roadway may extend to a greater length (see diagram).

- A weight platform, measuring no more than 2 inches × 4 inches, must be built into the roadway near the center of the bridge. In this area toothpicks may be overlapped and designed to either have weights set on it or suspended from it. The bridge must support at least 5 pounds.

- Only whole toothpicks may be used during construction. Any protruding segments may be trimmed off.

- The bridge may be spray painted and/or decorated with flags, etc.

Example: This suspension bridge has its main support structure above the roadway (as contrasted with the bridge shown on page 186).

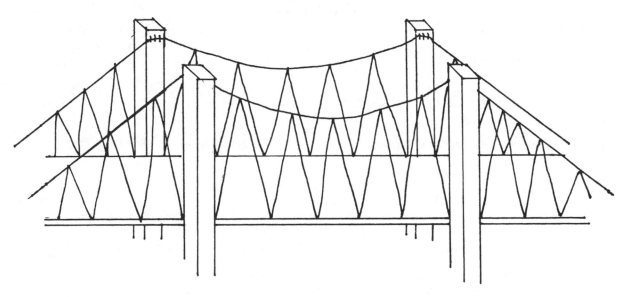

Extensions:

1. Students might draw pictures and note the special features of the following bridges:

- drawbridge
- cantilever bridge
- covered bridge
- suspension bridge
- arch bridge
- pontoon bridge
- truss bridge
- other bridges

2. Learners might research the history of bridges and prepare a written and/or a verbal report.

3. Some participants might be interested in comparing and contrasting important bridges. They might make a table noting the longest, highest, longest single span, oldest covered, most expensive, etc.

A BRIDGE WITH A BULGE

Grades 6–8

☒   total group activity
☒   cooperative activity
☒   independent activity

☐   concrete/manipulative
☒   visual/pictorial
☒   abstract procedure

Why Do It: To challenge the learners with an applied problem-solving experience that involves geometry, measurement, computation, and logical-thinking skills.

You Will Need: Pencils; paper; and a calculator (optional, but helpful).

How to Do It:

1. Share the following bridge-related situation with the learners, have them make initial estimates, draw a diagram, discuss possible solution strategies (see "A Problem-Solving Plan" located earlier in this Section), and then attempt to solve the problem.

> A long bridge has pilings only at the ends, and extends exactly 1 kilometer between them. The roadway on the bridge is perfectly flat, except during summer heat. On the hottest days the roadway expands a total of 2 meters and (since there are pilings at the ends) bulges upward. Assuming an even distribution, how high is the bulge?

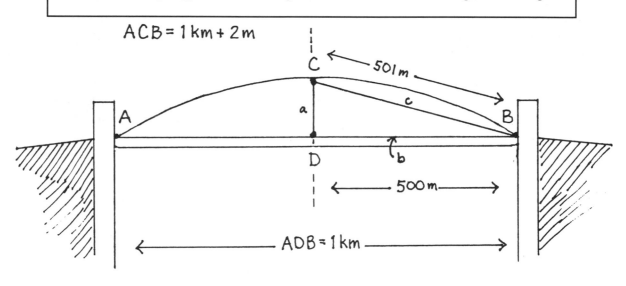

2. As the learners work on this problem they may, if necessary, be provided with suggestions regarding problem-solving strategies and/or clues. A good first strategy is to draw a diagram (see above) of the original bridge and superimpose on it the bulged bridge; it should also be labeled with letters for reference points and known distances. This is a good time to have the participants make some initial estimates. For instance, would the space between the original roadway and the bulged roadway allow enough space to drive a semi-truck, or walk under, or crawl under, or slip a hand between, or slide a sheet of paper into?

3. A discussion should follow noting that we know AB = 1 km and, therefore, both AD and DB must be ½ km or 500 m. We also know that, along the bulged surface, AB = 1 km + 2 m; thus, both AC and CB = ½ km + 1 m or 501 m. What we need to solve for is distance CD. Further discussion may bring forth some plausible solution strategies, but if not, provide the following clue. Draw a line segment CB (or AC) and ask how it might be helpful. Someone will almost certainly point out that we now have a right triangle BCD, and we may use the Pythagorean Theorem ($c^2 = a^2 + b^2$). In this situation c is approximately equal to CB (the hypotenuse), a = CD (one leg), and b = DB (the other leg of this right triangle).

4. At this juncture the learners should get ready and compute as follows:

$$c^2 = a^2 + b^2$$
$$(501)^2 = (a)^2 + (500)^2$$
$$251,001 = a^2 + 250,000$$
$$a^2 = 1,001$$
$$a = 31.6385 \text{ meters}$$

Thus, the bulge height is approximately *31 meters*. This solution will surprise a number of the participants, but it is essentially the correct outcome. (*Note:* The bulge curvature, when calculated, will yield a slightly different, but very close result.) A number of the learners may need to rethink and/or recalculate, and some may even need to build a scale model (see Extensions below), before they are certain.

Extensions:

1. Some students may need to build a scale model of this bridge situation in order to fully comprehend. To do so they might fasten cross pieces on a board so that there is exactly 1 meter (1000 mm) between them. Then have them cut a piece of stiff, but flexible material (perhaps balsa wood or sheet metal) to a length of 1002 mm and force it between the cross pieces. The result will be a scale model that looks and measures much like the diagram on page 188.

2. This same problem may be dealt with, if desired, using English measurement units. As such the bridge might measure 1 mile long and the expansion 2 feet.

3. Advanced students might be challenged to determine the bulge height for quite small expansions as 1 cm (or 1 in.) or less.

Section IV

LOGICAL THINKING AND SOME PUZZLES

Throughout our lives we all use reasoning to attempt to find correct answers. The scientist seeking an explanation for some natural occurrence, the toolmaker trying to design a tool for a specific job, the swimmer intent on improving her or his technique—each makes use of reasoning processes to solve their problems. Logic provides the tools to guide their reasoning in the right direction. The activities in this section will allow the learners to experience both deductive logic (beginning with general principles and then proceeding to the particular case under investigation) and inductive logic (beginning with a limited number of specific facts and deriving a general conclusion). In addition, a number of the included activities, even though they can be solved logically, are considered to be puzzles.

Selected activities from other parts of this book will also prove helpful as learners seek to develop their logical-thinking skills. Some of these are *Number Cutouts, Reject a Digit, Number Power Walks*, from Section I; *Chalkboard Spinner Games, Square Scores, Here I Am* in Section II; *Sugar Cube Buildings, Flexagons, Building the Largest Container, A Postal Problem*, and others from Section III.

STACKING ORANGES

Grades K–8

☒ total group activity
☒ cooperative activity
☒ independent activity

☒ concrete/manipulative
☒ visual/pictorial
☒ abstract procedure

Why Do It: To help players enhance their logical-thinking skills as they first seek hands-on and then abstract solution patterns for an everyday problem.

You Will Need: A bag of 35 oranges (or balls all of the same size) and 4 pieces of 2″ × 2″ × 18″ lumber for the base framework (or use heavy books).

How to Do It:

1. Tell the participants that for their new math job they will need to stack oranges, like grocery stores sometimes do. Ask how the orange stacks stay piled up; why don't they fall down? Discuss the concept that the stacks are usually in the shape of either square- or triangle-based pyramids. Then allow the students to begin helping with the orange-stacking experiment.

2. As they are sometimes easier to conceptualize, the players might begin piling and analyzing patterns when the oranges are stacked as square-based pyramids. Have them predict and then build the succeeding levels. The top (Level 1) will have, of course, only 1 orange. How many oranges will be required for the next level down (Level 2)? What about Level 3; discuss possibilities and then build it. How about Level 4? Since there aren't enough additional oranges to build a still larger base level (Level 5), how might we figure the number that would be needed?

3. It may be sufficient for young students to predict, build, and develop logical concepts for dealing with Levels 1 through 4. Older students, however, should likely get into the business of logically analyzing the orange-stacking progression. Thus, from the top down, Level 1 = 1 orange; Level 2 = 4 oranges; Level 3 = 9 oranges; Level 4 = 16 oranges; Level 5 will require 25 oranges. How many oranges will be needed for Level 6, Level 8, or Level 10, or even Level 20? Write a statement or a formula that we can use to tell how many oranges will be needed at any designated level (see Solutions).

4. When ready, students might also be challenged with stacking oranges as triangular-based pyramids. With 35 oranges the participants will be able to predict, build, and analyze Levels 1 through 5. Then, how many oranges will be needed for Level 6, Level 10, etc.? As before, write a statement or a formula that we can use to tell how many oranges will be needed at any designated level (see Solutions).

Example: The students below have diagrammed the oranges needed at each level of a square-based pyramid stack. In addition, their comments reveal some of their logical thinking.

Extensions:

1. When finished with the orange-stacking experiments, the participants may, after washing their hands, be allowed to eat the oranges. (*Note:* Be certain that no one is allergic to oranges.) Also, prior to eating them, the oranges might be used in the same manner as the *Watermelon Math* activity.

2. The findings from both the square and triangular orange-stacking experiments might be set forth as bar graphs and then analyzed, compared, and contrasted.

3. Advanced students might be challenged to try orange stacks with bases of other shapes. What if the base was a rectangle using 8 oranges as the length and having a 5-orange width, etc.? In another situation, if 7 oranges formed a hexagon base, how many oranges would need to be in the level above it; how many would be needed to form a new base under it, etc.?

Solutions for the Rectangle-Based Orange-Stacking Experiment:

a. Initially, participants will often notice that Level 2 has *3 more* oranges than Level 1, Level 3 has *5 more* than Level 2, Level 4 has *7 more,* etc. This realization will allow them to figure out the number of oranges needed at any level, but the required computation will be cumbersome!

b. A more efficient method occurs when the participants realize that all of the Levels are square numbers. That is, Level 1 = 1^2 = 1 orange; Level 2 = 2^2 = 4 oranges; Level 3 = 3^2 = 9 oranges, etc.

Solutions for the Triangle-Based Orange-Stacking Experiment:
The hands-on stacking of oranges in triangular-based pyramids is quite easy to comprehend; however, as the following explanation notes, the abstract level logical thinking is a bit more complex. With this in mind, the participants will notice that Level 2 has *2 more* oranges than Level 1, Level 3 has *3 more* than Level 2, etc. Thus, it can be seen that the total number of oranges at any level is equal to the number at the prior level, plus the additional oranges needed at the "new" level (which, for the orange stacks, is the same as the level number). For instance, the total number of oranges required at Level 4 will be 6 oranges (the Level 3 total) plus 4 oranges (the additional oranges needed at Level 4, which is the level number) or 6 + 4 = 10 oranges. The following table may help to clarify matters:

Level (from the top down)	Number of Oranges
1	1
2	3 = 1 + 2
3	6 = 3 + 3
4	10 = 6 + 4
5	15 = 10 + 5
6	21 = 15 + 6
etc.	etc.

TELL EVERYTHING YOU CAN

Grades K–8

☒ total group activity   ☒ concrete/manipulative
☒ cooperative activity   ☒ visual/pictorial
☒ independent activity   ☒ abstract procedure

Why Do It: To investigate, compare, and contrast the logical likenesses and differences of varied mathematical phenomena.

You Will Need: A variety of exemplary materials (see Examples below) that have at least one attribute in common.

How to Do It:

1. Display two mathematical items that, at first glance, appear to have few, if any, similarities. For instance, the square design and the clock face shown above seem to have little in common, but let us logically analyze them for possible similarities. Help the students to see that: (1) ½ the square is shaded and ½ hour is indicated on the clock; (2) the clock face shows four quarter (or ¼) hours and the square is split into ¼ths; (3) they both occupy approximately the same amount of space (area); (4) the perimeter of the square and the circumference of the circle are "roughly" equivalent; (5) both show 360° as well as four 90° quarter sections, etc. Also, spend some time discussing ways these figures are clearly different. In many instances, the learners will suggest logical similarities and differences that the leader has not realized.

2. After one or two examples, suggest another mathematical phenomena and have the participants, verbally and/or in written form, *Tell Everything You Can* about the situation. Try some of the examples noted below and, once students are familiar with the process, have them make suggestions of their own for everyone to try.

Examples to Try: (*Note:* Some Possible Solutions are provided.)

1. *Tell Everything You Can* about 9, 16, and 25.

2. *Tell Everything You Can* about these two figures:

3. *Tell Everything You Can* about an orange.

4. *Tell Everything You Can* about these two graphs:

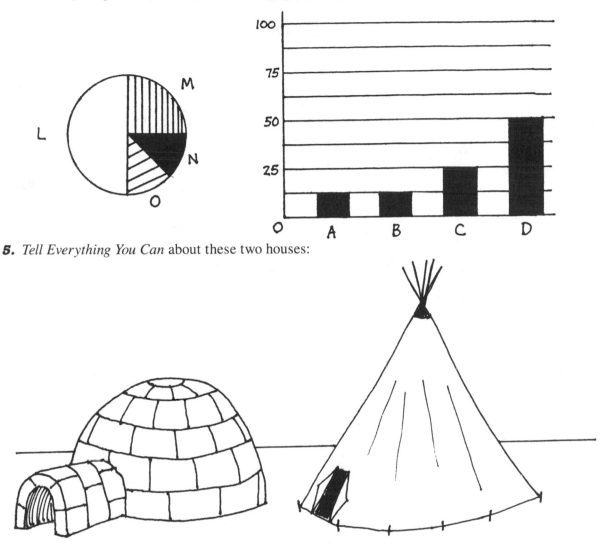

5. *Tell Everything You Can* about these two houses:

Possible Solutions: (*Note:* Numerous other answers are possible.)

1. *9, 16, and 25:* $9 + 16 = 25$; $25 - 16 = 9$; all are square numbers as $3^2 = 9$, $4^2 = 16$, and $5^2 = 25$.

2. *Circles:* The diameters are 1 in. and 2 in.; the circumferences are approximately 3.14 in. and 6.28 in.; at .785 sq. in. and 3.14 sq. in. the area of the smaller circle is ¼ that of the larger; the larger circle has about the same circumference as a ping-pong ball, etc.

3. *Orange:* It is almost the size of a baseball; the circumference measures as _____ in.; the peel is about ⅛ in. thick and when flattened out covers about _____ sq. in.; there are _____ segments inside and each is _(fraction)_ of the whole; there are _____ seeds inside, etc.

4. *Graphs:* Both are graphs, but one is a bar graph and the other, a circle graph. The values on the graph seem to correspond (as with L = ½ and D = ½; M = ¼ and C = ¼, etc.). The graph values could represent _____ .

5. *Houses:* Both are "primitive" houses; both have circular bases that allow maximum floor space; the tepee is shaped like a cone and the igloo like ½ a ball or sphere; the inside volumes for the tepee and the igloo could be found with formulas if we knew their linear measurements.

HANDSHAKE LOGIC

Grades K–8

☒   total group activity   ☒   concrete/manipulative
☒   cooperative activity   ☒   visual/pictorial
☒   independent activity   ☒   abstract procedure

Why Do It: To help students see that it is sometimes possible to use any of 3 or 4 different techniques to logically solve a single problem.

How to Do It:

1.   Introduce the learners to the "classic" handshake problem (see below). Have them predict possible answers and suggest how they think it might be solved.

> It is a tradition that the 9 United States Supreme Court Justices shake hands with each other at the opening session each year. As such, each justice shakes hands with each of the other justices once and only once. How many handshakes result?

2.   The initial prediction sometimes ranges from 9 to 81, and a variety of interesting solution procedures are often suggested. Since it is possible to solve this problem in at least 3 or 4 different ways, let's explore some possibilities.

a.   *Act It Out*—Ask 9 people to stand in a line. The first person in line should shake the hands of everyone else in line and then sit down; this will yield 8 handshakes, so an 8 needs to be recorded. The next person in line should shake hands with the remaining people and sit down; another 7 handshakes should be recorded. Continue this procedure of shaking hands and recording just until two people remain in line. These two shake hands and record the 1 handshake between them. The recorded handshakes are then totaled to equal 36.

b.   *Draw a Diagram*—Using an overhead projector or the chalkboard, place 9 large dots, to represent the 9 justices, around a large circle. Specify further that a line drawn between any two dots indicates one handshake. Begin with any selected dot and draw lines connecting it to all the other dots; this will yield 8 lines, so 8 handshakes need to be recorded. Select another dot and draw the possible lines; the outcome will be an additional 7 lines, so record 7 handshakes, etc. When finished 36 lines will be shown.

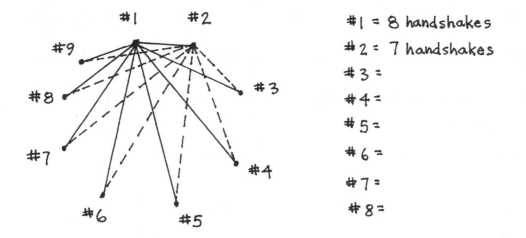

#1 = 8 handshakes

#2 = 7 handshakes

#3 =

#4 =

#5 =

#6 =

#7 =

#8 =

c. *Build a T-table*—Tables are often a help when organizing data and/or looking for patterns. In this table note that 1 person = 0 handshakes (no one to shake with), 2 people = 1 handshake, 3 people = 3 handshakes, etc. Also, as can be seen listed to the right of the T-table, a related pattern evolves.

Number of People	Number of Handshakes	
1	0	1
2	1	2
3	3	3
4	6	4
5	10	5
6	15	6
7	21	?
8	?	?
9	?	

d. *Use a Formula*—Advanced students might be asked to derive a workable formula of their own. However, many students, after experience with one or more of the previous methods, may benefit from seeing how a formula can determine the same solution(s) that they did. The following formula, where n = the number of people and H = the total number of handshakes, can be used to determine the answers to the justices handshake problem.

$$\frac{n(n-3)}{2} + n = H$$

Extension: See *A Problem-Solving Plan* for additional techniques that may be used in conjunction with logical-thinking problems.

MYSTERY OBJECT GUESS

Grades K–8

<table>
<tr><td>☒</td><td>total group activity</td><td>☒</td><td>concrete/manipulative</td></tr>
<tr><td>☒</td><td>cooperative activity</td><td>☒</td><td>visual/pictorial</td></tr>
<tr><td>☒</td><td>independent activity</td><td>☒</td><td>abstract procedure</td></tr>
</table>

Why Do It: To visually investigate and analyze the attributes of geometric 2- and 3-dimensional figures.

You Will Need: An overhead projector; a variety of small objects that will display interesting overhead projector images (as a paper clip, pen cap, soda can, nail, screw, clear plastic drinking glass, computer disc, belt buckle, cassette tape, nail clipper, fishing lures, various tools, etc.); and a file folder.

How to Do It:

1. Discuss with the participants the idea that we live in a geometrical 3-dimensional world, but we often see things in only 2-dimensions. For example, television and photographs both imply 3-dimensions, but actually show only 2-dimensions. Tell the learners that you will be using the overhead projector, from behind a standing file folder, to display flat or 2-dimensional views of different objects. As the image of each object is projected, note that it is their job to visually rotate the object in their minds and attempt to "see" it in 3-dimensions. At this juncture, it is a good idea to allow the learners to confer with each other, perhaps in cooperative groups, state what they think the object is, and why they think so. If more than one solution is suggested, conduct further discussion and then display a second view of the object. Conclude by allowing everyone to see the actual object and noting its geometric 2- and 3-dimensional attributes.

2. At the onset, begin with an easily identified object such as a paper clip. Then progress to a situation that is a bit more difficult. For instance, stand side by side, on their heads, a nail and a flat head screw; both will project as dark circles, but tell the students that these are 2 different objects. They may be confused, but then lay both on their sides and the grooves in the screw versus the straight sides of the nail should make the identification almost immediate. Finally, it may at times be necessary to display three views before identification can be accomplished. For example, a cassette tape (see Example below) set on its base will display a wide dark line segment with a bulge in the center portion, an end view will show a shorter line segment with a bulge at one end, and when laid on its side a rectangle with several small holes plus two openings showing drive sprockets can be seen.

Example: When displayed with the overhead projector, views 1 and 2 of this object may still leave the viewer with a "mystery." View 3, however, will allow most students to quickly identify the object as a cassette tape.

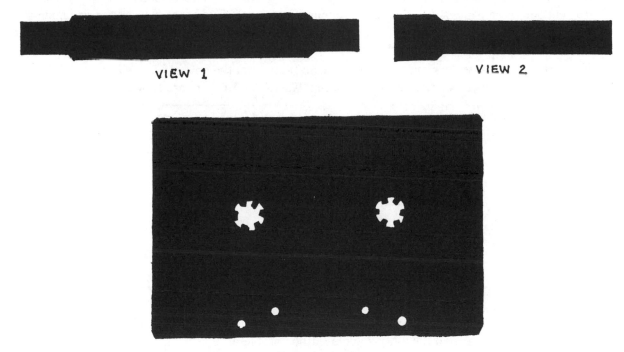

VIEW 1   VIEW 2

VIEW 3

Extensions:

1. Allow the participants to bring objects of their own to "secretly" project. Their peers (and the teacher) should attempt to guess the mystery objects.

2. Have the students do some mechanical drawing where they will learn to draw the different views of an object: front, top, side, etc.

3. Obtain some architectural blueprints for the learners to inspect. Note particularly the different views and other special features.

2- AND 3-D ARRANGEMENTS

Grades K–8

☒ total group activity   ☒ concrete/manipulative
☒ cooperative activity   ☒ visual/pictorial
☒ independent activity   ☒ abstract procedure

Why Do It: To discern usable 2-dimensional geometric arrangements and then determine which of
these might also become functional 3-dimensional containers.

You Will Need: Several sheets of grid or graph paper; a pencil; and scissors for each participant.
(For black-line masters of 1 in. or 1 cm graph paper see *Number Cutouts.*)

How to Do It:

1. Have the participants begin by exploring the following 2-dimensional problem. If they wish, they
may cut out graph paper squares to use as stamps. They should find as many usable arrangements as
possible, keep a record of them, and compare their own findings with those of the other participants.

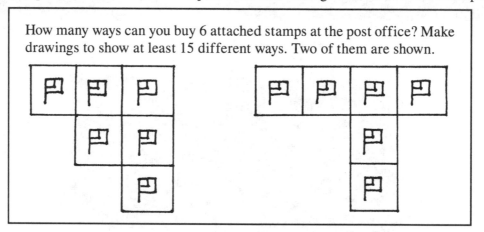

How many ways can you buy 6 attached stamps at the post office? Make
drawings to show at least 15 different ways. Two of them are shown.

2. After exploring the numerous stamp problem solutions, tell the participants to get ready to deal
with a related but slightly more difficult 3-dimensional problem. When doing so, the stamp drawings will be used, but each square in them needs to be thought of, instead, as a cardboard square.
With this in mind, present the following closed-box problem.

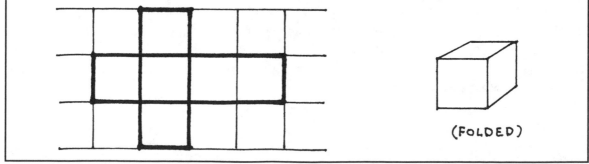

What are all possible 2-dimensional patterns, using 6 attached squares, that can be folded to
form closed boxes? Make drawings of your patterns on graph paper, cut them out, and fold
them along the edges to "prove" which patterns will work. One such pattern is shown.

(FOLDED)

Stamp Examples: The first drawing shows a possible stamp solution. However, because some of the stamps are not fully attached along the edges, the second diagram is not feasible.

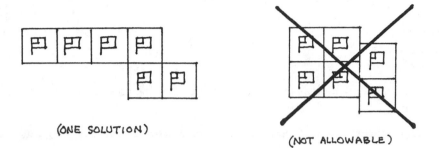

(ONE SOLUTION)   (NOT ALLOWABLE)

Box Examples: The first pattern shown can be folded into a closed box, but the second cannot.

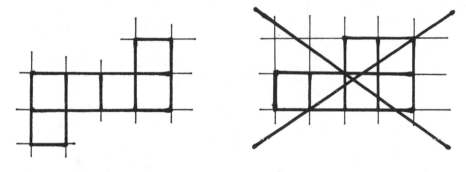

(A FEASIBLE BOX PATTERN)   (WILL NOT FOLD INTO A BOX)

Extensions:

1. In some countries of the world stamps shaped as triangles may be purchased. How many different ways might 4 triangular stamps be attached? Make drawings of the possibilities. Also, how many of these arrangements might be folded to form closed containers shaped as triangular-based pyramids *(tetrahedron)?*

2. Extend the activity to include a variety of 2-dimensional patterns that, when cut out and folded, can make selected 3-dimensional figures. Consider, for instance, dodecahedron, icosahedron, etc.

OVERHEAD TIC-TAC-TOE

Grades 2–8

☒ total group activity   ☐ concrete/manipulative
☒ cooperative activity   ☒ visual/pictorial
☐ independent activity   ☒ abstract procedure

Why Do It: To make use of logical-thinking strategies during activities that first utilize everyday game skills and later involve coordinate graphing.

You Will Need: An overhead projector; transparencies (marked as noted below); marking pens; plus graph paper and a pencil for each group.

How to Do It:

1. Organize the players into cooperative groups and designate jobs (as encourager, clarifier, recorder, speaker, etc.). Then, using the overhead projector, play one or two regular tic-tac-toe games to see that everyone is properly carrying out his/her job.

2. Display a Super Tic-Tac-Toe grid (see projected grid above) and explain that the game ends only when all spaces have been filled with team marks. Further, points will be awarded as follows:

6 in a row = 4 points
5 in a row = 3 points
4 in a row = 2 points
3 in a row = 1 point

3. Encourage each group to try to determine and use strategies that will allow them to obtain the most points. Note that, at first, each group will be allowed up to 2 minutes to select and call out a location for their team mark, but that, shortly, the time will be shortened to 1 minute, or even 30 seconds.

4. After playing two or three Super Tic-Tac-Toe games, take time to discuss the strategies tried. Did they try to place their marks so that both ends were open? Did they try blocking the other team? Did they try to place marks a distance apart and then fill in the middle, etc.?

Extensions:

1. When ready, introduce (or review) the coordinate graphing procedures utilizing x- and y-axis locations. Then play Positive Quadrant Super Tic-Tac-Toe where the team marks are placed on the vertices (rather than in the spaces). For example, in the game below, Team "o" has marks at (1,2) and (1,3), and Team "x" has thus far placed them at (2,3) and (3,3). Since it is Team "o's" turn, they may choose to score by placing a mark at either (1,1) or (1,4); or they may choose to block by marking (4,3).

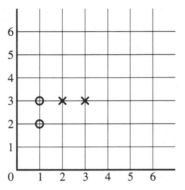

2. Play Four Quadrant Super Tic-Tac-Toe in the same manner as in Extension #1, except that both positive and negative coordinate locations must be considered. For instance, Team "o" has placed team marks at $(-1,4)$ and $(-3,2)$, and Team "x" has thus far placed markers at $(-2,-1)$ and $(-2,-4)$.

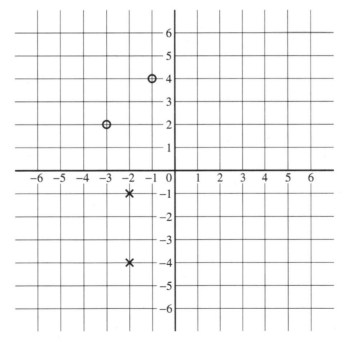

3. Finally, with players who are quite adept, allow three or four teams to play simultaneously on one large four-quadrant grid.

MAGIC TRIANGLE LOGIC

Grades 2–8

☒ total group activity
☒ cooperative activity
☒ independent activity

☐ concrete/manipulative
☐ visual/pictorial
☒ abstract procedure

Why Do It: To logically manipulate the same numbers to achieve multiple solutions and, at the same time, to practice mental mathematics.

You Will Need: A *Magic Triangle* with four number spots along each edge and the numerals 1 through 9 printed on markers small enough to fit into those spots; plus, for record keeping purposes, a "Magic Triangle Solutions" sheet (master copies provided).

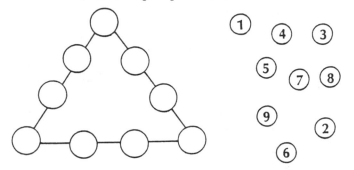

How to Do It: Tell the players that they are to place the numerals 1 through 9 in the number spots so that the sum of each edge of the triangle is the same. Let them know that there are several correct solutions, but that you aren't sure how many. Work one or two *Magic Triangles* together and then challenge them to find and record as many solutions as they can. This activity can be ongoing for several days or even weeks.

Example: Two *Magic Triangle* solutions are shown below (at least 10 more are possible).

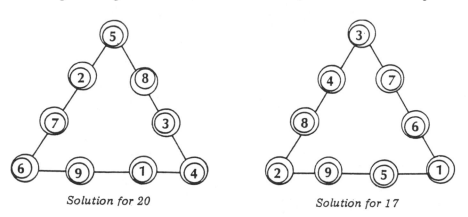

Solution for 20   *Solution for 17*

Extensions:

1. Challenge the players to determine the greatest sum possible.

2. What is the smallest possible sum?

3. Which sum found has the greatest number of different *Magic Triangle* combinations?

4. What other numbers will work to form *Magic Triangles?* (What of 23 through 31, etc.?)

MAGIC TRIANGLE

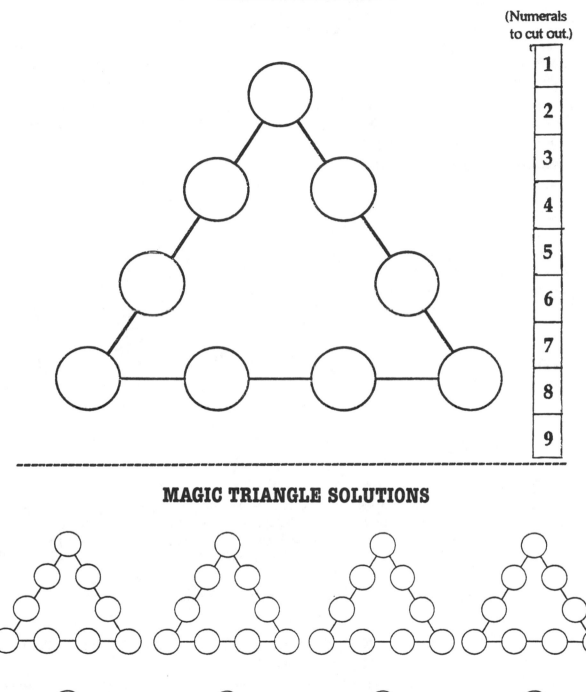

(Numerals to cut out.)

1
2
3
4
5
6
7
8
9

MAGIC TRIANGLE SOLUTIONS

207

PAPER CLIP SPINNERS

Grades 2–8

☒ total group activity
☒ cooperative activity
☒ independent activity

☐ concrete/manipulative
☒ visual/pictorial
☒ abstract procedure

Why Do It: To experience first-hand how the design of probability devices can affect the outcomes. The learners will design and test spinner surfaces that will increase the likelihood of certain outcomes and decrease or make impossible others.

You Will Need: Pencils, paper, and a paper clip for each participant. If desired, blank spinner surfaces may be duplicated and distributed (see copies on page 209). The leader might also use the overhead projector to display a variety of spinners.

COULD WE ALSO SPIN 13 IN 3 SPINS?

How to Do It:

1. Display and discuss the possibilities for a selected spinner. With the spinner shown above, for instance, is it possible to spin a sum of 10? (Yes, by spinning 5 and 5 again; or by spinning 3 + 3 + 4.) Could we spin 11? (Yes, with 5 + 3 + 3.) What different sums could we get with 1 spin; with 2 spins; with 3 spins, etc. Are there any sums we could not get?

2. Next, tell the participants that they will be making and testing their own *Paper Clip Spinners*. However, the spinners they design must follow certain rules, such as the following:

    • Each spinner must have 3 different numbers on it.

    • The sum of the numbers can equal 12 in 3 spins, but not in 2 spins.

    • (Option) The numbers are not equally likely to occur.

3. Allow the participants to work independently or in small groups as they design their spinner surfaces. Once completed, provide each person with a paper clip to use as the "pointer." To do so, lay the paper clip on the spinner surface so that one end overlaps the center point. Put the point of a pencil through the end loop of the paper clip and hold it on the center point with one hand. Use the other hand to flip the paper clip. The paper clip "pointer" will randomly point to different numbers.

4. Have the players try their spinners and keep records of their spins and totals. A table, such as the one on page 209, will help with record keeping. When finished with a specific number of tests, have the participants share and compare their findings.

Test #	Spin 1	Spin 2	Spin 3	Total
1				
2				
3				
4				

An Example to Try: Which spinner, shown below, will work with the following rules? Use the table to help determine possible outcomes and/or test a spinner.

- Each spinner must have 4 different numbers on it.
- The sum of the numbers must equal 15 in 3 spins.
- The numbers are not equally likely to occur.
- A number may be spun only once (respin as needed).

Test #	Spin 1	Spin 2	Spin 3	Spin 4	Total
1					
2					
3					
4					

Extension: Have the participants experiment with the rules and discuss how changes affect the probable outcomes. Also, have them design and test spinners with up to 10 numbers on them.

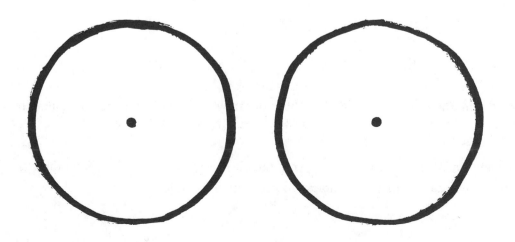

TRIANGLE TOOTHPICK LOGIC

Grades 2–8

☒ total group activity
☒ cooperative activity
☒ independent activity

☒ concrete/manipulative
☒ visual/pictorial
☒ abstract procedure

Why Do It: To enhance logical reasoning and pattern-seeking skills through a nonroutine problem-solving activity.

You Will Need: Toothpicks or straws.

How to Do It: Use 9 toothpicks or straws to make the same triangular shape the player in the illustration is using. Then answer the Questions and Extensions below. Answers to these questions may be found under Solutions; but *don't look* until you think you have the solution, or you are really stuck!

Questions and Extensions: Use toothpicks or straws to make the same triangular figure as the player in the illustration. Then, for each question, begin again with that same shape, except when directed otherwise.

  1. How many small triangles did the player in the illustration make with the 9 toothpicks?

  2. Show how you can remove 2 toothpicks to get 3 small triangles.

3. Remove 3 toothpicks to get 1 large triangle.

4. Remove 2 toothpicks to get 2 different-size triangles.

5. Remove 6 toothpicks to get 1 triangle.

6. Remove 3 toothpicks to leave 2 triangles.

7. Start with this shape ▽ ▽ ▽ and *move* just 3 toothpicks to get 5 triangles.

8. Start with the same shape as in #7 and move 2 toothpicks to make 4 triangles.

9. Use 12 toothpicks to make 6 congruent triangles.

Solutions:

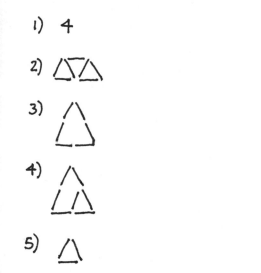

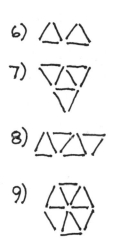

RECTANGLE TOOTHPICK LOGIC

Grades 2–8

☒ total group activity   ☒ concrete/manipulative
☒ cooperative activity   ☒ visual/pictorial
☒ independent activity   ☒ abstract procedure

Why Do It: To further enhance logical reasoning and pattern-seeking skills through a nonroutine problem-solving activity.

You Will Need: Toothpicks.

How to Do It: Use 12 toothpicks to make the same rectangular shape the player in the illustration is using; later questions will call for 24 toothpicks. Then solve as many of the Questions and Extensions as you can. (Some will require more thinking than those from the *Triangle Toothpick Logic* activity.)

Questions and Extensions: To begin, use 12 toothpicks to make the same rectangular shape as the player in the illustration. Then try to solve each problem and, if successful, use a pencil to sketch your solution on paper. Notice that some of the problems require more toothpicks and/or they become more difficult.

Problem Solving with Squares

1. Remove 2 to leave 3 squares.

2. Remove 2 to leave 2 squares.

3. Remove 4 to leave 2 squares.

4. Remove 4 to leave 1 square.

5. Remove 1 to leave 3 squares.

6. Move 4 to make 3 squares.

7. Move 3 to make 3 squares.

8. Use 12 toothpicks to make 6 squares.

9. Use 12 toothpicks to make 6 congruent squares.

Perimeter and Area

10. Make a rectangle with a perimeter of 10.

11. Make a rectangle with an area of 4.

12. Make a rectangle with a perimeter of 12 and an area of 5.

Advanced Toothpick Problems (24 toothpicks needed)

13. Remove 5 to leave 5 squares.

14. Remove 5 to leave 3 squares.

15. Remove 7 to leave 2 squares.

16. Remove 2 to leave 6 squares.

17. Remove 3 to leave 2 squares.

18. Find the minimum that can be removed to leave no squares.

19. Remove 3 to leave 4 squares.

20. Remove 2 to leave 4 squares.

21. Move 3 to make 6 squares.

22. Move 4 to make 6 squares.

23. Move 2 to make 4 squares.

24. Move 1 to make a perfect square.

25. Move 4 to make 3 squares.

26. Move 3 to make 3 squares.

27. Move 4 to make 2 squares.

Solutions:

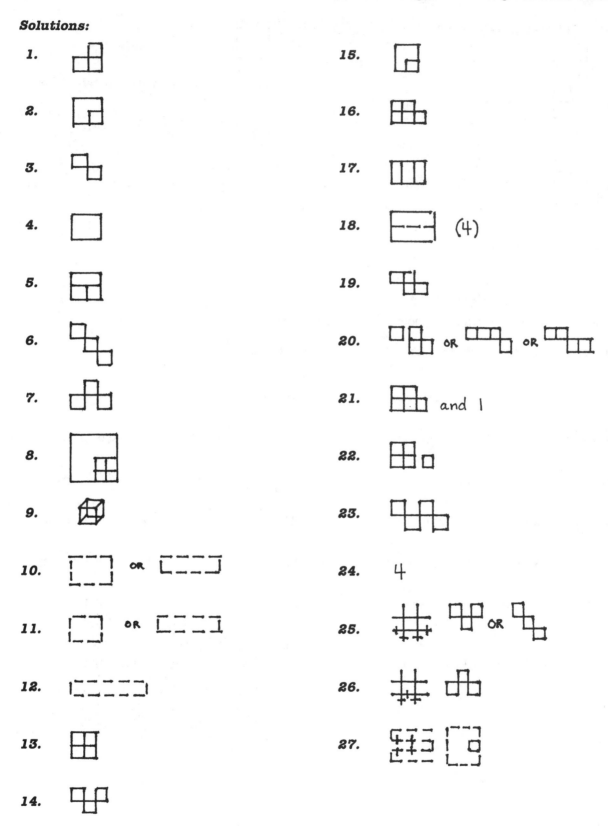

1.

2.

3.

4.

5.

6.

7.

8.

9.

10.   OR

11.   OR

12.

13.

14.

15.

16.

17.

18.   (4)

19.

20.   OR   OR

21.   and 1

22.

23.

24.   4

25.   OR

26.

27.

WHAT GRAPH IS THIS?

Grades 2–8

☒ total group activity ☐ concrete/manipulative
☒ cooperative activity ☒ visual/pictorial
☒ independent activity ☒ abstract procedure

Why Do It: To investigate graphs and what they mean from a logical, but reverse perspective.

You Will Need: Various graphs that focus on everyday events or other situations of which the participants should have a knowledge.

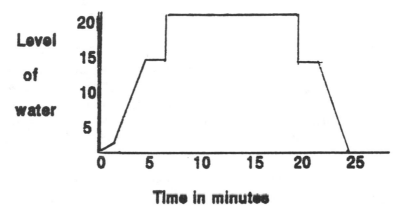

How to Do It: Display a copy of a graph minus the title and other information that would identify exactly what it portrays. Together with the participants, note the type of graph, the structure of the graphed information, whether there are numbers or other information along axes, etc. Then ask, "What might this be a graph of?" For instance, the line graph above notes an activity that many people participate in every day. From the axes information it can be told that water and time are involved. What graph is this? *(solution given later)*

Examples to Try: (Possible solutions are found later.)

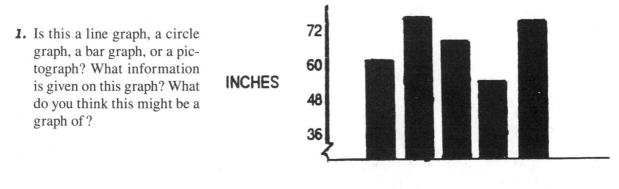

1. Is this a line graph, a circle graph, a bar graph, or a pictograph? What information is given on this graph? What do you think this might be a graph of?

2. In this pictograph † = 5 students. Can you tell what this graph shows?

Ms. Johnson	† † † † †
Mr. Evans	† † † † † †
Mr. Romero	† † †
Mr. Smith	† † † †

Extensions:

1. The graphs utilized in other portions of this book may also prove to be helpful at this time. Of interest might be those developed in conjunction with the activities Tired Hands, Four-Coin Statistics, and Tell Everything You Can.

2. Have students explore media sources for graphs. They might bring line, bar, circle, pictographs, etc., from newspapers or other sources to discuss with the group. (Note: Such graphs may also "tie in" with studies in science, social studies, etc.)

3. The learners might construct their own graphs and try them out on the other group members (and the teacher). When doing so, have them see if they can portray the same information in several different types of graphs.

Possible Solutions:

- The situation noting water and time is a line graph portraying someone taking a bath in a bathtub. During the first minute only the hot water faucet is turned on; then the water is regulated and run for another 3 minutes to fill the tub; for 2 minutes the water is level; then the bather gets into the tub, raising the level again, and takes a bath for 12 minutes; the bather steps out of the tub and towels off for 3 minutes; and finally, the drain is opened and it takes 2 minutes for all the water to drain.

- Example #1 displays a bar graph of the heights (in inches) of 5 people.

- Example #2 shows a pictograph indicating the number of students in particular classes. Ms. Johnson has 25, Mr. Evans has 30, Mr. Romero has 15, and Mr. Smith has 20 students in class.

FOLD-AND-PUNCH PATTERNS

Grades 2–8

☒ total group activity   ☒ concrete/manipulative
☒ cooperative activity   ☒ visual/pictorial
☒ independent activity   ☒ abstract procedure

Why Do It: To investigate sequential patterns, determine their relationships, and be able to predict further outcomes.

You Will Need: Four or five sheets of paper (such as discarded computer paper) for each participant (or each cooperative group) and several paper punches. Also, duplicate record-keeping charts (as those shown below) or have students sketch their own.

(FIGURE A)   (FIGURE B)

How to Do It:

1. Begin by having the participants consider paper folds and thicknesses. "For zero folds, how many thicknesses of paper do you have? Next, fold your paper in half (Figure A) and tell how many thicknesses you have now. Fold it in half again (Figure B), and how many thicknesses are there now? Fold the paper a third time. Now, make a chart (see below) to show the number of thicknesses for each fold. Continue the table to 10 folds. Also, if you can, write a relationship statement (or a rule or a formula) that will tell us the number of thicknesses for a given number of folds."

Paper Folds and Thicknesses

Folds	0	1	2	3	4	5	6	7	8	9	10
Thicknesses	1	2	4	8							
Rule Applied											

(For a completed chart and a rule, see Solutions)

2. If and when the participants have successfully dealt with paper folds and thicknesses, have them consider the slightly more difficult *Fold-and-Punch Patterns.* "If you have a sheet of paper with zero folds and you punch it once, how many holes will result? If you fold it in half and punch once again (remember that your paper already had 1 hole from punching it with no folds), what will the total number of holes be? Make a sketch (Figure C) of this situation. If you fold it in half again and make one more punch, what number of holes are now in the paper? Make a sketch (Figure D) of this new situation. Also, make a chart to show the total number of holes for each fold. Finally, see if you can write a rule or formula that will tell the total number of holes punched for any given number of folds."

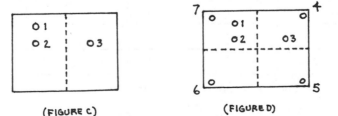

(FIGURE C)   (FIGURE D)

Paper Folded in Halves and Holes Punched

Folds	0	1	2	3	4	5	6	7	8
Holes Added	0	2	4	8					
Total Holes	1	3	7	15					

(For a completed chart and a rule, see Solutions)

5. Allow the participants to note their findings and state, in their own words, the patterns found. Finally, they should discuss how they could apply the relationships, rules or formulas that were derived.

Extension: After the students have solved the problems noted above, have them investigate what will happen when the paper is folded in thirds, instead of halves. Have them predict, sketch expected outcomes, punch holes, record their findings on a chart (see below), and try to derive a rule.

Paper Folded in Thirds and Holes Punched

Folds	0	1	2	3	4	5	6
Holes Added	0	3	9	27			
Total Holes	1	4	13	40			

(For a completed chart and a rule, see Solutions)

Solutions:

Paper Folds and Thicknesses

Folds	0	1	2	3	4	5	6	7	8	9	10
Thicknesses	1	2	4	8	16	32	64	128	256	512	1024
Rule Applied	2^0	2^1	2^2	2^3	2^4	2^5	2^6	2^7	2^8	2^9	2^{10}

Rule: The number of paper thicknesses = 2^n where n = number of folds.

Paper Folded in Halves and Holes Punched

Folds	0	1	2	3	4	5	6	7	8
Holes Added	0	2	4	8	16	32	64	128	256
Total Holes	1	3	7	15	31	63	127	255	511

Rule: The holes added = 2^n where n = number of folds + 1.

Paper Folded in Thirds and Holes Punched

Folds	0	1	2	3	4	5	6
Holes Added	0	3	9	27	81	243	729
Total Holes	1	4	13	40	121	364	1093

Rule: The holes added = 3^n where n = number of folds + 1.

COORDINATE CLUES

Grades 2–8

☒ total group activity
☒ cooperative activity
☒ independent activity

☐ concrete/manipulative
☒ visual/pictorial
☒ abstract procedure

Why Do It: To actively introduce and/or reinforce applied coordinate graphing.

You Will Need: Index cards or paper of three different colors (such as green, pink and white); a marking pen; and masking tape.

How to Do It: Write large size numerals 0 through 9 on the green cards. Repeat this process on the pink cards. Tape these cards to two adjacent classroom walls so that they can be used to designate coordinate locations. For instance, (0,0) will be in a corner and (5,5) should be near the center of the room, etc. Next, write sequential clues on the white cards and hide all but the first one at their appropriate coordinate locations. Put them in interesting locations such as under a book or taped to the bottom of a table. Put the first card at (0,0); it might read, "You are at (green 0, pink 0). For your next clue go to coordinate (green 6, pink 3). There is a surprise waiting IF you can find your way to the end of the coordinate trail." The students may work independently or in small groups as they seek each clue and then proceed to the next. At the end of the coordinate clue trail, each student might receive a simple surprise such as a paper badge labeled COORDINATE CLUE EXPERT, a coupon excusing him or her from one math problem, etc.

Example: The players shown above have found some of the COORDINATE CLUE locations and the messages at each.

Extensions:

1. Play *Four Quadrant Coordinate Clue.* To do so, the (0,0) location will need to be at the center of the classroom (or playground) and the messages placed at positive and/or negative coordinate graph locations as noted below.

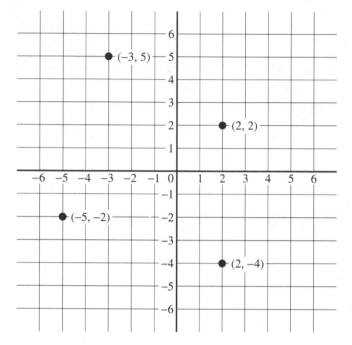

2. Able students might write clues and set up their own Coordinate Clue Trails.

3. Play *Three-Dimensional Coordinate Clue* in a manner similar to *Four Quadrant Coordinate Clue* (see Extension #1) except that vertical coordinates and messages are also needed. As such, some messages might be taped to light fixtures or suspended with string from the ceiling and/or placed in the basement or on a lower floor.

PUZZLERS WITH PAPER

Grades 2–8

☒ total group activity   ☒ concrete/manipulative
☒ cooperative activity   ☒ visual/pictorial
☒ independent activity   ☒ abstract procedure

Why Do It: To actively engage learners in geometry activities that appear to be tricks, but have logical solutions.

You Will Need: Index cards; typing paper; a roll of wide adding machine paper; tape; pencils; rulers; scissors; and a highlighter.

How to Do It:

1. The participants will be involved with three paper geometry activities. Depending on the time available, the activities may be attempted singly or all may be done during one session.

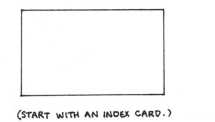

(START WITH AN INDEX CARD.)

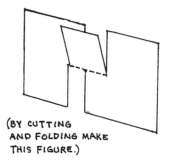

(BY CUTTING
AND FOLDING MAKE
THIS FIGURE.)

2. For the *first paper puzzler* activity, provide each person with an index card, a ruler, a pencil, and scissors. Their challenge is to cut and fold the index card so that it appears as shown above. If some of the participants are successful, allow them to share their method with others; if not, provide a clue or two. Clues might include: (1) You will make just three cuts; or (2) the cuts will be made to a center fold, etc. (Solution later.)

3. The *second paper puzzler* challenges the players to cut a piece of typing paper in such a way that a loop large enough for them to step through will be created. They will need one sheet of $8\frac{1}{2} \times 11$ inch typing paper, rulers, pencils, and scissors. If a clue is needed, have the players make a picture frame cut on three edges of the paper (see page 221); then suggest that some of the additional cuts needed can be started at the picture frame cut, but some cannot. If the participants consider this clue carefully, they will be able to determine a logical solution. (See Solutions.)

4. Moebius Strips provide a *third type of paper puzzler*. These strips are probably best analyzed in two phases—the *$\frac{1}{2}$ Phase* and the *$\frac{1}{3}$ Phase*.

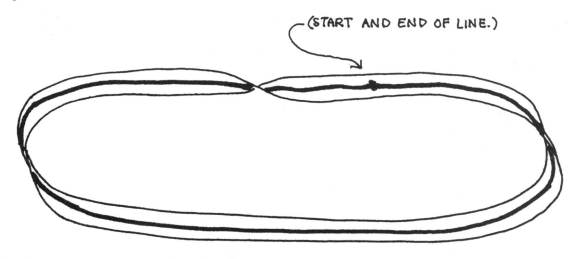

(START AND END OF LINE.)

To consider a *$\frac{1}{2}$ Phase Moebius Strip,* a length of adding machine paper (about 5 ft.), tape, a highlighter (or a pencil), and scissors will be needed for each participating individual or group. The construction directions are: (1) bring the ends of the paper tape together to form a large loop; (2) twist one end of the loop $\frac{1}{2}$ turn (180 degrees); (3) tape the ends together. The participants now have a loop with a twist in it or a Moebius Strip. To logically analyze their $\frac{1}{2}$ Phase Moebius Strips, consider the following activities and questions:

a. Use a highlighter (or a pencil) to draw a line down the middle of your $\frac{1}{2}$ Phase Moebius Strip. When doing so, do not lift the highlighter from the paper. What happened with the line?

b. Predict what will happen if you cut along the line that you drew down the middle of your $\frac{1}{2}$ Phase Moebius Strip. Use scissors to make that cut. What happened?

c. What will happen if you cut down the middle of the "new" strip that you created? Make the cut and tell what really happened.

d. A short review—At what times was the paper strip a true moebius (having a $\frac{1}{2}$ turn or 180 degrees)? When did it become non-moebius? How did these changes affect the outcomes?

Consider next a *$\frac{1}{3}$ Phase Moebius Strip.* Construct it exactly as you did the $\frac{1}{2}$ Phase Moebius Strip (see directions above) and respond, with one major difference, to questions a and b. The major difference is that the line should be drawn $\frac{1}{3}$ of the way in from an edge and the cut should be made along that line. Something different will happen. What do you predict the outcome to be? Is the result completely moebius, or is a portion of it non-moebius? Can you explain why?

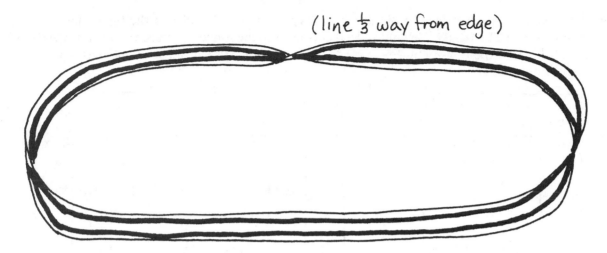

(line ⅓ way from edge)

Extensions:

1. Ask the participants, "Where, in everyday life, are moebius strips commonly used?" Also, "What is the advantage in using a moebius belt, rather than a regular belt?"

2. Imagine cutting around a moebius strip ¼ of the way in from an edge. Predict the result. Then do the cutting. What did you find?

3. Take a piece of paper tape, give it a full twist (360 degrees) and tape the ends together. What do you predict will happen if you cut ½ of the way from an edge? ⅓ of the way? ¼ of the way? Try it and do the cutting. What happened? Repeat the experiment using three half-twists (540 degrees). Repeat it again using four half-twists (720 degrees). What did you find for odd-numbered twists? Even-numbered twists? Keep records of your findings.

Solutions:

1. *First paper puzzler:* Make 3 cuts as shown, fold the center tab up and crease it along the dotted line, hold the tab straight up, and give one end of the index card a ½ twist (180 degrees).

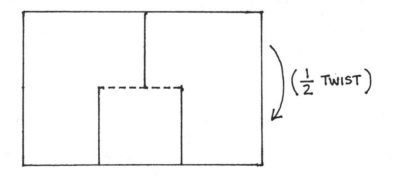

(½ TWIST)

2. *Second paper puzzler:* Make a picture frame type cut along 3 edges of the typing paper (indicated below). Then make 5 evenly spaced cuts in from the longest picture frame cut. Also make 6 cuts in from the non-picture frame edge (see below). Spread the segments into a loop and step through it.

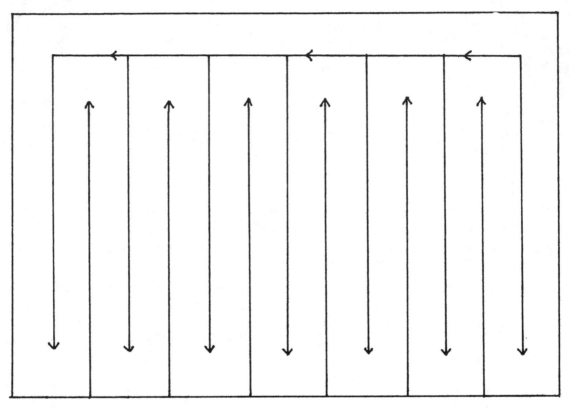

3. *½ Phase Moebius Strip:* (1) The line will meet itself; as such, there is just 1 line and therefore, this moebius strip has just 1 side. (2) When cut down the middle, a single "new" strip twice as long and ½ as wide results; further, the "new" strip is non-moebius. (3) When cut down the middle, the "new" non-moebius strip splits into 2 strips that are linked together.

4. *⅓ Phase Moebius Strip:* (1) The continuous line will miss itself on the "first pass," but will meet itself on the "second pass." (2) When cut ⅓ the way in, the result will be a small "fat" loop interlinked with a longer "narrow" loop. The "narrow" loop is non-moebius and the "fat" loop is moebius. Further, the "fat" loop is the center of the original moebius strip and the "narrow" one is the outside edge of it.

5. *Extension #1:* Moebius strips are in common use as conveyor (and other) belts, where they will, theoretically, wear twice as long as regular belts. The reasoning for this is that the wear is distributed evenly to all portions of a moebius belt, whereas a regular belt wears only on one side.

CREATE A TESSELLATION

Grades 4–8

☒   total group activity   ☒   concrete/manipulative
☒   cooperative activity   ☒   visual/pictorial
☒   independent activity   ☒   abstract procedure

Why Do It: To allow learners to explore regular tessellations and then to create M. C. Escher-type tessellations of their own.

You Will Need: A large sheet of light-colored drawing or construction paper that is fairly stiff; a small square of tagboard (about file folder weight) which measures 2½ inches on a side; tape; pencils; scissors; rulers; and colored markers. Some examples of Escher-type tessellations (from encyclopedias, other resource books or art files) may also prove to be helpful.

How to Do It:

1. Initially the learners might search out and explore the many regular tessellations that are found in everyday locations. (*Note:* A tessellation of a geometric plane is the filling of the plane with repetitions of a figure in such a way that no figures overlap and there are no gaps.) Such everyday tessellations are most often made with regular polygons as squares, triangles and hexagons; for example, ceramic tile patterns on bathroom floors, brick walls, or chain link fences.

2. Next, explore some examples of the Escher-type tessellations and tell the participants that they will be learning the logical procedures for developing similar tessellations of their own. When ready for the construction phase, it is suggested that everyone work together as they create their first tessellations; that is, the participants (even though they will likely use different designs) should complete Step 1 together, then Step 2, etc. These steps are outlined in the Example below.

3. Following completion of their first tessellations, engage the participants in a discussion of the "motion" geometry that they accomplished. In this instance they cut out segments and then used a "slide" motion to move them to their new location. (In other instances of "motion" geometry, such cutout segments might be "flipped," "turned," "stretched," or "shrunk.") As such, this discussion, involving the logic of creating tessellations, should include questions as, "What happens when you _____ ?" and "What might happen if _____ ?" Finally, allow the participants to try out some of their ideas as they attempt to create more tessellations.

Example: To create your first tessellation follow the steps noted on page 226.

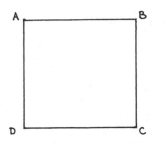

Step 1: Label your tagboard square A, B, C, D as shown.

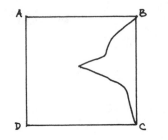

Step 2: Draw a continuous line that connects vertex B with vertex C and cut along that line.

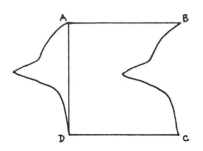

Step 3: Slide the cut-out piece around to the opposite side, place the straight edge BC against AD, and tape them together.

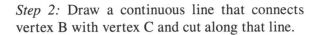

Step 4: Draw a continuous line that connects vertex D with vertex C and cut along that line.

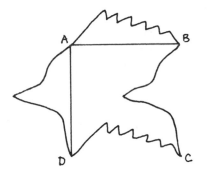

Step 5: Slide this cut-out piece around, from the bottom, and place it on top, with the straight edge DC against AB and tape them together. Your tessellation pattern is now complete.

(*Note:* See the completed bird-like tessellation on page 225.)

Step 6: Place the pattern on your drawing paper and trace it. Then slide the pattern (up, down, left or right) until it is against a matching edge and trace again. Continue until the entire drawing paper is filled with repeating patterns. You may use colored markers to emphasize your tessellation pattern.

Extensions:

1. The students might create tessellations to depict important events, holidays, etc.

2. Create tessellation book covers, laminate or protect them with clear self-stick vinyl, and mount them on the participants' personal or school books.

3. Create a large tessellation (beginning perhaps with a 2½ foot piece of cardboard) and cover an entire wall.

PROBLEM PUZZLERS

Grades 4–8

☒ total group activity	☐ concrete/manipulative
☒ cooperative activity	☒ visual/pictorial
☒ independent activity	☒ abstract procedure

Why Do It: To enhance logical thinking and mental math skills while enjoying some mathematical tricks.

You Will Need: Collect a series of *Problem Puzzlers* (see samples below). You may wish to duplicate some of the selections for individual or small group use.

How to Do It:

A. *Problem Puzzlers* may be shared verbally or in a duplicated format. In general, however, the shorter problems are presented orally by the teacher and the longer ones distributed to the students for close scrutiny. Thus, this first group of *Problem Puzzlers* should be presented orally. The answers are found under Solutions.

1. Take two apples from three apples and what do you have?

2. If an individual went to bed at 8:00 P.M. and set the alarm on a wind-up clock to get up at 9 o'clock in the morning, how many hours sleep would he get?

3. Some months have 30 days, some 31; how many have 28?

4. If your doctor gave you three pills and said to take one every half hour, how long would they last?

5. There are two U.S. coins that total 55¢. One of the coins is not a nickel. What are the two coins?

6. A farmer had 17 sheep. All but 9 died. How many does the farmer have left?

7. Divide 30 by one-half and add 10. What is the answer?

8. How much dirt may be removed from a hole that is 3 feet deep, 2 feet wide, and 2 feet long?

9. There are 12 one-cent stamps in a dozen, but how many two-cent stamps are in a dozen?

10. Do they have a fourth of July in England?

11. A ribbon is 30 inches long. If you cut it with a pair of scissors into one-inch strips, how many snips would it take?

12. How long would it take a train one mile long to pass completely through a mile-long tunnel if the train was going 60 miles per hour?

B. Some other *Problem Puzzlers* that are more lengthy or that require pencil-and-paper computations are cited below. The solutions are given.

1. Suppose you have a 9 × 12 foot carpet with a 1 × 8 foot hole in the center, as shown in the drawing. Can you cut the carpet into two pieces so they will fit together to make a 10 × 10 foot carpet with no hole?

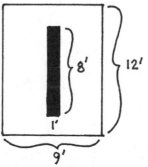

2. *Johnson's cat:*

> Johnson's cat went up a tree,
> Which was sixty feet and three;
> Every day she climbed eleven,
> Every night she came down seven,
> Tell me, if she did not drop,
> When her paws would reach the top.

3. *Horse trading:* There was a sheik in Arabia who had three sons. Upon his death, and the reading of the will, there came about this problem. He had 17 horses. One-half (½) of the horses are willed to his first son. One-third (⅓) are willed to his second son, and ⅑ are willed to his third son. How many horses will each son receive?

4. *Rivers to cross:* There is an old story about a man who had a goat, a wolf, and a basket of cabbage. Of course, he could not leave the wolf alone with the goat, for the wolf would kill the goat. And he could not leave the goat alone with the cabbage, for the goat would eat the cabbage.

   In his travels the man came to a narrow foot bridge which he had to cross. He could take only one thing at a time across the bridge. How did he get the goat, the wolf, and the basket of cabbage across the stream safely?

5. *Jars to fill:* Mary was sent to the store to buy 2 gallons of vinegar. The storekeeper had a large barrel of vinegar, but he did not have any empty 2-gallon bottles. Looking around, he found an 8-gallon jar and a 5-gallon jar. With these 2 jars he was able to measure out exactly 2 gallons of vinegar for Mary. How?

6. *A vanishing dollar:* A farmer was driving his geese to market. He had 30 geese, and he was going to sell them at 3 for $1. "That is 33⅓¢ apiece," he figured, "and 30 times 33⅓¢ is $10."

   On his way to market, he passed the farm of a friend who also raised geese. The friend asked him to take his 30 geese along and sell them, too; but, since they were large and fat, he wanted them sold at 2 for $1. "That is 50¢ apiece," the farmer said to his friend, "so your geese will bring 30 times 50¢, or $15."

   After leaving his friend, the farmer figured, "It would be a lot simpler to sell all 60 geese at a single price. Now 3 for $1 and 2 for $1 are the same as 5 for $2."

   So the farmer decided to sell all the geese at the rate of 5 for $2. And that's exactly what he did.

   On his way home he gave his neighbor the $15 due him. Then he thought, "When I get home, I'll give my wife the $10 that I got for our geese."

   But when he looked in his pocket, he was surprised to find that he had only $9 instead of $10.

   He looked all over for the missing dollar, but he never did find it. What became of it?

Solutions:

A. Answers to *Problem Puzzlers* presented orally.

   1. 2 apples
   2. 1 hour
   3. all

4. 1 hour

5. 50¢ piece + nickel

6. 9 sheep

7. 70

8. None—the hole has no dirt itself.

9. 12

10. yes

11. 29 snips. The last two inches are divided by one snip.

12. Two minutes. From the time the front of the train enters the tunnel to the time the back of the train leaves the tunnel, the train must travel two miles. At 60 mph, the train is going a mile a minute.

B. Answers to *Problem Puzzlers* that are more lengthy or that require pencil-and-paper computations.

1. The original carpet might be cut as shown below. Then slide the top portion to the left 1 foot and down 2 feet. The result will be a 10 by 10 foot carpet that can be sewn together or glued down.

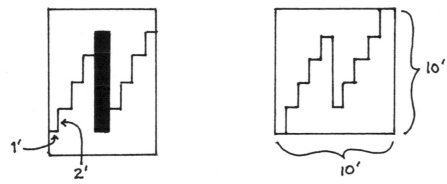

2. *Johnson's cat:* Each day the cat went up 11 feet and came down 7. So she moved 4 feet a day. In 13 days the cat climbed 4 × 13, or 52 feet; then on the 14th day her paws reached the top, since 52 + 11 = 63.

3. *Horse trading:* Possible solutions:

$$\tfrac{1}{2} \times 17/1 = 8\ \tfrac{1}{2} = \quad 9 \text{ horses for 1st son}$$
$$\tfrac{1}{3} \times 17/1 = 5\ \tfrac{2}{3} = \quad 6 \text{ horses for 2nd son}$$
$$\tfrac{1}{9} \times 17/1 = 1\ \tfrac{8}{9} = \underline{\ 2} \text{ horses for 3rd son}$$
$$\phantom{\tfrac{1}{9} \times 17/1 = 1\ \tfrac{8}{9} = } 17 \text{ horses}$$

4. *Rivers to cross:* Takes goat across; returns. Takes wolf across; brings back goat. Takes cabbage across; returns. Takes goat across.

5. *Jars to fill:* (Call 8-gal. jar A and 5-gal. jar B.) Fill B; empty B into A. Fill B. Fill A from B. There are 2 gallons left in B.

6. *A vanishing dollar:* $10 + $15 = $25

$$5 \text{ for } \$2 = 40¢ \text{ each}$$
$$60 \times 40¢ = \$24$$

DART BOARD LOGIC

Grades 4–8

☒   total group activity   ☐   concrete/manipulative
☒   cooperative activity   ☒   visual/pictorial
☒   independent activity   ☒   abstract procedure

Why Do It: To mentally manipulate number sums in an effort to determine possible gameboard solutions.

You Will Need: Dart boards (or sketches of them) with several different number scoring patterns. For some students, duplicated copies of the dart boards and markers will also prove helpful.

How to Do It: Place a dart board in front of the classroom (or sketch one on the chalkboard or use an overhead projector) and play a practice game. When three darts, for instance, are thrown at the target shown above, what scores are possible? List possibilities including the greatest and least scores, all achievable scores plus the addition showing how, and discuss scores within the range (if any) that cannot be achieved. When ready, have the players consider the same target again, but this time with four darts. They may work in cooperative groups or individually, but when finished hold a group discussion of the "new" possibilities. Have them next consider the possible outcomes for two darts; for five darts; for six darts; are there patterns for even or odd numbers of darts?; etc.

Example: These students are considering the logical outcomes for 5 darts that all hit the target shown.

Extensions:

1. Try the dart board target shown here and answer the following questions: (1) For 6 darts, which of these scores are possible—4, 19, 28, 58, 29, 35? (2) What is the range of scores—the greatest and least? (3) List all possible scores and "prove" their correctness by showing the related addition (as $30 = 3 + 3 + 5 + 5 + 7 + 7$)? (4) What kind of numbers were all of the achievable scores for 6 darts; and why? (5) If 5 darts were thrown instead, what scores would be possible and why?

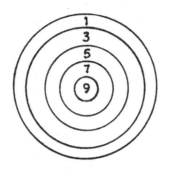

2. Have the participants design targets of their own and specify the number of darts to be thrown. Allow them to try the proposed dart boards on each other, but also have summary discussions as to the logical possibilities and especially the "whys"!

ANGELICA'S BEAN LOGIC

Grades 4–8

☒ total group activity
☒ cooperative activity
☒ independent activity

☒ concrete/manipulative
☒ visual/pictorial
☒ abstract procedure

Why Do It: To help players enhance their logical-thinking skills as they look for solution patterns.

You Will Need: About 30 beans per player (or group) plus pencils and paper.

How to Do It: The group leader should read *Angelica's Bean Logic* story to the group, provide beans, and allow the participants to work together or individually to seek solutions. When a solution is found, it should be displayed (perhaps with an overhead projector) and recorded. The solver(s) should share her/his solution procedures.

Angelica's grandfather always liked to tell her stories or have her try to solve puzzles. One day he said, "If you will count out 24 beans for me, I will show you some interesting tricks. I'm going to arrange the beans around a square with 3 in each group (see below). That way you have 9 beans along each side of the square. Now what you must do is take 4 beans away and rearrange the rest so that you will still have 9 beans along each side of the square. Let me see if you can do it."

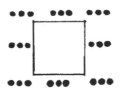

Example: The students below have worked out one solution for *Angelica's Bean Logic* problem. Can you find two additional solutions? (*Note:* Further solutions are given later.)

Extensions:

1. Place the 24 beans around the square in groups of 3, as was done originally. However, this time add 4 beans and still show 9 beans along each edge. Remember, the original configuration was:

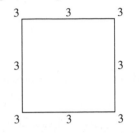

2. Try bean square arrangements with 12 and/or 15 beans along each edge and see what patterns are possible.

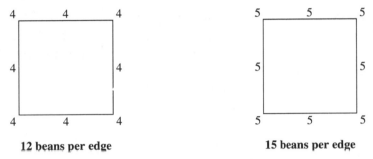

12 beans per edge   15 beans per edge

Solutions:

1. *Initial Bean Logic Problem* (show 9 beans along each edge after removing 4):

2. *Extension #1* (add 4 beans and still show 9 on each edge):

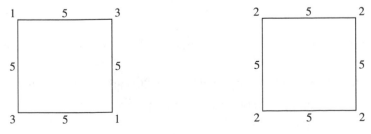

LINE IT OUT

Grades 4–8

☒   total group activity   ☒   concrete/manipulative
☒   cooperative activity   ☒   visual/pictorial
☒   independent activity   ☒   abstract procedure

Why Do It: To determine the logical intersection points of lines in a plane.

You Will Need: A "Line It Out" record-keeping sheet and a pencil with an eraser. Toothpicks or straws may also be used as optional aids. Suggested solutions, for the leader, are also provided.

How to Do It: Line It Out may be tried individually or "attacked" as a cooperative effort. At the onset, the leader should help the players solve two or three of the problems. Some, such as Problem A-0, which calls for 2 lines with no intersections, can readily be solved with parallel lines. Others, such as Problem C-1, which asks for 4 lines with only one intersection, are sometimes more challenging (see Examples below). Once the participants understand the activity parameters, challenge them to find solutions for as many of the remaining situations as they can. (Note: Remind the players that lines go on forever and do not end within the boxes shown; thus, an intersection outside the box must "count" as part of an answer.)

Examples: Shown below are Line It Out solutions for Problems A-0, C-1, and D-5.

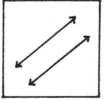

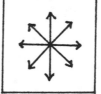

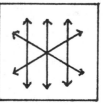

Show 2 LINES with
NO INTERSECTIONS

Show 4 LINES with
1 INTERSECTION

Show 5 LINES with
5 INTERSECTIONS

Extensions:

1. A challenge question: With 5 lines (as in problem set D), is it possible to have more than 10 intersections?

2. Have able students create their own problem sets E through I for 6 through 10 lines.

3. Another challenge question: What solution(s) might be offered if these same Line It Out questions were considered in a 3-dimensional setting?

LINE IT OUT

MATERIALS: You may wish to use flat toothpicks to help you complete this worksheet.

DIRECTIONS: Sketch an example in each box. Are some impossible? Some may be done several different ways. If using toothpicks, students may need to be reminded that lines extend in both directions.

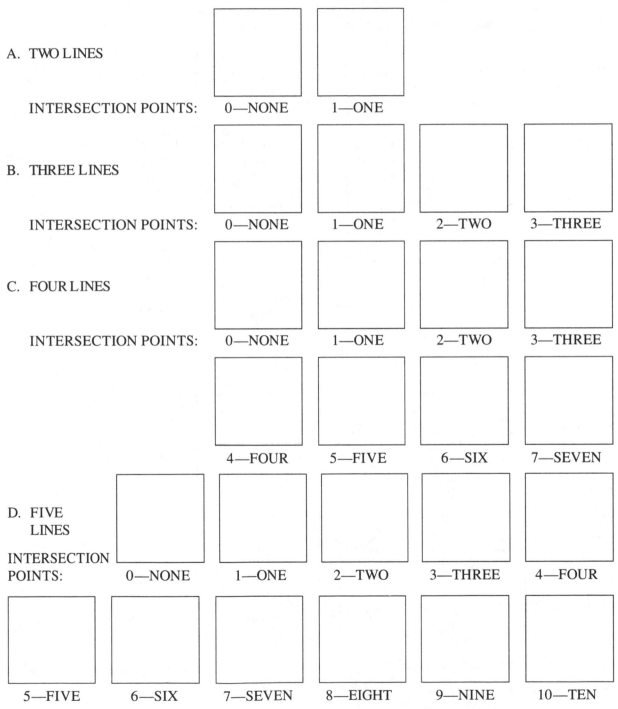

A. TWO LINES

INTERSECTION POINTS: 0—NONE   1—ONE

B. THREE LINES

INTERSECTION POINTS: 0—NONE   1—ONE   2—TWO   3—THREE

C. FOUR LINES

INTERSECTION POINTS: 0—NONE   1—ONE   2—TWO   3—THREE

4—FOUR   5—FIVE   6—SIX   7—SEVEN

D. FIVE LINES

INTERSECTION POINTS: 0—NONE   1—ONE   2—TWO   3—THREE   4—FOUR

5—FIVE   6—SIX   7—SEVEN   8—EIGHT   9—NINE   10—TEN

235

Some Solutions:

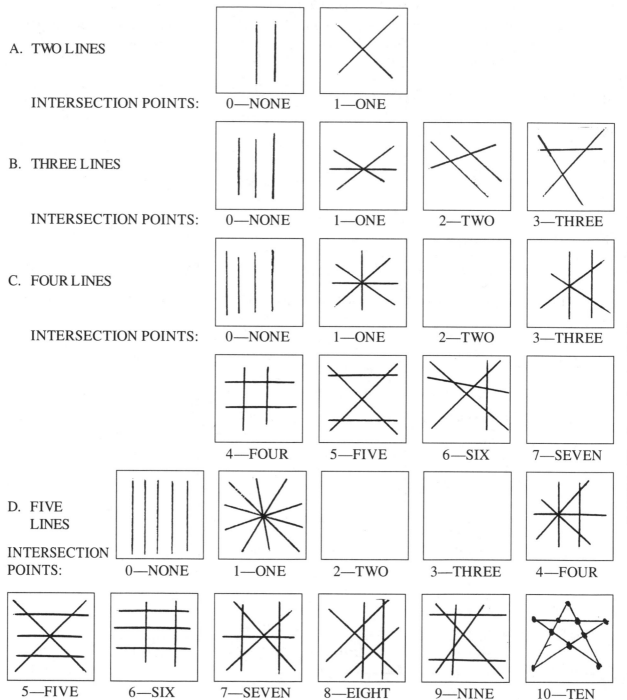

A. TWO LINES

INTERSECTION POINTS: 0—NONE 1—ONE

B. THREE LINES

INTERSECTION POINTS: 0—NONE 1—ONE 2—TWO 3—THREE

C. FOUR LINES

INTERSECTION POINTS: 0—NONE 1—ONE 2—TWO 3—THREE

4—FOUR 5—FIVE 6—SIX 7—SEVEN

D. FIVE LINES

INTERSECTION POINTS: 0—NONE 1—ONE 2—TWO 3—THREE 4—FOUR

5—FIVE 6—SIX 7—SEVEN 8—EIGHT 9—NINE 10—TEN

CALCULATOR SOLUTION LOGIC

Grades 4–8

☒   total group activity
☒   cooperative activity
☐   independent activity

☐   concrete/manipulative
☐   visual/pictorial
☒   abstract procedure

Why Do It: To provide the learners with an experience that combines inductive logic with calculator clues.

You Will Need: An overhead projection calculator that has an automatic constant feature (see Note below) is preferred when working with a large group or the whole class. Alternately, if it is to be a small group activity, a calculator will be needed for each group.

How to Do It: Calculator Solution Logic is played most effectively as a group activity that utilizes an overhead projection calculator. (Note: The calculator must have an automatic constant feature. To check, try the following problem.) To play, the teacher or leader enters (in secret) a problem such as 75 divided by 75 equals 1 and displays the 1 on the overhead screen. The learners are then told that the number they are to find, with the fewest possible guesses, is between 1 and 100. Further, as their guesses are entered, the calculator will give them clues. When the correct number is identified, the calculator will again display 1. For example, if 40 were guessed and entered (enter only 40 =) the display would read .5333333; if 50 were tried, the display would become .6666666; for 80, it becomes 1.0666666; for 74, it becomes .9866666; and for 75 the display is 1, so the hidden number has been determined!

Example: The students are trying to logically determine the secret calculator number between 1 and 1000. The teacher had secretly entered 412 ÷ 412 = in the overhead calculator and had displayed the 1 to the students. Their statements suggest some of their logical thinking.

Extensions:

1. Advanced students might try working with decimals. For example, tell them the calculator number is between 1 and .001. Then secretly enter, perhaps, .876 ÷ .876 = and display the 1. If the first guess was .500 (or as .5) the display would read .5707763. Should a student respond that is about 57% of the number we are seeking, she/he has a good grasp of the situation. Allow them to do some figuring on their own and see if they can determine .876 in just a few tries.

2. If other calculator work is desired the activities Beat the Calculator and Upside-Down Displays might be tried.

DUPLICATE DIGIT LOGIC

Grades 4–8

☒ total group activity
☒ cooperative activity
☒ independent activity

☐ concrete/manipulative
☐ visual/pictorial
☒ abstract procedure

Why Do It: To logically manipulate and compute duplicate digits in an effort to determine whether multiple, single, or no solutions are possible.

You Will Need: Problems that can be presented on an overhead projector, the chalkboard, or as duplicated copies.

How to Do It:

1. Present the players with the following problem. Tell them that A, B, C, D, etc., are different digits. Then challenge them to solve it in every possible way.

   ```
    AAA        111
   +BBB       +222        (This is one solution. Also show all other ways to solve it.)
    CCC        333
   ```

2. After the participants have shown and discussed all possible solutions for the initial problem, present them with another that will "stretch" their logical-thinking abilities a bit further. Begin by asking which of the suggested solutions are not possible and why.

   ```
    AAA       Are all, some, or none of these duplicate digits possible
    BBB       solutions for DDD? Explain why.
   +CCC
    DDD        111   222   333   444   555   666
   ```

3. Have the players also determine and list all of the possible solutions. Then, they might also consider the problem noted below and whether it can be solved.

Extensions:

1. Try Duplicate Digit Logic for subtraction. Consider the following problems. Have the players determine all possible solutions.

$$
\begin{array}{cc}
\text{AAA} & 999 \\
-\text{BBB} & -111 \\
\hline
\text{CCC} & 888
\end{array}
$$
(This is one solution. Also show all other ways to solve it.)

2. When doing Duplicate Digit Logic look for palindromic (reversible) products. Two problems with palindromic outcomes are shown below. What others are possible?

$$
\begin{array}{r}
33 \\
\times 11 \\
\hline
33 \\
33 \\
\hline
363
\end{array}
\qquad\qquad
\begin{array}{r}
222 \\
\times 111 \\
\hline
222 \\
222 \\
222 \\
\hline
24642
\end{array}
$$

3. Which division Duplicate Digit Logic problems have answers (quotients) with no remainders? Two examples are shown below. Are there other possibilities? List and discuss them.

$$
\begin{array}{r}
4 \\
222\overline{)888}
\end{array}
\qquad\qquad
\begin{array}{r}
3 \\
333\overline{)999}
\end{array}
$$

4. While no longer focusing on Duplicate Digit Logic, the activities for students may be extended to include problems such as the following. (Some solutions are noted below.) After such experiences, the participants may wish to create problems of their own.

Each letter stands for a different digit.
Find addition problems that work.

$$
\begin{array}{r}
\text{DOG} \\
+\text{CAT} \\
\hline
\text{TOAD}
\end{array}
$$

Solutions: Some solutions to Extension #4 (there are others):

$$
\begin{array}{rrrr}
302 & 403 & 706 & 807 \\
+741 & +621 & +351 & +261 \\
\hline
1043 & 1024 & 1057 & 1068
\end{array}
$$

STRING TRIANGLE GEOMETRY

Grades 4–8

☒ total group activity
☒ cooperative activity
☒ independent activity

☒ concrete/manipulative
☒ visual/pictorial
☒ abstract procedure

Why Do It: To construct geometric patterns in a hands-on manner and to logically analyze the outcomes.

You Will Need: About 3 yards (or meters) of string; measuring devices (rulers or yard or meter sticks); masking tape; pencils; paper; and scissors for each group of learners.

How to Do It:

1. Organize the class into groups of two to four students and give them a piece of string approximately 3 yards long, about 10 inches of masking tape, a pencil, and scissors. Then instruct them to cut ⅓ to ½ of their string off and to tape it to some flat surface (a table top, chalkboard, the floor, etc.) in the form of any type of triangle. They should then label the vertices A, B, and C by writing in pencil on the tape at those locations (see the illustration).

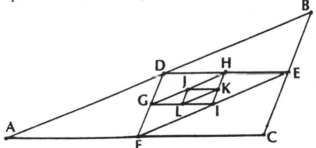

2. Next, have the students locate the midpoints of each edge by any means that they desire (measuring, folding string, etc.). They should then connect those points with string and label the new vertices D, E, and F. When this is completed ask, "What shapes can now be seen?"

3. Now find the midpoints of the new triangle DEF and use string to connect them. Label these points G, H, and I. Repeat the process one more time and label it triangle JKL. Then proceed to ask leading questions (answers are provided) such as:

   a. How do triangles ADF and DBE compare?

   b. What can be said about triangles GHI and ABC?

   c. How many triangles the size of JKL are contained in triangle ABC?

   d. If triangle JKL was subdivided one more time into triangle MNO, then how many triangles of that size would be included in triangle ABC?

   e. Can you determine a rule that will tell how many of the smaller triangles will result from each successive subdivision?

   f. What figures, other than triangles, are delineated by your strips?

4. When the students have exhausted most of the possibilities, from finding edge midpoints and connecting them to subdivide the original triangle inward, suggest that they change their focus to extending the triangle outward by multiples. To accomplish this, let us begin with triangle *PQR* (see illustration below). Then extend *PQ* to *S* so that *PQ* = *QS;* and *PR* to *T* so *PR* = *RT.*

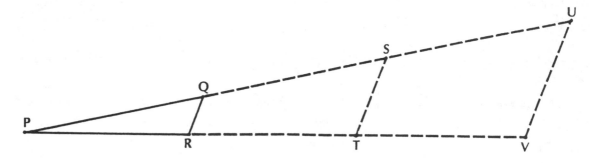

5. Now ask questions such as:

   g. How many triangles the size of *PQR* would fit into *RQST?*

   h. Triangle *PST* is how many times larger in area than triangle *PQR?*

6. Then extend the sides of the triangle one multiple further so that *SU* = *PQ* and *TV* = *PR.* Now proceed to ask further questions such as:

   i. How many triangles the size of *PQR* would fit into triangle *PUV?*

   j. Can you determine a rule that will tell us how many triangles the size of the original one (triangle *PQR*) there will be each time you expand outward by another multiple?

7. Activities with string and tape have certain advantages over pencil-and-paper geometry constructions. For one thing they allow, in fact encourage, students to work their problems together in an everyday-life type of problem-solving situation. Also, the students must handle and measure the string in a "concrete" fashion. Furthermore, the students are applying their geometric identification and labeling skills to another medium. Thus, the utilization of String Geometry for work with many geometric constructions is recommended.

Solutions:

   a. *ADF* is congruent to *DBE*

   b. *ABC* is similar to and 16 times larger than *GHI*

   c. 64

   d. 256

   e. multiply by 4 for each new subdivision

   f. *JKIL, DECF,* and *DHIG* are parallelograms, *FDHI* is a quadrilateral, etc.

   g. 3

   h. 4

   i. 9

   j. Square the number of the original triangles plus the multiple extensions; thus, $1^2 = 1$ for triangle *PQR;* $2^2 = 4$ for triangle *PST;* $3^2 = 9$ for triangle *PUV;* and continue with 4^2, 5^2, 6^2, 7^2, etc.

A POTPOURRI OF LOGICAL-THINKING PROBLEMS, PUZZLES, AND ACTIVITIES

Why Do It: To provide the participants with a wide variety of logical-thinking experiences.

You Will Need: A variety of easily obtained materials as cited within each of the activities that follow.

How to Do It: See the individual activities below. Solutions are provided.

1. Plan a Circuit Board

Grades K–8

☒ total group activity
☒ cooperative activity
☒ independent activity

☒ concrete/manipulative
☒ visual/pictorial
☒ abstract procedure

Many (perhaps most) of today's electronic circuits are printed rather than wired. As such, these circuits become 2-dimensional or plane geometry problems. On the circuit board illustrated right, the task is to *connect terminals A and A, B and B, and C and C with printed electronic circuits that do not touch.* Should the electronic paths touch each other, or an incorrect terminal, they will cause a "short circuit" and the device will malfunction. Your job then is to draw circuit paths that connect the A terminals, the B terminals, and the C terminals without causing a short circuit.

2. 22 Wheels and 7 Kids

Grades K–8

☒ total group activity
☒ cooperative activity
☒ independent activity

☐ concrete/manipulative
☒ visual/pictorial
☒ abstract procedure

Twenty-two wheels brought seven kids to school. They either walked, rode bicycles, or came in cars or trucks. Draw a picture to show one way the kids may have gotten to school. Figure out and list all of the ways you can think of. Discuss your findings with someone else and/or the whole group. (**Extensions:** What are the possibilities for 24 wheels and 8 kids? For 30 wheels and 9 kids, etc.?)

(AN 18-WHEELER PLUS 2 BICYCLES)

3. Candy Box Logic
Grades 2–8

☒   total group activity
☒   cooperative activity
☒   independent activity

☒   concrete/manipulative
☒   visual/pictorial
☒   abstract procedure

Design candy boxes that will hold 36 pieces and have no extra space. What are all the possible ways for boxes that hold one layer? What additional designs are possible for two layers? For three layers? For more layers? Draw pictures of your boxes and/or use blocks to show the different ways. (**Extensions:** What are the possibilities for 12 candies? For 30 candies? For 48 candies, etc.?)

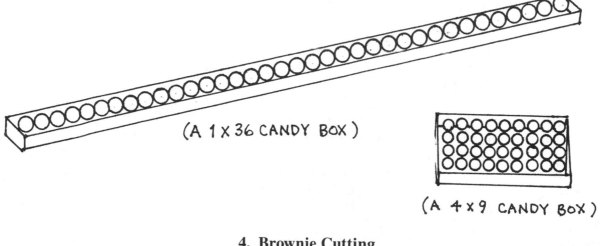

(A 1 X 36 CANDY BOX)

(A 4 X 9 CANDY BOX)

4. Brownie Cutting
Grades 2–8

☒   total group activity
☒   cooperative activity
☒   independent activity

☒   concrete/manipulative
☒   visual/pictorial
☒   abstract procedure

In a few minutes I am going to give you a brownie. Once you have completed a math job with it, you may eat the brownie. Your job will be to *divide the brownie into 32 equal pieces with the least number of cuts.* Plan how you will do it (you might draw a diagram) and when ready I will provide each of you with one brownie and a knife (be careful with it). Then, before anyone gets to eat, share how you divided your brownie, and we will sketch the different methods on the chalkboard.

5. Making Sums with 0-9

Grades 2–8

☐ total group activity
☒ cooperative activity
☒ independent activity

☐ concrete/manipulative
☐ visual/pictorial
☒ abstract procedure

Each person will need a 3-digit addition job sheet (as shown below) and matching 1-digit number cards 0-9. Have each player remove one number card, perhaps 3, and then *use each of the remaining digits to construct a workable addition problem.* Find and list as many problems as you can. (**Extensions:** Remove a different digit and find more workable problems. Create similar problems for subtraction, multiplication, or division.)

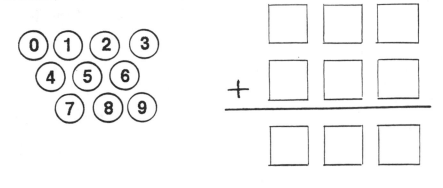

6. Upside-Down Displays

Grades 2–8

☒ total group activity
☒ cooperative activity
☒ independent activity

☐ concrete/manipulative
☒ visual/pictorial
☒ abstract procedure

Your math job will be to use a hand-held calculator to devise upside-down messages. (An example is noted below.) First figure out what letter(s) each number 0-9 looks like when viewed upside down. Then, create words or short messages from those letters. Next, determine calculator computations that will yield the upside-down displays that you planned. Finally, try your upside-down messages on other players.

$440 \times 7 = 3080$, but when read upside down we find a musical instrument

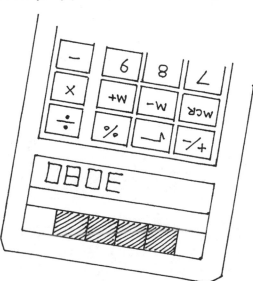

7. Coin Walk
Grades 4–8

☐ total group activity
☒ cooperative activity
☒ independent activity

☒ concrete/manipulative
☒ visual/pictorial
☒ abstract procedure

To take a random coin walk you will need 1 coin, a piece of graph paper, and different colored pencils or crayons. Begin at the lower left corner of your graph paper and, for each toss of the coin, mark 1 unit to the right for a "head" or 1 unit up for a "tail." Predict where your random coin walk graph will end. Then, keep tossing your coin and recording the outcomes until the coin walk trail reaches an edge. Repeat the experiment 2 or 3 times using different colored pencils. What logical statement might you make about coin tosses?

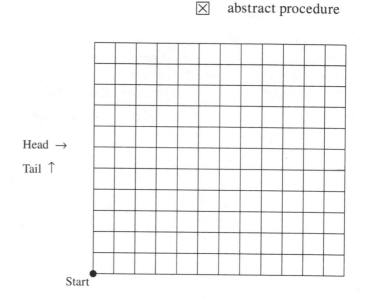

8. Dice Plotting
Grades 4–8

☐ total group activity
☒ cooperative activity
☒ independent activity

☒ concrete/manipulative
☒ visual/pictorial
☒ abstract procedure

Logical thinking and chance events both play roles during a *Dice Plotting* game. Each two players will need a pair of red dice, a pair of green dice, a coordinate graph (see below), and pencils. The first player rolls 4 dice; 2 red and 2 green. She chooses 1 red and 1 green die, and marks the point they represent on the graph with an "X." The second player then takes a turn and marks an "O" on the graph for his selected dice location. Once a graph location is marked, it belongs to that player. The winner is the player to get 4 in a row horizontally, vertically, or diagonally.

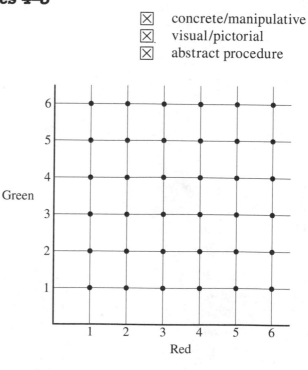

9. Coin Divide
Grades 4–8

☐ total group activity   ☒ concrete/manipulative
☒ cooperative activity   ☒ visual/pictorial
☒ independent activity   ☒ abstract procedure

Place 18 coins, perhaps pennies, on grid paper as shown below. Challenge the players to mark "fences" along the grid lines so that each fenced-in space has the same area and contains 3 coins.

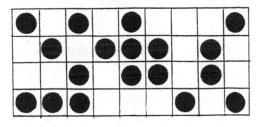

10. Animal Pens
Grades 4–8

☐ total group activity   ☒ concrete/manipulative
☒ cooperative activity   ☒ visual/pictorial
☒ independent activity   ☒ abstract procedure

A farmer has sheep in 3 large pens (A, B, and C). He needs to separate them in such a way that each animal will be in a pen of its own, but he has only 3 lengths of portable fencing that he can use inside each of the large pens. Use just 3 straight portable fence sections (you might want to use toothpicks) inside each of the large pens to separate the sheep so that each is in an individual pen.

The farmer also had another "strange" pen situation. He told his friends that he had 15 pigs in 4 square pens in such a way that each pen contained an odd number of pigs. The friend said that was impossible, but then went to look and found it to be true. How had the farmer penned his pigs?

11. 12 Days of Christmas

Grades 4–8

☒ total group activity   ☐ concrete/manipulative
☒ cooperative activity   ☒ visual/pictorial
☒ independent activity   ☒ abstract procedure

According to the popular Christmas song, the following gifts were received successively during the 12 days of Christmas:

1st Day	Partridge in a Pear Tree
2nd Day	Turtle Doves
3rd Day	French Hens
4th Day	Calling Birds
5th Day	Golden Rings
6th Day	Geese a Laying
7th Day	Swans a Swimming
8th Day	Maids a Milking
9th Day	Ladies Dancing
10th Day	Lords a Leaping
11th Day	Pipers Piping
12th Day	Drummers Drumming

Can you determine:

1. What was the total number of gifts?

2. How many of the gifts were birds? (*option:* state as a fraction or percent)

3. How many gifts included people? (*option:* state as a fraction or percent)

4. What portion of the gifts were jewelry?

12. Rubber Sheet Geometry

Grades 6–8

☐ total group activity   ☒ concrete/manipulative
☒ cooperative activity   ☒ visual/pictorial
☒ independent activity   ☒ abstract procedure

Topology is geometry where the points, lines, and angles are permitted a great deal of motion. Figures in topology can shrink, stretch, bend, or be distorted. Because of this, topology has been nicknamed "Rubber Sheet Geometry." You will be using *Rubber Sheet Geometry* to investigate maps and mapping situations.

Several pieces of thin translucent rubber about 6 × 6 inches (may be obtained from drug stores, or cut up rubber gloves); markers that will write on the rubber; thumb tacks; cardboard; a globe; several types of map projections; and several figures or logos for tracing will be needed. Begin by placing the rubber over a logo and tracing it. Then pull and stretch the rubber and observe what happens to the logo. The logo's length and width can be altered, straight lines can be curved, etc., but the identifying portions, though distorted, remain in the constant relative positions.

Now try a similar globe and map activity. Place your rubber sheet on a world globe and trace a portion of it, perhaps North America (include lines of longitude and latitude). Then place the rubber sheet on a piece of cardboard and stretch it until the longitude lines are parallel and perpendicular to the lines of latitude and secure the rubber with thumb tacks. The image created is a commonly utilized projection most often termed a Mercator map. (**Extensions:** Other types of projections might be researched and constructed. Included might be azimuthal, conic, cylindrical, or homolographic projections.)

13. How Long Is a Groove?

Grades 6–8

☒ total group activity	☒ concrete/manipulative
☒ cooperative activity	☒ visual/pictorial
☒ independent activity	☒ abstract procedure

Obtain a large bolt and inspect the threading or groove on it. What is the total length of that groove? How might you find out? What is the diameter of the bolt? Is the diameter in the groove the same? Could you make a calculation from these figures? Could you use string to find the circumference for 1 rotation? How many rotations does the groove make? Calculate and compare your findings with someone else's. Use a long piece of string and wrap it through the entire groove, mark it, unwrap it, measure it, and compare it to your calculations. How close were you? (**Extensions:** Use similar, though not as concrete, methods to determine the length of a groove on a long-playing vinyl record or the length of tape in a cassette tape.)

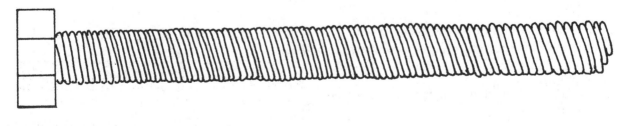

Solutions to Selected Potpourri Activities:

1. *Plan a Circuit Board*

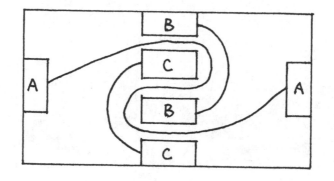

2. *22 Wheels and 7 Kids:* Any workable solution is acceptable. The following are possibilities:

- 4 kids came in separate cars + 3 rode bicycles = (4 × 4) + (3 × 2) = 22
- 5 kids came in cars + 1 rode a bicycle + 1 walked = (5 × 4) + (1 × 2) + 0 = 22
- 5 kids rode in my Dad's 18 wheeler + 2 rode bikes = 18 + (2 × 2) = 22

3. *Candy Box Logic:* The 1-layer boxes for 36 candies will range from 1 by 36, to 2 by 18, to 3 by 12, to 4 by 9, to 6 by 6 arrangements. (*Note:* The participants are, of course, dealing with all of the multiplication facts for 36.)

4. *Brownie Cutting:* 12 and 13 cuts are quite interesting, 10 cuts is the usual solution, but the most efficient solution is 7 cuts.

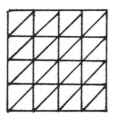

13 CUTS

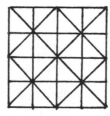

12 CUTS

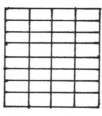

10 CUTS

7 CUTS WITH
1 SIDE CUT

6. *Upside-Down Displays:* A few additional calculator computations that yield upside-down messages are:

- 52043 ÷ 71 and get a snake-like fish   EEL
- 159 × 357 − 19025 and get a beautiful young lady   BELLE
- 161616 ÷ 4 and get what Santa might say   h0h0h0
- 2101 × 18 and get the name of a good book   BIBLE
- 73^2 + 9 and get a honey of an answer   BEES

9. *Coin Divide:* The following is one solution.

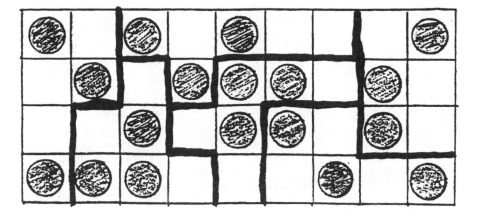

10. *Animal Pens:* The following are possibilities for separating the sheep in pens A, B, and C.

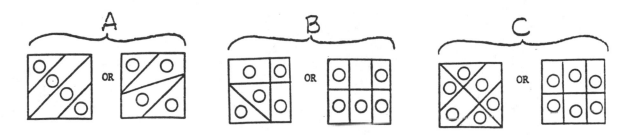

The pig pens might have been situated as shown below: